the interpreted world

Praise for the book

'This fully revised and updated edition of Spinelli's classic introduction to phenomenology should be essential reading on all person-centred, existential and humanistic trainings, and any other counselling or psychotherapy course which aims to help students develop an in-depth understanding of human lived experience. With a new chapter on phenomenological research, discussion of contemporary developments in the field, and an integration of Spinelli's own contributions to existential-phenomenological theory and practice, this book is sure to remain a key text for many years to come.'

Mick Cooper, Senior Lecturer in Counselling,
University of Strathclyde; author of *Existential Therapies* (Sage, 2003).

'As the foundational world-view of "modernity" lapses into philosophical and practical incoherence, existential-phenomenological thinking will surely play a key role in informing the new meta-paradigm that will eventually replace it. From its masterly descriptions of R.D. Laing's view of the schizoid split and Rogers' humanism to its carefully respectful but incisively critical interrogations of psychoanalytic, cognitive behavioural and humanistic theory, this book's rich insight into the lacunae of modern psychological thinking illustrates the contribution that existential phenomenology can make to founding a coherently mature Psychology that is both fully human(e) and responsibly "scientific" in the best sense of that term. More specifically, in his welcome and careful clarification of the distinctions between humanistic and existential-phenomenological approaches, Spinelli opens up the potential for a truly formidable "third force" in psychology that takes us beyond the limitations of cognitive behaviourism and psychoanalysis. At last there is the real prospect of a constructive dialogue between the major schools of psychology, in which, to quote Spinelli, phenomenological psychology can make a "pivotal contribution to increased communication and substantial rapprochement between all the contemporary systems in psychology". For this reason alone, this book could fittingly be compulsory set reading on all undergraduate-level psychology and post-graduate counselling/psychotherapy courses.

In sum, The Interpreted World is a comprehensive, intelligent and highly readable introduction to this vitally prescient field of thought; and in opening up existential phenomenology so ably and engagingly, it makes an important contribution to the momentous evolutionary developments in human consciousness that the transcendence of "modernity" will most surely entail. For as Spinelli himself writes, what is under fundamental challenge here is "the stance of an isolationist self-centred, self-focused way of being and relating that runs rampant throughout our culture" – and to the transformation of which existential-phenomenological thinking can make a possibly decisive contribution.'

Richard House, PhD, Magdalen Medical
Practice, Norwich and Steiner Waldorf teacher;
author of *Therapy beyond Modernity* (Karnac, 2003).

'This is by far the most monumental, erudite, comprehensive, authoritative case that existentialism and phenomenology (a) have a rightful place in the academy; (b) are tough-minded bodies of thought; (c) have rigorous scientific foundations; (d) bequeath a distinctive school of psychotherapy and counselling; and (e) are just as good as the more established systems of psychology.'

Alvin R. Mahrer, PhD, University of Ottawa, Canada;
author of *The Complete Guide to Experiential Psychotherapy* (Bull Publishing, 2003).

the interpreted world

an introduction to phenomenological psychology

second edition

ernesto spinelli

 SAGE Publications

London ● Thousand Oaks ● New Delhi

First edition published 1989
Reprinted 1992, 1994, 1995, 1998, 1999, 2000, 2002, 2003
This second edition published 2005

SAGE Publications Ltd
1 Oliver's Yard
55 City Road
London EC1Y 1SP

SAGE Publications Inc.
2455 Teller Road
Thousand Oaks, California 91320

SAGE Publications India Pvt Ltd
B-42, Panchsheel Enclave
Post Box 4109
New Delhi 110 017

British Library Cataloguing in Publication data

A catalogue record for this book is available
from the British Library

ISBN 1 4129 0304 1
ISBN 1 4129 0305 X (pbk)

Library of Congress Control Number: 2004095886

Typeset by C&M Digitals (P) Ltd., Chennai, India
Printed and bound in Great Britain by Athenaeum Press, Gateshead

Contents

Preface to the second edition   ix

Preface to the first edition   xiii

Introduction   1

1   An introduction to phenomenological theory   5

2   The phenomenological method   19

3   The perception of objects   35

4   The perception of others   59

5   The perception of self   75

6   Existential phenomenology   103

7   Phenomenological research   128

8   Existential psychotherapy   143

9   Phenomenological and humanistic psychologies:
    similarities and contrasts   176

10 Phenomenology and the major systems in psychology   186

11 A critical overview of phenomenological psychology   202

References   219

Index   232

This text is dedicated to
Philip K. Dick
a writer of phenomenological marvels
and to
Maggi Cook
who allowed me access into her world

Preface to the Second Edition

... and even the noticing beasts are aware
that we don't feel very securely at home
in this interpreted world...

Rainer Maria Rilke, *The Duino Elegies*,
my emphasis

Most of the authors I know, myself included, don't tend to re-read their books once they are published. Occasionally, we might have a sentence or a paragraph quoted in someone else's book, or, as is most common in my case, as part of a trainee's essay or dissertation. My own most common reaction to such events is that of surprise.

Sometimes, the surprise is pleasant: 'Gosh! I didn't think I could have ever expressed something as elegantly as that!' More often, the surprise is one of despair: 'How could I have ever written such a clumsy convoluted sentence?' and, on occasion, the surprise is, more than anything else, amazement in that the quote has revealed that this exciting and novel idea I'd scribbled down in haste last week and around which a whole new text might be written, was actually all there in something more than rudimentary form in a book I have not looked at in years.

All of which is a rather long-winded way of stating that my shock in re-reading the whole of the first edition of this book, while containing elements of each of the three reactions just mentioned, revealed yet another: 'How could I have been so naïve and arrogant to have assumed that I was capable of writing such a book?' I know better now. Still, for better or worse, if it hadn't been for that combination of naïvety and arrogance this book would have never come into existence. And here I go again.

The first edition of *The Interpreted World* was published almost exactly 15 years to the day that I am sitting down to write this new preface. It had taken something like 18 months to get it from its original draught to its final one. It was my first published book as well as the first that I had written using a word processing programme. I had worked on the book during what is likely to be my nearest equivalent to that 'splendid isolation' with which Sigmund Freud was so enamoured. Just after I had begun it, I had resigned from a secure, usually enjoyable, combined Lecturing and Counselling post in an international college so that I could set out on a rather uncertain road determined to extend my psychotherapeutic practice both in a private capacity and in the NHS. I was 40 years old. It was time to get on and know better my chosen profession and those colleagues who, I supposed, shared interests similar to my own.

During 1988 I was invited to attend the inaugural meeting of what would become *The Society for Existential Analysis (SEA)*. I had met Emmy van Deurzen, the initiator of the event, informally, once before. I had read, and had valued, Emmy's first book *Existential Counselling in Practice* (1988), and was thrilled to have been asked to participate in this new attempt to place existential psychotherapy on the therapeutic map in the UK. That my book, like Emmy's, was being published by SAGE helped to add to the allure of 'a movement' beginning to find its way. Fifteen years later, that possibility of a movement has not only established its credibility, it has earned a degree of respect and acceptance within the allied professions of psychotherapy, counselling and counselling psychology which I doubt any of us who attended that inaugural meeting would have permitted ourselves to imagine. Today, on the other hand, it is difficult to imagine how frail and tentative those initial steps were and, as well, how united we were in our enterprise. It is a measure of how much we have grown and how far we have established ourselves as an organization that we are able to survive inter-personal divides and animosity and that we can accommodate differing emphases and competing conclusions. I can't speak for anyone else but, personally, I am proud of our shared efforts. Though some of us took, and continue to take, positions of leadership, SEA's achievements, and their impact, are cheapened if reduced to their being identified with one or a select group of individuals. If those of us who responded to the challenge contributed to its advancement in different ways, we still all contributed equally.

Today, Emmy's book, published in 1988, and my own have been joined by a substantial number of works written by a variety of authors who have identified themselves as existential-phenomenological theorists and psychotherapists and who share a common affiliation to SEA. For some, like Mick Cooper (2003), whose book *Existential Therapies* has sought to delineate the correspondences and variations between diverse existential schools in Europe and North America, it makes sense to speak of a 'British School' that is distinct in its emphases and tenets. There may be a great deal of sense in this view, though it seems to me to be somewhat apt in that existential paradox sort of way that that of the three people who are currently most closely identified with the first wave of this 'British School' – Emmy van Deurzen, Hans W. Cohn and myself – not one of us is British born, though each, for his or her own diverse reasons, chose to make something more or less approximating 'a home' in Britain.

The 'second wave' at least is more mixed. Along with Mick Cooper, others such as Martin Adams (2002), Simon du Plock (1997, 2002; Cohn and du Plock, 1995), Nick Kirkland Handley (1996), Mike Harding (1999; 2003), Diana Mitchell (2002), Ian Owen (2002), Darren Wolf (1999) and Sarah Young (1993) are British born. Representing the still substantial number of emigrés in this second wave are Ismail Asmall (1997), Harriett Goldenberg (1998), Lucia Moja-Strasser (1996), Simona Revelli (1998) and Freddie Strasser (1999; Strasser and Strasser, 1997). What appears to be something like the beginning of a 'third wave' becomes even more internationally fascinating as it includes within it authors such as Alison Strasser (Strasser and Strasser, 1997) who were born in but have subsequently left Britain, emigrés who are about to or have already returned to their countries of origin (Madison, 2002; Rennie, 2001), as well as authors who have never actually lived or trained in Britain. In this latter cluster I include, in particular, Dr Bo Jacobsen (2003) and 'The London Group' who are both based in Denmark. Many of the writings of these authors, and a great many more, can be found in *Existential Analysis,* the SEA journal.

I count myself lucky to know as colleagues and friends the great majority of these people, as well as many more who have not been named owing to restrictions of space. What disagreements we may have on aspects of theory and practice do not extend to the dismissal of each other as persons. Equally, though the interpersonal disagreements between myself and Emmy van Deurzen remain something of an 'open secret' within the SEA and the wider UK psychotherapeutic community, it is also the case that what differences in theoretical interpretations there may be between us, these are far outweighed by their similarities – as Mick Cooper has shown and as is revealed by the fact that the training institutes with which each of us is currently associated employ many of the same tutors and supervisors. As such, what 'silence' there may be between Emmy and myself is counterbalanced by the open colloquium between our institutes' tutors and trainees.

So, 15 years later much has changed and much of that is undoubtedly for the better. And what of this book you now hold in your hands? How has *it* changed?

Most obviously, I have added a new chapter on phenomenological research. I am indebted to David Rennie for having made me aware of the significance of this gap. Second, I have sought to emphasize far more clearly the fundamental principle of *intentionality* or *inter-relation* from which all phenomenological ideas are developed. This emphasis brings the book nearer to my current stance as a phenomenological psychologist and existential psychotherapist and, I believe, succeeds in making the arguments presented throughout more coherent and consistent. In line with this, I have also substantially revised my summaries of Heidegger and Sartre and added a brief discussion on Buber whose profound insights on inter-relationship became a little clearer to me in the years following the publication of the first edition. I think that readers will also find that this second edition is a little more critical of psychoanalytic theories and a little less so of cognitive-behavioural theories than was the previous one. The passage of time has also clarified for me something more of the different interpretations that exist between the underlying philosophical principles of humanistic and phenomenological psychologies and I have sought to express this herein.

What *hasn't* changed? Well, first and foremost is that very clear sense of regret at how much of significance has been left out; if anything that sense has grown all the more acute this second time around. What also haven't been altered or amended are the great majority of discussions of and references to research examples that amplify the points under investigation. I followed a strict policy that more up-to-date references would be adopted only if these provided significant amendments in, or re-evaluations of, the research material in question. As such, where it matters I have alerted readers to new developments or provided some discussion of shifts in theoretical emphases or practice that are relevant to the focus of this text. Finally, what has also not changed that certainly matters the most to me, professionally and personally, is the value, respect and sense of connection I continue to retain for phenomenological inquiry in its various expressions and emphases. As my understanding of phenomenology deepens, I see more and more how it is a philosophy that requires commitment at a lived or embodied level. I hope that readers will be able to access something of this sense of commitment.

I am grateful to all who have helped me to write this book and hope that they will not be too disappointed with the result of their efforts. I am most particularly grateful to all the trainees with whom I have discussed many of the themes of this book over the years and who have challenged me to clarify, rethink, struggle. And, with sadness and respect, I am grateful to, and salute, those SEA colleagues who particularly touched my life and who have passed away in the intervening years between editions: Kahldun Nahr, Margaret Nelson, Gigi Gatti-Doyle, Peter Stehle and Hans Cohn.

As a final comment regarding changes that I have made to this new edition, I would like to direct readers' attention to the new cover that has been designed. The images that appear on it were taken by me with a digital movie camera. The larger background image was shot on a beach in Cape Tribulation, Australia; the series of inset shots is of a lakeside scene – water, rocks, plants – from Yosemite National Park, California. The images were 'solarised' and 'negative/positive reversed' while being filmed. Nonetheless, the camera simply recorded what was there, but from a more intensified perspective; no post-production 'magic' was carried out. When I first saw what I had recorded, I immediately thought of the cover to this new edition of *The Interpreted World* since the images captured scenes from a very ordinary, if attractive, natural setting (the world) but through their intensified 'interpretation' revealed a very different and alien world to us. The structures that make up and create this novel world are exactly the same as those that create our more ordinary images of the natural world, including the 'ordinary' perspective we might take on the scene in question. As such, I thought that the images express pictorially precisely that which the book seeks to express in words.

Preface to the First Edition

Of the various regrets in my life, one that comes back to haunt me, on occasion, is my, now long-ago, choice not to pursue philosophy as my area of academic specialization.

Ironically, it was an introductory course in philosophy which led me to psychology. Unlike what we might now expect to make up the ingredients of an undergraduate-level introductory philosophy course – a touch of Plato, a smattering of Aristotle, some Kant for the sake of confusion, and a hint of Nietzsche just to flavour the whole concoction – in place of all such, I was made to read Freud.

If this strikes the reader as being somewhat unusual, I must clarify that I sat this course in 1968 – a time when the unusual was taken for granted.

In any case, having been presented with the writings of one of the very few true geniuses in my profession, I was beguiled into becoming a student of psychology. I was not a brilliant student; far from it, in fact. Often uninterested, frequently disappointed, I don't know to this day why I persisted. Still, persist I did, even if, always at the back of my mind, there remained a hint of a serious gap, a missing element, in all that I learned.

Over the intervening years, I've discovered that numerous others seem to have arrived at a similar conclusion. Among them, many of my students (usually the best in their class) have confided in me that they're not really certain why they remain in this field either, especially since the gap between what it claims to offer and what it actually delivers seems unbridgeable.

This text represents my attempt at relieving some of this shared dissonance. As will become apparent, it seems to me that a *phenomenological* perspective in psychology offers the possibility of reconsidering many established psychological issues and concerns in ways which are both original and illuminating. More importantly, perhaps, phenomenology seems to bring a breath of fresh air to how we think about 'doing' psychology.

Having taught an introductory course on phenomenological psychology on a yearly basis over the past eight years, I've been rewarded with the newly rediscovered enthusiasm for psychology expressed by the great majority of students who have taken it. Their comments, and the superior standard of much of their submitted work, provided me with the necessary energy and determination to reformulate my lectures into a text which, in its wider accessibility, may invigorate and enlighten a greater audience.

Like most authors, I've found the writing of this book to be a challenge. Firstly, because it is the first extended piece of non-fiction that I've ever attempted. Secondly, and of far greater personal significance, because it has forced me to confront that source of regret – and weakness – that I mentioned earlier.

For, more than any other system in psychology, the foundations of phenomenological psychology are firmly grounded in philosophy. As aware as I am of my philosophical deficiencies, it remains necessary for me to examine and argue a number of important philosophical propositions. I hope that my attempts to present such arguments do not earn me the enmity of philosophers.

To the students and friends who, in their unique ways, have encouraged me throughout the writing of this text, my heartfelt thanks. May they decide that their efforts have been worthwhile.

Introduction

We need a language adequate to the times we inhabit.

Michael Ignatieff

As odd as it may seem to non-psychologists, the study of *consciousness* held little appeal for psychology throughout most of the twentieth century. Dismissed as unworthy of scientific examination by behaviourists, devalued in favour of the unconscious by psychoanalysts, reduced to physiological artefact, and remodelled to suit electronic parallels, our species' conscious experience of the world (and of itself, of course) has received short shrift from psychologists.

Indeed, for many years, the only authors who treated consciousness seriously and openly, without need to explain or defend their seemingly perverse fascination with the subject, were Continental European philosophers who, in what might have seemed to be their attempts to test the perseverance and mettle of their readers, insisted on presenting their ideas in a language so arcane and rarefied that it made the decyphering of the Dead Sea Scrolls seem like the simplest of tasks. The most ardent (and, arguably, obscure) among such writers were philosophers belonging to an approach that has come to be labelled *phenomenology*.

Initially, phenomenologists took their principal task to be the exploration of conscious experience, not for its own sake, but in order to expose how our consciousness imposes itself upon, and obscures, 'pure' reality so that they might, ultimately, *bracket* (or set aside) the biases of their seemingly 'naturally-oriented' observations and arrive at a more adequate approximation of 'what is'. These academic pursuits soon came to be recognized as the principal focus of what has since become the *transcendental* branch of phenomenology. Its main ideas relevant to psychology are discussed in Chapters 1 and 2.

An alternative branch – *existential phenomenology*, or *existentialism* – arose as a result of the refocusing of phenomenological investigation onto the very meaning of existence (Lee and Mandelbaum, 1967; Moran, 2000). As such, the principal task of existential phenomenology became the exploration of the potentials for freedom and the unavoidable limitations inherent in human beings' experience of themselves as *beings-in-the-world*. I will discuss some of the principal ideas of existential phenomenology most relevant to psychology in Chapter 6.

Not surprisingly, the concerns of both branches of phenomenology intrude upon most (if not all) of the major subject areas of psychology. The ideas of transcendental phenomenology, for instance, can be shown to have significant impact on a variety of topics centred on the study of *perception*. Chapters 3, 4 and 5 examine various aspects of this vast area.

In addition, phenomenology has played a pivotal role in the development of novel *research methodologies* focused upon all facets of distinctly human experience. Chapter 7 provides an introduction to the foundational principles of phenomenological research.

Similarly, certain key ideas of existential phenomenology have had a major impact upon *psychotherapy* and *counselling psychology*, as I will attempt to demonstrate in Chapter 8.

Although phenomenological psychology is far from being a recent development, and, increasingly, has become an accepted component of both undergraduate and graduate programmes in psychology, psychotherapy and counselling psychology, there still remains a general confusion as to its principal concerns and direction. This confusion is further aggravated by the tendency to lump together phenomenological and *humanistic* psychologies as though they were one and the same system. While it is true that both share similarities in their realms of discourse, and that humanistic psychology is indebted to an overwhelming degree to certain foundational tenets of phenomenology, there are also major differences between these approaches. I will attempt to clear up some of this confusion in Chapter 9.

More generally, in spite of criticisms from representatives of the remaining major contemporary psychological systems, the phenomenological approach can both clarify and expose the (often hidden) biases and assumptions within these systems, and in their practical applications, and may well provide the means towards the development of a more unified psychological science. Chapters 10 and 11 provide a more detailed discussion of these issues.

There exists a wealth of literature on both transcendental and existential phenomenology as *philosophical* systems. These writings are often of obvious importance to phenomenological psychology. Nevertheless, as well as being a source of strength, the link between phenomenology as a philosophical system and phenomenological psychology has helped to minimize the latter's impact upon psychology. Phenomenological philosophers are notorious for the obscurity of their language and the convoluted manner in which they express their ideas (Heidegger, for example, is a perfect case in point), so that, at first, it may seem that phenomenology's central arguments are not likely to be easily grasped, or correctly understood, by non-philosophers and might, as a result, be seen to be of limited and dubious value.

This text seeks to present the relevant philosophical arguments in a manner which is accessible to non-philosophers and which directly relates them to psychological concerns. In order to achieve this aim, I have attempted to keep this text as jargon-free (or 'reader-friendly', as some might say) as possible and have sought to provide both experimental studies and clarificatory examples drawn from everyday experience in order to illuminate potentially difficult arguments which might otherwise be easily misunderstood by readers new to the subject. I realize that, in doing so, I run the risk of irritating those who are more advanced in their understanding of the principal concerns of the area, but I hope that such readers will see their necessity and tolerate (or simply skip) them.

All this is not to suggest that there exist no relatively recent texts which deal adequately with phenomenological psychology in general or with specific topics and themes that have been examined from a phenomenological perspective.

Raymond J. McCall's *Phenomenological Psychology* (1983), Ronald S. Valle and Mark King's *Existential-Phenomenological Alternatives for Psychology* (1978), Hubert Dreyfus's *Husserl Intentionality and Cognitive Science* (1982) as well as Henryk Misiak and Virginia Sexton's *Phenomenological, Existential, and Humanistic Psychologies: a Historical Survey* (1973) remain excellent and essential overviews of phenomenological psychology. Don Ihde's series on phenomenology, including *Experimental Phenomenology* (1986a), *Consequences of Phenomenology* (1986b) and *Expanding Hermeneutics* (1998) are more appropriate for advanced readers, but are well worth the effort.

In like fashion, Hans Cohn's *Existential Thought and Therapeutic Practice; an Introduction to Existential Psychotherapy* (1997) and Mick Cooper's *Existential Therapies* (2003) join Maurice Friedman's *Worlds of Existentialism: a Critical Reader* (1964), R.D. Laing's *The Divided Self* (1960/1970), Rollo May's *Existential Psychology* (1969a), Emmy van Deurzen-Smith's *Existential Counselling in Practice* (1988) and Irvin Yalom's *Existential Psychotherapy* (1980) in providing highly accessible introductions to the existential branch of phenomenology.

At the same time, however, it seemed to me that there still remained a need to present phenomenological psychology's unique focus and approach to a representative number of key psychological issues in a clear and systematic manner so that its distinctive characteristics could be more accurately understood and assessed. Many writers, for example, have assumed that phenomenological psychology dismisses experimentally derived findings from psychological research and takes, in general, an anti-research stance. This is far from being the case – as I will seek to demonstrate in Chapter 7.

Although the issues I will discuss might well be informative to a general readership, this text is principally aimed at both psychologists and those who apply various aspects of psychology in their profession. As such, as well as being of possible value to introductory courses which deal specifically with phenomenological psychology, or that examine the various contemporary systems in psychology, many (if not all) of its topics should also be of use to trainee and practising psychotherapists and counsellors, as well as to members of the various caring professions and to medical and nursing staff. Wherever it seemed both valid and useful, I have employed brief therapeutically oriented examples drawn from my own phenomenologically oriented practice. A possibly realizable personal hope is that this text might open the way for a greater number of courses, or course-sections, whose focus is upon phenomenological psychology.

Though I began this Introduction by referring to the role of 'consciousness' in psychology, I do not wish to mislead the reader into thinking that the sole, or even principal, concern of this text, as was the case with early, now virtually forgotten, introspectionist theories in psychology, lies in the exploration of the components and structures of subjective experience.

Even if the question of consciousness remains the starting point of all phenomenological investigations, the central focus of phenomenological psychology rests, more properly, with the analysis of how all of us arrive at *unique interpretations* of our experience by means of both innate, or species, invariants, imposed by our biology and experientially derived social constructs and frameworks. Perhaps paradoxically, but central to phenomenological inquiry, such an approach has increased substantially the adequacy of our understanding of the *shared* qualities and features of our species.

1

An Introduction to Phenomenological Theory

Pure logical thinking cannot yield us any knowledge of the empirical world; all knowledge of reality starts from experience and ends in it.

A. Einstein, P. Podolsky, N. Rosen

As human beings, we attempt to make sense of all our experiences. We strive to impose meaning upon the world. In our awareness and acceptance of this immense capacity, we are led, ineluctably, to an underlying issue that poses perhaps the most basic of all philosophical questions: What is real? At first, the answer to such a question might seem to be absurdly simple to provide, and indicative of the unnecessarily pedantic obscurity of much that passes as philosophical enquiry.

A typical reply to such a question might proceed in the following manner: if I look around my room, I see (among other objects) books, a desk, a chair, a pen. Similarly, I can look out of my window and observe people walking down the street, other houses, flowers, shrubs, trees and so forth. All these things are real to me in that I believe them to be independent of my consciousness. If I were to die suddenly at this moment, I assume that these objects would continue to exist since I view them as having an existence that is separate to my own. Their physical properties and their independent existence lead me to declare them as being real.

This theory of reality, which the vast majority of us in the West take to be so patently obvious that we imagine it to be not theory but fact, has led us to posit the existence of an *objective reality*. The notion of an objective reality adopts the view that there are real objects in the world that exist independently of our conscious knowledge or awareness of them. In addition, it argues that we have direct access to them through our brain and senses. Whether organic or man-made, they exist as separate entities, separate structures. What we perceive as being 'out there' *is* actually there; it is objectively real.

Like much of modern philosophy, the system known as *phenomenology* questions this viewpoint in an attempt to clarify it. It asks us first to consider the possible assumptions and biases that have led us to our conclusion so that we may be more certain of its accuracy. As a result of such probing, representatives of scientific fields as diverse as cognitive science, neurophysiology, sociology, theoretical physics and psychology have arrived at an intriguing, not to say disturbing, conclusion (Farber, 1962).

Stated simply, this conclusion argues that true reality is, and will forever remain, both unknown and unknowable to us. Instead, that which we term reality, that is, that which is experienced by us as being real, is inextricably linked to our mental processes in general, and, in particular, to our in-built, innate human species capacity to construct meaning.

This view is the starting point to phenomenological enquiry.

The Origins of Phenomenology

The term 'phenomenology' is partly derived from the Greek word *phainomenon* (plural: *phainomena*). *Phainomenon* literally means 'appearance', that is, 'that which shows itself'. Philosophers generally define 'phenomena' to mean 'the appearances of things, as contrasted with the things themselves as they really are'. The world, as we experience it, is a phenomenal world.

Immanuel Kant, who remains among the most influential of the post-Classical Western philosophers, took as the cornerstone of his philosophical speculations precisely this contrast and argued from it that our mind cannot ever know the thing itself ('the noumenon', to employ Kant's terminology), but can only know it as it appears to us – the phenomenon. As such, the true nature of reality, for Kant, was not only far from being obvious, it was beyond our ability to understand and to experience directly.

Although the term 'phenomenology' was coined in the mid-eighteenth century, and several noteworthy philosophers (such as Kant, Hegel and Marx) employed it at various times in the course of their writings, the philosophical school known to us as phenomenology only originated in the early years of the twentieth century.

When Edmund Husserl (1859–1938), its founder, adopted the term, he supplied it with new meaning and significance. Husserl wanted nothing less than to develop a science of phenomena that would clarify how objects are experienced and present themselves to our consciousness. Husserl's hope and stated aim was 'to reform philosophy, and… to establish a rigorously scientific philosophy, which could provide a firm basis for all other sciences' (Misiak and Sexton, 1973: 6).

In an attempt to fulfill this aim, Husserl developed an approach to investigation that is generally known as the *phenomenological method*. Husserl was not its inventor, nor can it be said that he was the first philosopher to employ it, but he refined and specified its conditions and purpose, and raised the method to the status of a fundamental philosophical procedure that would become the cornerstone of his approach.

As we will see in the following chapter, the phenomenological method focuses on the data (or phenomena) of consciousness in order to clarify their role in the process of meaning-construction, and, as well, attempts to set them aside – or 'bracket' them – in order to arrive at a more adequate (if still necessarily incomplete) knowledge of reality.

Transcendental and Existential Phenomenology

Husserl's attempts form the basis of one strand of phenomenology – *transcendental phenomenology* – of which he remains the most prominent exponent. However, it would be wrong to identify all of phenomenology as being solely, or even principally, Husserlian. Of equal, if not greater, philosophical and psychological significance is the second major branch known as *existential phenomenology* (or, more commonly, *existentialism*), that was principally influenced by the writings of Husserl's university assistant, Martin Heidegger (1889–1976).

As such, it is more helpful and accurate to consider phenomenology not strictly as a school of thought possessing a set body of agreed-upon tenets, but, rather, as an investigative approach that encompasses a variety of similarly focused perspectives whose shared concerns are directed towards a methodologically structured investigation of our experience of the world.

I will consider the main ideas that impact upon psychology from both of these major strands of phenomenology in this text. For the moment, however, let us remain with the Husserlian transcendental strand since, as well as historically preceding existential phenomenology, it supplies us with the central arguments presented by phenomenologists on the issue of reality.

The Phenomenological View of Reality

As I stated at the beginning of this chapter, the objects that we perceive (including, of course, the people, or others in general with whom we interact, as well as ourselves) exist, in the way that they exist, through the meanings that each of us gives them.

For example, the book that you are currently reading appears to you to be real, you see it as being separate, inhabiting a different space to that which you inhabit; it is a concrete entity. In your meaning system, it is 'a book'. But what is it *really*? If, for some inexplicable reason, your vocabulary, your language, your meaning system, were suddenly to be deprived of the meaningful term 'book', what would it be that you held in your hands? What is it that you would perceive? It would certainly be 'something', but the definition or meaning given to that 'something' would have as much to do with you, and the meaning system that you employ, as it would have with the thing itself.

Phenomenologists argue that this interpretational process must be acknowledged in our statements about reality. Indeed, phenomenologists suggest that, in our everyday experience of reality, this process is to all intents and purposes indivisible from the reality being perceived. Reality, as far as each of us experiences it, *is* this process.

That our interpretations of reality turn out to be seemingly more or less correct is dependent upon any number of factors. For instance, they may be correct or incorrect only insofar as one culture has provided a different meaning system to that imposed by another culture for the object being perceived.

So, for example, were I a representative from a Stone Age society, who is confronted, suddenly, with an object which you, as a representative of your society, have labelled as being 'a book', it would be highly unlikely that I, too, would label it in the same way. I would certainly perceive 'something', but my interpretation might be that the object was some type of weapon, or a rather unusual stone, or perhaps even a previously unseen food product.

Whose interpretation is the correct one? Whose reality is truly real? For each of us, the object would have a reality that was dependent upon our meaning-derived interpretation of it. As such, to argue the case for a non-interpetatively-derived 'correct' or 'incorrect' statement of reality is highly misleading. Our conclusions are relative – based as they are upon a number of variables, including those of socio-cultural diversity. Ours is a phenomenal reality, and, as such, it remains open to a multiplicity of interpretations.

Nevertheless, though phenomenologists avoid terms like 'correct' and 'incorrect' when considering interpretations of reality, they still recognize that, at times, the meanings construed by individuals will be at great variance with those which (to some degree at least) are shared by others – perhaps even the majority of others.

For example, an individual suffering from what could be termed 'paranoid delusions' might imagine, indeed might be convinced, that the nurse who was coming to provide him with medication is actually about to make an attempt upon his life. Not surprisingly, he might take steps to avoid the danger. This interpretation might be judged as being wrong, or even 'crazy', by the nurse, or by most other people. Would not phenomenologists be shown to be unnecessarily pedantic if they were to argue otherwise?

The Problem of 'Correct' Interpretations of Reality

Phenomenologists deny the possibility of any final or completely 'correct' interpretations since such would presuppose that we had direct knowledge of an ultimate reality. But we do not; our interpretations, far from being certain, remain open to alternatives in meaning. What most of us term a 'correct' interpretation is not based upon external, objective laws or 'truths' that have been universally ascertained. Rather, our judgement is influenced, to a great degree, by consensus viewpoints agreed upon by a group of individuals, or by a whole culture.

If we return to my example of the person suffering from paranoid delusions and deliberate upon the issue phenomenologically, we would note that, like that person, we have also carried out an act of interpretation that led to an imposed meaning upon our experience. We are likely to have assumed, for instance, that our experience is in some way normal, that our perceptive faculties are in some way superior, more in touch with what we have labelled 'reality', than those of the person suffering from paranoid delusions. Our studies, our background, our teachings and lessons as counselling or clinical psychologists and psychotherapists, have given us the knowledge to interpret behaviour as being normal or abnormal; it is this knowledge that now makes meaningful for us the extraordinary behaviour of this person. Our stance assumes that our conclusions are not based upon interpretations of reality but are accurate reflections of objective reality.

Phenomenologists would argue that such a stance is likely to prevent useful, constructive communication and interaction with our 'paranoid' patient. Indeed, initially at least, our dismissal of his interpretation would almost certainly lead him to be further convinced of the 'correctness' of *his* stance. This is not to say that phenomenologically-oriented psychotherapists would not initiate some form of 'intervention'. However, as I will seek to show in Chapter 8, any such interventions would not be based upon mistaken assumptions concerning 'correct' interpretations of reality.

A phenomenological view does not deny that, to some degree, many of us do, indeed, partially share similar interpretations of reality. Important research demonstrating just how much we do share in our mental frameworks and models of experience is available in abundance and is not being discounted nor disputed. Indeed, phenomenologists place equal importance upon structured investigations that seek to clarify our understanding of the interpretative *invariant structures* shared by all members of our species. From a phenomenological perspective, it is these invariant structures that provide the foundational bases upon, or set of conditions through which, our unique interpretations of reality are formed.

All that is being argued for now is that, regardless of how singular or generally shared our interpretations of the world may seem to be, they remain *interpretations*.

Meaningless Experience

Any behaviour that at first appears to us as being inexplicable, or meaningless, is disturbing to us; it is a basic aversive stimulus. Its meaning *must* be uncovered so that, in our ability to explain, we can relax mentally. So long as the meaning or explanation we provide for our experience is suitable or acceptable to us as an explanation, it will be able to remove or, at least, reduce the disturbance we experience.

Let me provide an example in order to make this point as clear as I can. Imagine that you are looking at a surrealist painting. Let us say it is that famous painting *Time Transfixed* by Magritte which, among other things, depicts a train emerging from a fireplace. Looking at it, the first question that springs to mind might be: 'what is this painting about? What does it mean?'

In an attempt to answer this question, you might construct any number of hypotheses and theories that focus on the symbolic significance of the objects in the painting. You might conclude for example, that the train represented Magritte's penis, that the fireplace in some way evoked memories in Magritte of his mother, and of his relationship with her, and that, therefore, the painting was an expression of a universal Oedipal complex.

Alternatively, you might approach the problem from another angle. You might argue that the painting was, in fact, about the role of perspective in Western art, and that this was Magritte's attempt to explain its rules in the most original of ways.

Whatever the explanation would be (and there have been many forthcoming!), in the end, your conclusions as to the meaning of the painting would be dependent on which interpretations were satisfactory enough to reduce the tension you experienced as a result of your confrontation with meaninglessness.

Let me take things a step further. What would happen if you were unable to provide a satisfactory or acceptable meaning to your experience? Imagine now that, instead of looking at a painting by Magritte, you are standing in front of an abstract painting, and that, like many people, you dislike abstract art. When asked why, you explain that it's because you don't understand it, or because you don't know what it's supposed to mean, or because you can't see why abstract painters don't employ figurative elements with which to make their statements. All you see are colours and vague shapes that have no meaning.

Due to the growing anxiety and irritation that this meaningless experience evokes, you might declare that abstract art is, in some way, less acceptable, or less worthy, than figurative art. Indeed, you might go so far as to declare that it might not be 'art' at all and, hence, that your inability to find its meaning is because there is no meaning to it to begin with. This conclusion would itself be a meaningful explanation – and, if accepted, would remove or reduce the tension being experienced.

Alternatively, you might conclude that there was, indeed, a meaning to the painting but that you were incapable, at this point in time, of discerning it. The assumption of a currently hidden meaning open to future revelation would be enough to reduce tension, at least temporarily.

Meaning, then, is implicit in our experience of reality. We cannot tolerate meaninglessness. Through a variety of in-built species invariants and experientially derived mental frameworks, we attempt to stamp our experiences with meaning. Once again, however, it is important to remember that, whatever the meaning arrived at, it cannot be concluded that it is a final true or 'correct' reflection of reality.

Subjective versus Objective Reality

At this point, readers might well be concerned that the phenomenological argument is leading to the conclusion that reality is a purely *subjective* process. That is, that nothing other than mental constructs exists. Is this what phenomenologists conclude?

The recurring controversy concerning the separation between external reality and subjective consciousness, and how the two might interact within each of us, has plagued Western philosophy and psychology for centuries. For some, objects exist independent of the mind; for others, nothing exists other than the mind. Psychologists and philosophers have tended to side with one viewpoint or the other. To rephrase this issue phenomenologically, we can say that we are concerned with the difference, if any, between the appearance of things and what those things actually are (that is, 'the things themselves').

Initially, it was the stated aim of transcendental phenomenology to examine, expose and separate any such differences. If phenomenologists could find the true things themselves, that is, the ultimate reality that was separate and independent from our mind, then they could tell us what objective reality truly was. The rallying cry of early transcendental phenomenologists was: 'To the things themselves!' By this, they made it absolutely clear (at least to other philosophers) that their aim was to set out the means by which the ultimate, true nature of reality would be disclosed.

It should come as no surprise that they were unable to fulfil this aim. Modern phenomenology admits that it cannot tell us what the true nature of reality is, nor will it ever be able to do so. Indeed, it argues that no human-created system – be it scientific or philosophical – will ever be able to do so. Still, though phenomenologists cannot provide us with an answer to this question, their attempts to clarify and examine experienced, or phenomenal, reality provide a resolution to the continuing debate concerning objective and subjective reality that is, I believe, both simple and elegant.

Phenomenology's Stance on the Problem of Reality

As an example of phenomenology's proposal regarding the problem of reality, let me pose yet another art-related hypothetical situation. Imagine that you are in an art gallery walking past a series of paintings that hang from one of its walls. Imagine that you are attracted to one particular painting and stop in front of it in order to pay it closer attention. Perhaps you focus upon a certain element that intrigues you, or note the title of the painting, the name of its painter, and so on. You might even say something like: 'this is the painting that I've been meaning to see for years, but have seen only in textbooks, and now I can see the real thing'. Eventually, having satisfied yourself, you move away and walk on to the next painting.

What happens to the painting? Does it continue to exist as it did when you perceived it? Or is that particular perceived painting no longer in existence?

Phenomenologists would begin to answer the question by pointing out that the painting has physical substance. There is clearly some kind of 'raw matter' which acts as stimulus to our sensory-based perceptions of the painting. At a macroscopic level, we could argue that the painting was made up, to some extent, of the wood that forms its frame, of the canvas, of the oils, the pigment and so forth. This is its raw material. Although what that material might actually be in any ultimate atomic, or sub-atomic, sense remains unknown, whatever reality that painting has lies in this raw stimulus matter.

However, phenomenologists would also argue that the painting that you perceived, indeed the painting that anyone perceives and from which then walks away, can never be perceived again in exactly the same way as it was initially perceived. Even though the painting in its raw state continues to exist, insofar as the basic materials that make it up continue to exist, the perceived painting exists in the way it does only at that moment of perception.

What phenomenologists propose, then, is that our experience of reality is always made up of an interaction between the raw matter of the world, whatever that may be, and what might be broadly called 'our mental faculties'. We never perceive only raw matter; just as, similarly, we never perceive pure or 'raw' mental phenomena. We always experience the interpreted reality that emerges from the *interaction* or *inter-relatedness* between the two.

Each of us, as a representative of our species, develops, both through maturational processes and through social experience, increasingly complex mental frameworks (or 'schemata', as some developmental and cognitive psychologists might label them) through which we interpret and respond to the raw stimuli that bombard our senses.

As members of the human species, we share the same psycho-biological processes and mechanisms – the invariant structures mentioned before – that serve as the common underlying 'givens' through which life experiences are interpreted. At the same time, each of us is subject to any number of specific and individual events and circumstances that make up our own distinctive and particular life experiences. Through the combination of the two, each of us constructs a unique interpretation of the world.

To return to my example of the painting you perceived in the art gallery, the viewpoint just outlined would argue that your experience of the painting was shaped both by species shared interpretational structures and by those specific and unique interpretative tendencies or biases that reflect and express to your particular life experiences. Indeed, should you return to it at another point in time, your experience of the painting would not (and could not) be the same as it was in the first instance, since in returning to it you would now be adding to your previous 'schema' for that painting and, through this fresh experience, you would be altering its previous context and relations.

While as a species we share those mechanisms that provide the means by which we can interpret reality, our actual interpretations of reality can be seen to be not only unique, but also can be shown to be 'plastic' or open to re-interpretation in their meaning.

The 'Raw Matter' of Reality

Our contemporary scientific hypotheses as to the ultimate make-up, or reality, of the 'raw matter' of the world are principally dependent upon our current theories of physics. As advanced as they may be, these theories remain incomplete and undergo continual – and major – revision.

Much to their credit, a substantial number of physicists have pointed out that physics, like all other sciences, is subject to the mental faculties of the individuals who have provided its theories. As such, whatever physics has to say today, or will ever state, about 'the raw matter' of the universe cannot be final or categorical since physics is itself 'tainted' with the experiential biases and limitations of all-too-human theoreticians. This conclusion can be seen to be in keeping with the phenomenological view of reality.

There is a physical reality which remains separate from our consciousness, and which, in this sense, can be labelled *objective reality*. Equally, however, we do not have direct access to that reality, nor can we, in any sense, ever know it as it actually is. All we can do is acknowledge its existence and construct theories that might provide approximations of its nature and mechanics. In the end, however, we are forced to concede its mystery.

Edmund Husserl and the Development of Phenomenology

The acknowledged founder of the philosophical school known to us as phenomenology was the German philosopher Edmund Husserl (Smith and Woodruff Smith, 1995). Husserl was born in 1859, in Moravia (now the Czech Republic), which was, at the time, an annexed state of the Austro-Hungarian Empire. Husserl's initial academic interests lay in mathematics and the natural sciences, including psychology. Indeed, while a student at Leipzig, he attended a series of lectures given by Wilhelm Wundt, a leading proponent of experimental psychology, but found them to be distinctly unimpressive. If anything, Husserl emerged from these lectures even more convinced that mathematics was far more worthy of his attention and interest. He continued studying mathematics in both Berlin and Vienna where his dissertation on mathematical problems led to a PhD in 1883.

Although he returned briefly to Berlin, by 1884 he was back in Vienna where, under the growing influence of the philosopher Franz Brentano, he began to engage in studies that would interest him for the remainder of his life. Brentano's lectures (which, incidentally, were also attended by the young Sigmund Freud and played an intriguing role in the eventual development of psychoanalysis (McGrath, 1986)) revolutionized Husserl's thought. Central to Brentano's philosophy was a key idea that would eventually become known as *intentionality*. As I will discuss later, this term remains *the* central assumption of phenomenology.

So influential was Brentano's philosophy upon Husserl, that it is generally acknowledged to be the principal forerunner of the phenomenological movement. Indeed, Husserl (1965) specifically declared his indebtedness to Brentano by referring to him as his one and only teacher of philosophy. On a more personal level, Husserl's strong missionary zeal in promoting the ideas of phenomenology was a direct outcome of Brentano's influence (possibly because the latter, who had initially trained to enter the priesthood, was by all accounts a charismatic lecturer). Though they would eventually part company intellectually (Brentano could not accept – or, perhaps, appreciate – a number of Husserl's ideas), the two men remained friends for life.

Husserl was appointed Full Professor of Philosophy at the University of Freiburg in 1916; he would remain there until his enforced eviction by the Nazis. During these years, and for the remainder of his academic career, he wrote extensively on phenomenology and gave lectures on it in London, Prague, Vienna and Paris. His principal assistant at Freiburg was Martin Heidegger, who later succeeded him in the post and who would himself provide pivotal contributions to phenomenological theory. Husserl died in Freiburg in 1938.

Phenomenology's Fundamental Issues

In his attempt to explore and examine how we construct our reality, Husserl provided phenomenological psychology with two fundamental principles: the notion of *intentionality* as the basis to all mental experience, and the *noematic and noetic foci of intentionality* as 'shapers' of our experience.

Intentionality

For Husserl (1931a; 1931b) the basis to all our meaning-based constructs of the world lay in the fundamental inter-relationship between consciousness and reality (or 'the world') which he labelled 'intentionality'.

The term 'intentionality' is taken from the Latin *intendere*, which translates as 'to stretch forth'. Franz Brentano (1995) first alluded to the idea of intentionality in order to clarify his assertion that a real physical world exists outside our consciousness and that, as such, all consciousness is always directed towards the real world in order to interpret it in a meaningful manner.

Husserl adapted Brentano's idea by arguing that, for human beings, consciousness is always consciousness *of some thing* in that the most basic interpretative act of human consciousness is to experience the world in terms of objects, or things (Gurwitsch, 1966; 1982). For instance, if I am conscious that I am worried, then I am worried about some thing; if I am confused, I am confused about some thing; if I react, I react to some thing; and so forth. Even if I did not know what the specific 'thing' was, or even if the 'thing' to which I reacted was imaginary, my attention would focus upon the eventual identification of 'some thing'.

We have no idea whether 'things in themselves' truly exist. All we can say is that, as human beings, we are biased toward interpretations that are centred upon an object-based or 'thing-based' world. Whatever sense we make of the world is intentionally derived. Our earliest, most primitive relations and interpretative interactions rely upon the object distinctions we establish and build up over time.

The process of intentionality points out that, as humans, we never have direct access to, or knowledge of, the real world as it is. Since ours is an object world, it can be stated that, even at the most basic level of consciousness, an interpretative act has occurred. Through intentionality, the sensory data at our disposal, which respond to the unknown stimuli emanating from the physical world, undergo a basic, unavoidable 'translation' or interpretation that leads us to respond to the stimuli as if they were objects.

When phenomenologists speak of intentionality as 'the mind stretching forth into the world' and translating its stimuli into phenomenal objects, they are presenting (in spite of the scientific awkwardness of their language) an argument which is both profound and, unfortunately, not always easy to grasp. Perhaps a simple example will clarify their point.

Imagine that you are directing your attention to an object, say, a television set. As we have already seen, the meaning you have given to that object, the functions you ascribe to it, the interest in or pleasure you desire from it and so forth are dependent upon various experiential sociocultural variables through which you have 'set' your mental framework, or schema, for 'a television set'. As such, your 'knowledge' that what you see before you is 'a television set' is not the straightforward result of your direct access to external reality but rather, has come about through a complex of interpretations linked to your experience of, and dealings with, the world. The object 'a television set' is a phenomenal object.

As such, you might now rightly ask: well, what is this object (which I have labelled 'a television set') really? If I were capable of setting aside, or *bracketing*, all the additional meanings and functions that I've invested upon it, what would be left? Unfortunately, your question cannot be answered in any complete or final sense. Phenomenologists argue that it will never be possible for us to know the 'ultimate reality' of any object, be it 'a television set' or whatever else, precisely because we are limited by the intentional relationship through which we experience an object world. The very question '*What* would be left?', in its reference to 'some thing', makes clear the intentional boundaries in our experience.

Through the term 'intentionality', then, phenomenologists point out a basic *invariant* relationship that exists between the real world and our conscious experience of it. Unable to bracket this relationship, we are forced to acknowledge, through it, the undeniable role of interpretation that lies at the heart of all our mental experience.

At its most basic level of understanding, intentionality is simply the referential or directed nature of consciousness. All consciousness, Husserl writes over and over, is consciousness of *some thing*. At this level of understanding, intentionality is a descriptive term for that most basic of our world-interpreting processes. In this sense, intentionality refers to the first, most basic interpretative mental act – that of 'translating' the unknown raw stimuli of the real world, to which our senses have responded, into an object-based (or 'thing'-based) reality.

At a deeper, and more significant level however, intentionality has been described as the *foundational correlational rule of phenomenology* (Ihde, 1998). In this sense it can be seen that intentionality takes account of the inter-relatedness and interdependence of what in a modern empiricist tradition has been called 'subject' and 'object'. From the standpoint of Husserlian intentionality, neither term makes sense in and of itself, and neither term can, in fact, emerge as meaningful if isolated from the other. Intentioanlity argues that subject and object co-constitute, or bring meaning to, one another (Ihde, 1998).

Noema and Noesis

The phenomenological notion of intentionality points out that we carry out a basic (and invariant) interpretational step of translating the unknown stimuli of the world into things, or objects. Intentionality, then, can be seen to focus consciousness initially on some *thing* in the world (regardless of what that 'thing' may actually be in its real state).

Husserl suggested that every act of intentionality was made up of two experiential foci, or 'correlational poles' (Ihde, 1986a and b: 43), which he labelled *noema* and *noesis* (Husserl, 1929; 1931a; 1931b; 1948/1973). 'For what is experienced, as experienced, he used the term *noema* or noematic correlate, and for the mode of experiencing… he used the term *noesis* or noetic correlate' (Ihde, 1986a and b: 43). Noema, then, refers to the *directional* element of experience; it is the object (the *what*) towards which we direct our attention and upon which we focus. Noesis, on the other hand, is the *referential* element of experience; it is the mode (the *how*) through which we define an object. As the American philosopher Don Ihde (1986a: 43) points out: 'this internal correlation within experience may seem trivial and obvious – if I experience at all, I experience something and in some way'.

As a simple example of the different emphases given by the noematic and noetic constituents, consider the following situation. Two individuals are attending a political rally. They both hear a speaker presenting a speech dealing with nuclear disarmament and taking the stance that unilateral disarmament would be a serious and dangerous error. The first individual agrees with the speaker's sentiments and claps loudly and enthusiastically at the conclusion of the talk. The second individual, sympathetic to unilateral disarmament, becomes increasingly irritated by the arguments being presented and boos the speaker at the end of the speech.

The noematic focus, that is, the 'what' of the experience, is made up from the content, or argument, of the speech heard by each individual. The noetic focus, on the other hand, contains those referential elements dealing with 'how' each individual's various cognitive and affective biases add further elements of meaning to the experience. Together, the noematic and noetic foci lead each individual to interpret the experience of the political rally in a different and unique manner, and, as a consequence, to respond to it in their disparate ways.

There is a tendency within psychology to obscure or minimize the significance of this correlation either by focusing exclusively upon the noematic focus or by minimizing the unique experiential variables that add to any individual's noetic focus. This may be due to the fact that although we can, in theory, distinguish between the noetic and noematic foci, in practice the two are not fully distinct from one another. None of us can approach any experience in our life, past or present, without instantaneously evoking both foci. For instance, were I to ask you to remember any experience from your past, whatever it was that you remembered would not be merely the events contained in that experience, that is, its items (the noema), but, in addition, the way you today claim to have experienced them (the noesis).

As a result of clarifying the noematic and noetic foci in all intentional acts, the phenomenological assertion that all experiences are, at best, only partially shareable should become clearer. Human species-shared invariant interpretational 'givens' may well provide a partial similarity in separate individuals' experiences. Nevertheless, the foci (particularly the noetic focus) retain individually-determined variables that limit the extent to which any experience can be said to be shared between individuals.

It may appear initially to readers that phenomenological psychologists are interested only in the unique and unshareable differences in each individual's experience of the world. This would be a mistaken conclusion and should not be seen to be either explicitly or implicitly minimizing or invalidating the great number of important studies dealing with the shared and invariant structural features of human experience. Nevertheless, phenomenologists are at pains to point out that, although there may well be a substantial degree of 'shareability' in our experiences, there remain a variety of factors which, ultimately, point to the uniqueness in each individual's experience. To employ an analogy from nature, although the structure of all snowflakes is determined by the same six rules, each emergent snowflake retains a unique design. It is simply because experimental research in science (and in psychology in particular) has tended to focus upon the study of shared features and has either dismissed or diminished the importance of the unshared variables in experience that phenomenologists emphasize the latter in their studies. It is not because unique factors in themselves hold greater significance; phenomenologists are simply redressing the balance and, in so doing, are increasing the adequacy of our theories.

All mental acts, then, can be seen to be intentional. Our consciousness is always object-directed or of 'some thing'. This most basic of interpretative acts always contains two foci – the noematic focus which directs our experience towards 'some thing', and the referential, or noetic, focus which provides the broadly attitudinal mode through which we experience 'some thing'.

Consider, as an example, this very book which you are currently reading. Through intentionality, the (primarily) visual and tactile sensory responses to the unknown 'raw matter' are experienced in terms of 'some thing' or object. Through the noematic and noetic foci, that object is not only further interpreted as 'a book', but is also referentially defined in any number of ways (for example, the book is easy/difficult, interesting/boring, important/insignificant and so on). As a phenomenal object, the book each of us experiences is a product of both shared and unshared variables; via the noematic and noetic constituents of our intentional inter-relationship with the book, each of us experiences a unique approximation of what it may really be. Further, the impact of subsequent lived experience will affect the relative 'openness' or plasticity of either or both of these constituents such that, over time, each of us may experience alternative unique approximations of what the book may be. Finally, as will be discussed in later chapters, this same inter-relation serves to provide each of us with a unique approximation of who the 'I' who experiences the book may be.

The concept of intentionality, and its noematic and noetic foci, led Husserl to the development of a specific approach designed to clarify the interpretational factors contained within every experience. This approach has since become usually referred to as the *phenomenological method*. Just what the phenomenological method consists of and what its implications may be for psychologically related issues is the principal concern of the following chapter.

2

The Phenomenological Method

The idea had occurred to me that maybe what we see is not real. That it is somehow – I don't know what the alternative to 'real' is... There's a state of things being semi-real.

Philip K. Dick

Husserl's initial analyses led him to conclude that our experience of the world is a unique intentional construct containing both directional (noematic) and referential (noetic) foci. On this basis, he argued, it was to be the principal task of phenomenology to find the means to strip away, as far as possible, the plethora of interpretational layers added to the unknown stimuli to our experience in order to arrive at a more adequate, if still approximate and incomplete, knowledge of 'the things themselves'. In order to achieve this aim, Husserl proposed a *phenomenological method* of investigation which could be applied to all analyses of experience. This method became the primary basis for all conclusions arrived at by transcendental phenomenologists.

Though clearly of central importance to phenomenology in general, its primary value to phenomenological psychology differs slightly from the original function ascribed to it by Husserl, who sought to employ the method in order to strip away the variants of experience and so to arrive at a clearer understanding of its invariants. Phenomenologically oriented psychologists (among others who seek to apply a phenomenological orientation to their respective fields), on the other hand, apply the phenomenological method for the principal purpose of identifying and clarifying the variables, or variants, of experience so that they may be more adequately controlled as far as may be possible in the variety of studies undertaken by the different systems in psychology, and, also, so that their role in influencing (and limiting) the interpretations and conclusions arrived at by psychologists may be made more explicit.

Because this text deals with the phenomenological orientation within psychology, my account of the phenomenological method will limit its focus on this latter concern. Whatever its primary goal, however, the phenomenological method is carried out in much the same way. As a way of discussing its principal implications, it can be considered as being composed of three distinguishable, though interrelated, steps (Grossmann, 1984; Ihde, 1986a, 1986b).

Step A: The Rule of Epoché

The first step has become known as the rule of epoché. This rule urges us to set aside our initial biases and prejudices of things, to suspend our expectations and assumptions, in short, *to bracket* all such temporarily and as far as is possible so that we can focus on the primary and immediate data of our experience. In other words, the rule of epoché urges us to impose an 'openness' on our immediate experience (what I have termed as 'un-knowing' elsewhere (Spinelli, 1997) so that our subsequent inter-pretations of it may prove to be more adequate).

For example, imagine that you are about to meet someone for the first time and that you have been told certain things about this person by others so that, even before your meeting, you have built up a number of expectations and reservations about the person. Chances are that your eventual initial experience of that person will have been already 'set' and constrained by these biases. And, as is often the case under these circum-stances, your judgements and conclusions about the person may well turn out to be both inadequate and imbalanced.

On the other hand, were you to follow the first step of the phenomeno-logical method, you would attempt to bracket these biases as far as was possible for you so that you had more of an open mind about the person and so that your subsequent conclusions would be based more upon your immediate and unbiased experience of the person rather than upon prior assumptions and expectations.

Nonetheless, as phenomenologists themselves have pointed out repeat-edly (Merleau-Ponty, 1962; 1964) no final or complete act of bracketing can ever be achieved, nor should we trust any claim to have done so. Even so, while it remains impossible for us to bracket all biases and assump-tions, we are certainly capable of bracketing a substantial number of them. In addition, even when bracketing is not likely or feasible, the very recognition of bias lessens its impact upon our immediate experience.

Step B: The Rule of Description

The second step in the phenomenological method is known as the rule of description. The essence of this rule is: 'describe, don't explain'.

Having 'opened up to the possibilities' contained in our immediate experience as far as is possible through the rule of epoché, we are now urged not to place another type of limitation upon our experience by immediately trying to explain or make sense of it in terms of whatever theories or hypotheses we may tend towards.

Instead, the rule of description urges us to remain initially focused on our immediate and concrete impressions and to maintain a level of analysis with regard to these experiences which takes description rather than theoretical explanation or speculation as its point of focus. Rather than step back from our immediate experience so that we may instantly 'explain it', transform it, question it or deny it on the basis of preconceived theories or hypotheses which stand separate from our experience, the following of the rule of description allows us to carry out a concretely based descriptive examination of the intentional variables which make up our experience.

What value might there be in adopting this step? As an example, consider the hypochondriac who, worried over his health, immediately responds to any variety of somatic experiences by imposing (often incapacitatory) misinterpretations which are dependent upon the medical hypotheses at his disposal. From a phenomenological perspective, a hypochondriac is an individual who has failed to apply the rule of description because, rather than seek to describe his somatic experience in concrete terms, he jumps to abstract, disease-model explanations and theories which provoke levels of anxiety which may well be as debilitating as his hypothetical illness.

In keeping with the conclusions regarding the inherent limits of the first step of the phenomenological method, phenomenologists have pointed out that similar limits exist for the second step as well. A purely descriptive account remains an impossibility since no description is altogether free of explanatory components. Hence, the rule of description aspires to an ideal that cannot be achieved. Nevertheless it seems reasonable to me to argue that explanations may be seen to run along a continuum ranging from 'concrete descriptive' to 'abstract analytical'. The former are derived from and specific to any immediate sensory-based experience; the latter are conceptual generalizations which seek to explain or make an experience meaningful within the boundaries of a set theory or hypothesis.

Step C: The Rule of Horizontalization (the Equalization Rule)

The third step in the phenomenological method is known either as the rule of horizontalization or, alternatively, as the equalization rule. Having stuck to an immediate experience which we seek to describe, this rule further urges us to avoid placing any initial hierarchies of significance or importance upon the items of our descriptions, and instead to treat each initially as having equal value or significance.

In the act of simply reporting in a descriptive manner what is consciously being experienced while avoiding any hierarchical assumptions with regard to the items of description, we are better able to examine an experience with far less prejudice and with a much greater degree of adequacy.

In a sense, phenomenologists urge us to treat each bit of initial experience as if we have been given the task of piecing together some gigantic jigsaw puzzle without the prior knowledge of what image the completed puzzle depicts. In such a situation, it is clear that we cannot say from the outset that any one piece of the jigsaw is any more important or valid than any other, and so, initially at least, if we are to succeed in our task, we must treat each piece as having equal significance. In the same way, phenomenologists argue that if we are to embark on any worthwhile attempt to make sense of the gigantic jigsaw puzzle that is our mental experience of the world, we must, as far as is possible, avoid making immediate, misleading, hierarchically based judgements. Once again, no complete or fully-realized horizontalization of phenomena is possible. Nonetheless, the attempt at horizontalization permits a means whereby we may refrain from imposing questionable and biased hierarchies of significance upon our investigations, or at the very least, allowing ourselves a greater degree of caution in adhering too closely or uncritically to the immediate hierarchies that we may have imposed upon our investigation from its earliest stages.

The Practice of the Phenomenological Method

Taken together the three steps outlined above make up the phenomenological method. It should now be clearer that while the metaphor of 'steps' was a useful means by which the phenomenological method could be presented, the method itself should not be understood as following a 'one-two-three' step approach. Indeed, each 'step' is, more accurately, a particular *point of focus* that is taken, rather than an entirely independent activity that can be wholly distinguished from the remaining two. Nonetheless, as an initial means by which to train oneself to adopt a more adequate phenomenological attitude towards an investigation, the three steps serve a useful introductory function. As I will argue in subsequent chapters of this text, when applied to psychological and psychotherapeutic concerns the method provides significant contributions and important clarificatory insights. For the moment, however, to ensure that the reader has understood the phenomenological method, I want to provide two straightforward examples in order to demonstrate how it might be applied in any experience.

As my first example, I will outline a personal experience from my pre-phenomenological past which demonstrates the problems that might be encountered when not applying the phenomenological method.

A number of years ago, a friend phoned me up in a state of deep distress. She explained that she'd just broken up with a long-standing boyfriend, was feeling miserable and wanted a shoulder to cry on. I, dutifully, obliged. Towards the end of our conversation, I happened to remind her that we'd both been invited to a mutual friend's party that night and that going to it might be the best thing for her. She said she'd think it over, thanked me and hung up.

I thought no more about her until that night when, upon entering the apartment where the party was being held, I saw her sitting in the middle of a small group of close friends. I couldn't hear what she was saying, but her facial expression and her body movements suggested to me that she was in a highly agitated state. Certainly, everyone around her seemed to be closely monitoring her every word and action. Suddenly, the girl erupted into a series of excited, spastic movements, grimaced and let out a loud wail. As I moved closer to her, I noticed that she'd begun to shed tears. Now thoroughly convinced that she was, once more, deeply upset, I rushed to her side, hugged her close to me, and offered words of condolence and endearment which I hoped would allow her to regain control of herself. Imagine my shock when, in response, the girl looked up at me with some surprise and indignation and asked whatever was the matter with me and just what was I going on about. Looking round at the others in the circle, I noticed for the first time that most of them also had tears streaming down their faces and that, more importantly, they too were looking at me as if they couldn't make sense of my behaviour.

Eventually, the situation was straightened out. I discovered that, contrary to my initial assumption, the girl had not become emotionally upset once more, but, rather, had just finished telling the group a particularly funny joke which had sent her, and most members of the circle, into paroxysms of unrestrained laughter which, not unexpectedly, had provoked tears.

What had I done to interpret the situation in such an inadequate fashion? Firstly, I had 'biased' my initial sighting of the girl with my preconceptions and hypotheses as to how she must be feeling under the circumstances – in other words, I had failed to bracket my beliefs and assumptions. Secondly, I had sought out an immediate explanation for the general behaviour I observed her enacting. Rather than pay closer attention to what she was actually doing, I had formulated a theory – based on my assumptions – that made sense of her behaviour. Thirdly, I had singled out certain variables – those which fitted my theory – and bestowed on them significance and importance, while, at the same time, I had neglected to consider or had minimized other variables, such as the fact that other members of the group had responded to the joke's denouement in ways highly similar to the girl's, because these did not fit my interpretation of events.

Had I, instead, followed the steps of the phenomenological method and bracketed my beliefs and assumptions, restrained myself from applying impulsive explanations and, instead, concentrated on the immediate data of experience, and treated each, initially, as having equal value or significance, I might well have arrived at a different conclusion – and prevented myself from suffering unnecessary embarrassment.

As a second example, I want to focus on how the phenomenological method can influence more imaginative, not to say imaginary, interpretations of experiences. Consider the following situation. You are on holiday in the country. After a very pleasant evening meal at a local restaurant, you start to make your way home. Walking down the deserted country lane, you come to a stretch of road with overhanging branches; because of the abundance of vegetation on either side of the path, it is particularly dark. Half-wishing you weren't alone, you quicken your steps. Suddenly, you hear a noise. Is it the sound of footsteps following you? Could it be some wild animal? Have you really stopped believing in ghosts and ghouls? Or is the noise simply the sound of twigs and leaves being displaced either by the wind or by your own footsteps?

What would you do were you to follow the phenomenological method in order to make sense of your experience?

Firstly, you would attempt to set aside any immediate biases or beliefs which might predispose you towards any one particular meaning or explanation of the event. Instead, you would, for the time being, remain open to any number of alternatives, neither rejecting any one as being out of hand, nor placing a greater or lesser degree of likelihood on the options available. Initially, you'd be open to all possibilities.

Secondly, in having opened yourself to all possibilities, your focus of attention is forced to shift away from theoretical explanations (since, for the moment, no one explanation is more adequate than any other) and, instead, must attend to the items of your immediate experience so that, through them, you might eventually have the possibility of putting your options to the test. As such, your task becomes one of describing the events of your experience as concretely as possible. For example, you might note that there is a wind tonight and that it is strong enough to be felt passing through your hair; you might also note that there are plenty of dry, fallen leaves upon the path and that the sound they make when being stepped on is reminiscent of the sound that initially startled you; equally, you might note that the stillness of the night allows you to make out the laughter and even some of the words of people who are still in the restaurant. Item by item, then, you build up a store of concrete information based upon your immediate experience.

Thirdly, having collected together a sufficient variety of items, it remains necessary for you to avoid placing any greater or lesser significance or value on each of them and, instead, to treat each, initially, as having equal importance. If you did not do so, you might 'skew' your eventual conclusion so that it proved to be far less adequate than it might have been. In other words, the sound of distant voices, for instance, is initially no more significant a clue than is the crackling sound of dry leaves.

Once you have followed the three steps, you are able to arrive at an explanation of your experience whose adequacy (or 'correctness') rests upon data closely derived from your immediate experience and not upon abstract, biased speculation. Your explanatory conclusion may emerge all at once, as in insight learning, or, alternatively, may come about slowly through the process of elimination of one possible explanation after another on the basis of its ability to make sense of each accumulated item of experience. Whatever the case, in the following of the phenomenological method, the eventual explanations or conclusions we arrive at, as well as any subsequent action we might initiate, can be seen to be more adequate (or, loosely speaking, veering towards correctness) in that they are primarily based upon data derived as closely as possible from direct experience.

The phenomenological method seeks to avoid the imposing of set beliefs, biases, explanatory theories and hypotheses upon our experience either at the very start of any examination or before it becomes useful to do so. Clearly, there can be no fixed point at which we can say that enough data have been accumulated and theories can now be initiated. Indeed, it is evident that some degree of theoretical speculation exists in even the most 'descriptive' accounts of experience. Nevertheless, this limitation does not diminish the power of the phenomenological method. For the concern is not so much that we theorize, but that we typically *fix* upon a theory and derive our explanations and subsequent actions from its (often inadequate) conclusions.

In general, the application of the phenomenological method allows all experiences to be considered as initially valid. Phenomenologists have labelled this consequence the *inclusionary/exclusionary rule* (Ihde, 1986a). This rule states that in our exclusion of any initial judgements and biases, we are including an openness, or receptivity, in all our experiences.

Similarly, the following of the phenomenological method forces us, in the initial stages of investigation, to treat all experiences as being equally real or valid, so that they may be exposed to examination. This *equal reality rule* (Ihde, 1986a) can only be applied temporarily since it has no fixed end-point and, as such, all investigations must, at some point or other, set a pragmatic limit to its application. Nevertheless, in being willing to follow this rule to some extent, investigators reduce the likelihood of imposing unnecessary judgements or biases on their initial observations. In doing so, they increase the adequacy of their conclusions.

The practice of the phenomenological method, at the very least, minimizes our tendency to rely exclusively upon any one theory throughout the whole of our investigation. Equally, in its claim to lead us not to correct or final conclusions, but, rather, towards increasingly adequate approximations or probabilities, it allows for a theoretical flexibility and 'open-mindedness' which is in keeping with the ideology – if not the practice – of science.

Upon consideration, it should become evident that the phenomenological method should be the basic rule of any form of structured enquiry – not least scientific enquiry. While psychologists might argue that this is indeed the case, I suspect that while it may be so in principle, in practice it is quite another matter. Indeed, I would suggest that the application of the phenomenological method reveals important weaknesses in the various systems of contemporary psychology. Since each system is committed initially and primarily to a specific theory and/or methodology, its tendency is to fix upon those variables which it deems to possess significance *because* they validate its theory and/or methodology and to minimize the significance of those variables which suggest inadequacies and limitations in the theory and/or methodology. I will discuss this point at greater length in later chapters.

Consequences of the Phenomenological Method

Husserl initially developed the phenomenological method in order that it might be applied as a means of resolving a number of fundamental philosophical issues. A discussion of many of these lies outside the scope of this text. Nevertheless, the use of the method led to several consequences which have direct relevance for a variety of psychological concerns. It is to these that we must now turn our attention.

Straightforward versus Reflective Experience

If we analyse the manner in which we experience any event from a phenomenological standpoint, we discover that, typically, we both combine and confound the experience of an event with the meaningful account or explanation that we give to it. The differences between the two are so rarely considered that we commonly assume them to be part and parcel of a unitary experience.

However, through the process of 'bracketing' in order to carry out the phenomenological method, we are led to a singular and inescapable discovery: in the process of any experience taking place, no explanation or description can be given; it is only *once the experience has occurred* that we may both describe and explain it to some degree of adequacy. Nevertheless, the experience itself, as it takes place, stands outside the realm of description or explanation. *We cannot describe any experience as it occurs, but only after it has occurred.*

For example, were I to state: 'tell me what is happening to you right now', you would note several important invariants in your attempted response to my question. First, whatever your response, the event to which it alluded would have already occurred. The 'now' experience you report is already a past event. No matter how much you tried, you could not experience an event and describe your experience of it simultaneously.

Further, whatever your response, it would be both partial and incomplete. You could not ever tell me *everything* that you had experienced in that 'now' moment for several reasons. Firstly, at any point in time, your senses are being bombarded by so many different stimuli that the vast majority would remain below your threshold of awareness. Secondly, even if it were possible for you eventually to become aware of each of these stimuli, it would probably take you the rest of your life to report them – and, even then, your report would almost certainly remain incomplete. Thirdly, you might not have the knowledge or vocabulary to describe all of your experiences. As such, whatever description you gave as your answer would never be as complete as the experience itself.

Phenomenological enquiry makes a clear distinction between the experience as it occurs and our interpretations of that experience. The former is commonly labelled *straightforward experience,* while the latter is usually referred to as *reflective experience.*

Straightforward experience is action-based; it is the activity of experience itself *as it occurs.* As such, straightforward experience is both timeless and ineffable. It is timeless because it always functions in the 'now' of any event. Time only enters when we attempt to describe or explain the experience. Equally, straightforward experience is ineffable. It cannot be talked about directly. Any statement of description or explanation of it occurs subsequent to the experience and is limited by the amount of explanation/description that is practically possible.

On the other hand, when we make various attempts to describe or explain what has been experienced, we enter the realm of reflective experience. Reflective experience requires some kind of system of communication, relies upon notions of time, and is therefore open to measurement. It is through reflective experience that we formulate meaning and construct the various hierarchies of significances contained within those meanings. In doing so, we eliminate from our interpretations of experience any number of variables that form our straightforward experience on the grounds that they are unimportant or unnecessary to communicate or are incommunicable simply because we are unaware of their existence or do not possess the language or means to describe them. Reflective experience allows us to communicate only a minute part of the sum total of any experience.

The more commonly-employed psychological term '*attention*' might help the reader to grasp the idea being presented. When we attend to an event, we are carrying out a hierarchy of significance through which we decide, on any number of grounds, just what is and is not of significance in our experience. We focus on certain items of experience and exclude others from our focus of attention.

Any theory that we care to formulate (including, of course, phenomenological theory) is the result of reflective experience since it is an attempt to provide some hierarchy of significance to any straightforward experience.

The Phenomenological 'I'

In distinguishing between straightforward and reflective experience, we are led to yet another intriguing implication derived from the phenomenological method. This is concerned with our notion of 'I' – our experience of self.

Typically when we think about the 'I' in experience, we often start from the assumption that the 'I' is the primary means to an experience, that the 'I' must be present in order for us to experience anything. Our very language is infused with such assumptions. We say, for instance, that 'I had this experience', or that 'I am now experiencing this', and so forth.

Although it is typical for us to assume that the 'I' must exist so that any experience can occur, phenomenologists question this assumption. They point out, for example, that one can note that in a great many experiences the 'I' becomes a conscious presence only once the experience has been completed. This is particularly apparent when we are involved in intense, emotional and/or repetitive behaviour. In activities such as jogging, gardening, carpentry, typing and so on which require repetitious physical movements and an increasing focus on the actions themselves, the subjective experience of 'I' diminishes to the point where there seems to be no 'I' there at all. Indeed, all that there seems to be is the activity itself, just 'the process of doing' wherein any sense of 'I' is temporarily lost.

If we consider sexual intercourse, which is both an intense and, in terms of its stimulatory focus, largely repetitive activity, there is, once again, the commonly reported experience of a temporary loss of any ordinary sense of 'I'. For a period of timeless time, at the very height of intensity during the act, all 'everyday I'-related (that is, self-conscious) experience seems to disappear. For some, there is the experience of a total loss of self as a result of an experienced 'merging' of the lovers' selves so that there is simply the action taking place. For others, the 'I' seems to become all-encompassing such that the distinction between 'I' and 'not I' (self and others) loses all meaning. In this case, the 'I' seems to become everything, unlimited – and, hence, undefinable.

It is only once the action has been completed that the 'I' comes once more into focus and begins its meaning-focused assessment of what has just occurred.

Husserl noted how minimal the experience of self-consciousness is during such instances (Ihde, 1986a and b). On further reflection, he realized an odd paradox: when we consider the most astounding, the most vital, the most involving experiences in our lives, those times when we felt the most 'alive', we are likely to find that here, too, the 'I' is minimally self-conscious; indeed, during such times there seems to be little, if any, 'I'-related experience at a reflective level. It is only once the experience has ended, when we return to it in order to give it qualitative and descriptive meaning, that the 'I' takes centre-stage. As such, Husserl argued that self-consciousness is the basic *structure* of reflective experience. While we undoubtedly can and do remain conscious through many events and experiences that direct us towards a more straightforward-experience-focused way of being, what distinguishes these is the temporary limiting or eradication of reflectively-focused meaning making and, with it, the temporary 'loss' of self or inability to distinguish self from other, or the world in general.

As a result of the phenomenological method, we are led to an inversion of the typical view we take concerning the role of 'I' in any experience. While we tend to assume, in a commonsensical manner, that the 'I' initiates our experience of things, transcendental phenomenologists posit that in the realm of straightforward experience there is no obvious 'I', certainly not at a conscious level. It is only when we reflect upon our experience, when we begin to analyse and attempt to make sense of it, that the 'I' appears and takes its central place as the (seeming) originator of experience.

This major re-analysis of the role of 'I', or self, in our experience will be explored further in Chapter 5.

'I' and 'not I': The Relationship between Self and Others

The analysis of the phenomenological 'I' has an immediate implication for the relationship between self and others, since it would seem that the phenomenological argument leads us to question whether any intentionally-constructed object (including, of course, self and others) truly exists *as a separate and distinguishable entity*, independent of one's conscious experience of it. That is to say, if our notions of self and others are intentional constructs, it would seem that they, too, cannot be viewed as being experientially independent of one another. Just as the 'I' is a product of reflective experience, so, too, must be 'others' (or, as phenomenologists prefer, 'not I'). Such a conclusion, of course, once again runs counter to our everyday assumptions.

Phenomenological theory argues that each of us can be described as a *being-in-the-world*. We are all beings-in-the-world in the sense that we all share an intentionally derived conscious experience of the world and ourselves, through which we make various distinctions such as those relating to notions of 'I' and 'not I'. Although we are all similar in the sense that we are all beings-in-the-world, each of us *experiences* being-in-the-world in a unique and unsharable way.

Since 'I' and 'not I' are intentional constructs, we cannot say what 'I' and 'not I' actually are in themselves. Each has a basis in material reality, but our experience of 'I' and 'not I' is not a direct experience of 'the things themselves', but of 'things as they appear to us' – we experience *phenomenal* versions of 'I' and 'not I'.

I will attempt to clarify this issue further in Chapters 4 and 5, where I will consider phenomenology's stance on the perception of others and the perception of self in greater detail. For now, what can be stated is that each of us, through intentionality, 'constructs' others, in the sense that we each experience others from a unique and, ultimately unsharable, viewpoint.

If, for example, I experience you as being intelligent or unintelligent, as female or male, as short or tall, or as whatever other defining characteristics I might wish to apply, all such characteristics can be seen to be products of *my* intentional interpretation of you and *not* of objective 'factual' statements relating to aspects of your being.

The example of interpersonal attraction should make this argument obvious. What makes someone attractive to someone else is the result of a unique set of intentionally derived conclusions. The physical features and characteristics that one person focuses upon as being significant determinants of someone else's attractiveness are (thankfully!) open to a great deal of individual variation within which any one conclusion cannot be said to be 'more correct' than the other.

However, the phenomenological argument does not end here; there is another implicit, and perhaps far more significant, issue concerning the status of others.

Upon consideration, it becomes evident that each of us *requires* the existence of others in order that we may be able to define ourselves. Restated phenomenologically, we would say that the 'I' requires the existence of the 'not I' in order for it (the 'I') to have any meaningful phenomenal reality. In other words, I can only know who I am by comparing some assumed aspect of myself to that which I have interpreted as existing in others. I cannot, for instance, state whether I am male or female, short or tall, intelligent or unintelligent, overweight or underweight, attractive or unattractive, without undertaking some kind of explicit or implicit comparison between those aspects as perceived in myself and in others.

Phenomenologists argue that the variables 'I' and 'not I' are inseparable in that each is equally necessary for the definition of the other. A world in which no separation between 'I' and 'not I' existed would be a unified, identity-less world. It would be a world at a straightforward level of conscious experience. Self consciousness, on the other hand, requires the separation of 'I' and 'not-I' as constructed through reflective experience. Several theoreticians (primarily oriented within the psychoanalytic school (Greenberg and Mitchell, 1983; Stern, 1985)) have argued that, at some point in our early development as human beings, some such 'split' in this unified pre-self-conscious world occurs and leads us to the development of an identity (an 'I') through the (defensive) comparisons we make with the newly constructed others (the 'not I's') in our world. This argument, compelling as it is, nevertheless remains open to debate and is difficult to substantiate in any empirical manner. Whether it is ever likely to be proven or disproven is doubtful.

Nevertheless, the phenomenological contention that at *some* point in time (be it anywhere between the moment of fertilization and some time during our infancy) each of us develops notions relating to our concept of 'I' as a result of our interactions with items of our experience which we have categorized as being examples of 'not I', remains unchallenged.

Phenomenological Invariants

The mutual definitional dependency between 'I' and 'not I' is a specific example of a more general phenomenologically-derived fixed and unchanging rule, or invariant, of experience known as the *figure/ground invariant* (Grossman, 1984; Ihde, 1986a, 1986b). I will have much more to say about this invariant in the following chapter, which deals with the perception of objects in more detail. For now, I merely wish to bring the notion of invariants to the reader's attention.

Many of the insights and conclusions arrived at by phenomenologists that I have outlined in this chapter reveal a number of basic invariants to our experience of the world. Intentionality and its noematic and noetic constituents are examples of experiential invariants.

Of the two main branches of phenomenology, it is transcendental phenomenology which places particular emphasis upon the examination and analysis of that which remains once the various biases of reflective experience have been 'transcended', or bracketed, as far as is possible. It employs the phenomenological method in order to arrive at those invariants of experience which (in much the same way as do proven mathematical equations) provide the fixed-rule boundaries which govern all investigations concerned with human experience. Since experiential invariants cannot be removed or bracketed, it is through their discovery that we become aware of the ultimate limitations to our ability to experience 'things in themselves'.

Phenomenological Investigation: A Summary

Phenomenology, like all Western philosophical systems, is concerned with the relationship between the reality which exists outside our minds (objective reality) and the variety of thoughts and ideas each of us may have about reality (subjectivity). How these two variables interact with each other is both the most fundamental and the oldest of philosophical issues.

Phenomenology presents a unique perspective on this problem; it argues that we experience the phenomena of the world, rather than its reality. All phenomena experienced by human beings are constructs, formed as a result of the invariant process known as intentionality. Through the inseparable correlational foci of intentionality – noema and noesis – we interpret the make-up of our phenomenal world and imbue it with unique, constantly-altering (or plastic) significance and meaning. Even the being whom we think we are, the 'I', undergoes this continual revolution.

Each person's experience of the world undoubtedly contains commonly shared variables. As members of the same species, we have the same innately determined biological mechanisms designed to allow specific interactions with the world. One basic shared – or invariant – mechanism is that we interpret the unknown material stimuli of the world as 'things' or objects. Similarly, various sociocultural influences tend to 'set' us into mental frameworks, or schemata, which limit the parameters of our experience. Nevertheless, as a result of the unique experiential variables in each of our lives, no individual experience can be fully shared by any two people. In this sense, each of us experiences a unique and solitary phenomenal reality.

At its most basic level, phenomenology presents itself as a science of experience. Experience, from a phenomenological perspective, includes within it all mental phenomena, such as wishes, memories, percepts, hypotheses, theories as well as their accompanying physical components. By employing a specific approach – the phenomenological method – phenomenologists attempt to arrive at increasingly adequate (though never complete or final) conclusions concerning our experience of the world. Similarly, through this approach, phenomenologists are able to describe and clarify the invariant structures and limitations that are imposed upon our experiences.

Such interests, of course, impinge upon psychological territory. What place is there for a phenomenologically derived approach to psychology? What would be its primary concerns and identifying characteristics?

Phenomenological Psychology

The place to be assigned to psychology in the phenomenological system was a problem that deeply concerned Husserl (1948/1973). However, as much as he was convinced that psychology and phenomenology had a great deal to contribute to each other, Husserl remained a severe critic of contemporary schools of psychology, admitting an inability to follow their literature and revealing a lack of familiarity with the experimental approaches to psychology being initiated in North America and Great Britain.

This conflict led Husserl to revise his views on the contributions and relationships between psychology and phenomenology several times and revealed his uncertainty as to the place of either approach with regard to the other (Misiak and Sexton, 1973: 12–15). Eventually, it became obvious that the only resolution to this problem was for him to develop an alternative, radical psychology. Husserl's lecture notes dating from the years 1925 to 1928 reveal the growing emphasis he placed on this problem. Calling his new system at first 'rational psychology' or 'eidetic psychology', Husserl eventually settled on the term 'phenomenological psychology'.

Husserl argued that the goal of phenomenological psychology was the application of the phenomenological method to psychological enquiry. As such, he theorized that any experimental studies from other psychological approaches could be accommodated to his developing theory. In translating phenomenological philosophy into a psychological system, Husserl 'loosened' some of the aims and strictures which formed the central emphases of his 'transcendental' system.

As is now generally agreed (Dreyfus, 1982; Misiak and Sexton, 1973; Valle and King, 1978), phenomenological psychology is principally concerned with the application of the phenomenological method to issues and problems in psychology so that an individual's conscious experience of the world can be more systematically observed and described. Any conscious act – such as perception, imagery, memory, emotion and so on – falls under the scrutiny of phenomenological investigation. In keeping with the rules of the phenomenological method, the focus of such a psychology is placed on the description (and acceptance) of current experience as a result of 'bracketing' as many assumptions, suppositions, theoretical explanations and habitual psychological biases as possible.

In its broadest sense, phenomenological psychology is distinguished by its central concern with the issue of intentionality-derived experience and its plethora of self/other-(or world-) focused manifestations. It can be contrasted with those psychologies that arise from various dualistically grounded assumptions – whether they be focused upon the dispassionate study of objectively observed behaviour or which place their focus of interest on mentalistic mechanisms of duality such as conscious/unconscious systems of mind.

Unlike other approaches, phenomenological psychology does not seek to invalidate the findings of other schools of thought; indeed, many phenomenologically oriented psychologists avoid formally defining it as a 'school' of psychology in the strict sense of possessing separate canons, hypotheses and interests from the other psychological schools. Most commonly, phenomenological psychology is presented as an *orientation* taken towards the examination of central psychological issues via the use of a specific methodology known as the phenomenological method.

In keeping with the general conclusions arrived at by previous authors (see, for instance, McCall, 1983; Misiak and Sexton, 1973; Valle and King, 1978), I would propose that phenomenological psychology contains a number of specific defining characteristics.

Phenomenological psychology places the analysis of our conscious experience of the world as its primary goal. Further, its focus of interest lies in the exploration of all human experience (from its inter-relational origins to its individualistic mental and behavioural manifestations) without recourse to implicit or explicit reductionist or associationistic assumptions, nor by 'the exclusive restriction of the subject matter of psychology to behavior and its control' (Misiak and Sexton, 1973: 41).

Instead, broadly derived from phenomenological philosophy, phenomenological psychology attempts an unbiased examination of conscious experience, via the application of the phenomenological method, in order to present a description of phenomena which is as free from experientially based, variational biases as is possible. Rather than seek to stand beside, or replace, existing systems in psychology, phenomenological psychology attempts (where possible) to complement them, and, in its application, to clarify or remove such systems' unnecessary and/or divisive biases and assumptions.

Deeply committed to structured enquiry, phenomenological psychology derives much of the data for its conclusions both from controlled studies carried out by researchers allied to the more empirically oriented approaches and from its own meaning-focused approach to research. In addition, as we will see, as it is not uncommon to find many inconsistencies in both the data and conclusions arrived at through experimental research in psychology, phenomenological psychology also often reinterprets such findings in order that it may both clarify the sources of such inconsistencies and provide a more 'bias-free' set of hypotheses and predictions. In doing so, it presents unique perspectives on the standard concerns of psychology and paves the way for more adequate, and unified, models of human beings.

Having laid this basic framework, I can now turn the remainder of this text over to specifically psychological issues. As my first area of investigation, I want to consider the perception of objects.

3

The Perception of Objects

If the doors of perception were cleansed, everything would appear to man as it is, infinite. For man has closed himself up, till he sees all things through narrow chinks of his cavern.

William Blake

Although the study of perception was once considered to be an area of investigation that could rely almost exclusively on neuro-biological data in order to advance and extend its theories, over the last 20 or so years it has become evident that such a view is no longer tenable. Richard Gregory, one of the acknowledged expert theorists and innovators in the scientific study of perception, pinpointed the continuing problematic state of research on object perception in his book *Mind in Science*:

> It is an amazing thought that all our sensations and experience, and so knowledge, come from signals running to the brain down tiny cables; that the brain does not receive light, sound or touch, or tickle, but only patterns in space and time of electrical impulses which must be read – decoded – before they can have reference to the world of objects. (1981: 202)

How the brain translates these electrical impulses into meaningful perceptions, what in-built mechanisms for translation (if any) the brain possesses and what their limitations may be are key issues of perceptual research. As I will seek to show in this chapter, a phenomenological analysis of object perception may clarify many current concerns and help to inform future research.

There have been three major, if conflicting, traditional approaches to the study of perception: *stimulus theory*, which seeks to find a physiological basis to, or correspondence with, every perceptual act; *Gestalt theory*, which emphasizes innate properties and tendencies in perception; and *inference theory*, which applies an empiricist perspective to studies of perception.

The stimulus school argues that 'for each type of perception... there is a unique stimulus or type of stimulus information. Thus there is no need to postulate such mechanisms as unconscious inference or spontaneous neural interaction to explain perception' (Rock, 1984: 12). Instead, the stimulus school seeks to find correlations between subjective sensations and external physical stimuli without having to posit intervening mental variables. In spite of the forceful arguments made in its favour by proponents such as J.J. Gibson (1950), this approach has been found to have limited explanatory value and, as we shall see, many experimental findings in perception pose serious problems for its wholehearted acceptance.

The Gestalt approach has been heavily influenced by philosophical conclusions first presented by Descartes (who argued that the mind possesses an innate knowledge of form, size and other properties of objects) and later extended by Kant (who theorized that the mind imposes its own subjective conceptions of time and space upon sensory data). Gestalt psychologists were among the first scientifically oriented theoreticians to posit the notion of an *organizational* element in perception (Koffka, 1935; Kohler, 1929). They argued that, unlike sensations, which are chaotic and unrelated to one another, perceptions are characteristically organized into wholes or units that are qualitatively different from the sum of their parts. Rather than assume that the organization of perception is somehow learned over time, the Gestalt approach theorized that our perceptions are organized at birth 'on the basis of innately given laws that govern unit formation...' (Rock, 1984: 11). While this theory has been very useful for the understanding of perceptual constancies and illusions, research has shown that it is, at best, only partially correct in its stance in that some amount of perceptual organization can be shown to be the result of learned experience (Rock, 1984).

Modern-day inference theories of perception have been derived directly from the writings of British empiricist philosophers such as Locke and Hume. Locke, for instance, argued that perception was, in essence, reflection; the characteristics of perception were 'out there' in the world, not within us. The mind was seen to be a kind of blank slate which received experiential impressions. As Locke himself wrote:

> Let us suppose the mind to be as we say, white paper void of all characters, without any ideas. How comes it to be furnished? Whence comes it by that vast store which the busy and boundless fancy of man has painted on it with an almost endless variety? Whence has all the materials of reason and knowledge? To this I answer in one word: from experience, in that all our knowledge is founded, and from that it ultimately derives itself. (Locke as quoted in Gregory, 1981: 339)

For many empiricists, perception was to be regarded as the passive acceptance of selective knowledge from the external world. However, as with the other schools, there exists a multitude of experimental evidence on both human and other laboratory animals that demonstrates the error of this viewpoint. Perceptual studies reveal inferential and predictive processes to be central in all acts of perception (Gregory, 1981; Rock, 1984); we do not merely react to sensory signals by rigidly associating them with past experiences; our interpretational processing is far more complex than that.

In keeping with the conclusion arrived at by Irvin Rock (1984) in his still invaluable overview of theories of perception, it can be argued that each school, on its own, contains serious inadequacies. As I will argue in this chapter, the phenomenological approach to perception presents a position which goes some way to reconciling various aspects of the three schools summarized above and, in particular, unifies much of the data arrived at by followers of the Gestalt and inference schools. Before considering phenomenology's views, however, I must first clarify some more basic issues.

Sensation and Perception

There has been some confusion in the past, especially among students not well versed in perceptual theories, in clarifying the distinction between sensation and perception.

Not all of human behaviour takes perception as its starting point. Reflexive responses, for example, have been shown to be direct reactions to external stimuli (Gibson, 1950). Such responses require no mediation, no learning, no conscious awareness. It is only when mediating processes *influence* responses that the issue of perception arises. The differences between sensory and perceptual processing are clearly delineated by Hebb:

> *Sensation* may... be defined as the activity of receptors and the resulting activity of afferent paths up to and including the corresponding cortical sensory area. *Perception* is defined as the activity of mediating processes to which sensation gives rise directly. Sensation is in effect a one stage process. Perception normally requires a sequence of stimulations. (1966: 257)

Inference in Perception

It is now generally accepted that the brain receives sensory information in the form of electrical signals that are carried by nerve fibres conducting at speeds close to that of sound. If, as was originally supposed, perceptions were the result of direct access to, and stimulus selections of, the physical world, then research in object perception would not need to posit the existence of any 'mediating processes'.

That such processes *are* considered is because it has been widely demonstrated that the progress from sensory input of physical stimuli to the perceptual analysis and reaction to such inputs requires a sequence of neuro-psychological 'interpretations'. Any act of perception depends upon a variety of inferences derived from the neural signals. Such inferences may be more or less adequate, but *never* complete, or completely true.

Just one (if important) experiment that demonstrates the inferential aspects of perception was reported by Heron et al. (1956). Heron and his associates instructed participants to peer into a tachistoscope (a now ancient instrument thanks to the electronic revolution which allowed visual material to be presented for very brief periods of time) and to gaze at a point in the centre of the screen. Participants were then informed that letters would appear on the screen for a brief period (1/100th of a second) and that their task was to report as many letters as could be recalled. Different groupings composed of four letters were presented. Some groupings occurred to the left of the fixation point, some to the right, and some were centred on the fixation point. These positional variations were random and participants were given no advance warning as to upcoming positions. Results revealed a consistency in the ordering of reports *regardless of the position of the letter patterns.* The selected order was: top left, top right, bottom left, bottom right – in other words, the order one must adopt in order to read English properly.

Significantly, participants perceived the groupings of letters in this order even though the individual letters were presented instantaneously. Accurate reports were highest for those letters which appeared at the top-left position (about an 80 per cent level of accuracy) and lowest for letters appearing at the bottom right position (about a 40 per cent level of accuracy). In addition, participants' experiential reports pointed out that the top-left letter was perceived as being more vivid than the top-right one and so on down the line.

From a sensory input standpoint, there was no reason why participants should perceive one letter as being more vivid than another, just as there was no reason why the top-left letter should be reported first and most correctly under nearly all circumstances. After all, when the groupings were arranged to the left of the fixation point, the right-hand letters became the nearest to the fixation point. Indeed, followers of the stimulus school would have predicted that, in this circumstance, the right-hand letters would be reported first and most correctly. But the data obtained failed to confirm this prediction; participants still reported the top-left letters first and most accurately.

The authors concluded that the perceptual process itself had imposed an order on the sensory input in a way that was obviously linked to the past experience of reading English. Confirmatory (if reversed) findings were reported by Mishkin and Forgays (1952), who carried out the experiment with participants who were skilled readers of Hebrew, a language properly read from right to left.

Perception, then, can begin to be best understood as a mediating process activity. Although a perceptual act may seem to have occurred instantaneous to sensation, experimental investigation reveals that a complex serial ordering of events takes place. Such research has demonstrated, convincingly, that the same sensory stimulus gives rise to completely distinct perceptions and that different stimuli can give rise to the same perception (Rock, 1984). Such results run counter to those hypotheses that suggest that perception is nothing more than a complex sensation.

As an example of the same sensory stimulus giving rise to variable perceptions, consider the *ambiguous figure* in Figure 1. This figure is often seen either as a bird bath (or vase), or as two faces. No eye movement is required in order to perceive both figures. Simply by fixing one's eye on the

Figure 1   Rubin's vase/faces ambiguous figure

black space between the two noses, or at the centre of the vase, the reader will find that a seemingly spontaneous reversal of images will occur.

The sensory process itself cannot account for this phenomenon. Extensive research in the area of ambiguous figures reveals both the fallibility of perceptual processes and the great degree of error of which such processes are capable. Indeed, studies of ambiguous figures have been among the major means at the disposal of researchers to develop an understanding of the kinds of inference and assumptions on which perception depends and from which we develop various schemata which influence future perceptual experiences (Eysenck, 1984; Neisser, 1967; 1976).

I will return to ambiguous figures later in this chapter. For now, I use them merely as particularly clear examples of the conclusion that variability is a general property of perception. Even relatively superficial consideration of everyday perceptual processing leads us to the same conclusion. In fixing upon any point in our immediate environment we may note how variable our perception is in its shift from one detail to another or from one perceptual range to another. While it may be proper to argue that sensory input sets limits on what may be perceived, nevertheless within these limits perceptual variability can be pronounced.

On the other hand, the various *perceptual constancies* that have been demonstrated and analysed by researchers in the field provide indisputable evidence for our ability to maintain the same perception without regard to any changes in sensory stimuli. The phenomenon of *brightness constancy* provides an important example of a situation where the stimulus varies while the perception remains the same.

Brightness constancy is best understood when we consider that, for example, a white object will still appear to be white regardless of whether it is in bright light or in dark shadow. That it *should* remain white seems, at first, such an obvious expectation that the oddity of this perceptual phenomenon escapes us until we begin to ask ourselves how this event could possibly take place.

The amount of light reflected by an object will determine its colour (as perceived by us). The greater the amount of light reflected, the whiter the object will appear; similarly, black objects are such because of the small amount of light that they reflect. And yet, to refer to an oft-quoted example, although a chunk of coal lying in the sunlight reflects much more light than a nearby strip of white paper lying in deep shadow, our perceptual experience reveals that the coal still looks black, and the paper white.

What influences our perception is our dependence on contrast. The coal may be reflecting a good deal of light, but it reflects much less than do the objects that appear around it. Under experimental conditions where contrasting variables have been controlled, the coal will appear to be bright silver. Equally, a sheet of white paper in a contrast-controlled, dark environment will look dark grey (Rock, 1984). It should be noted that the recognition of the significance of contrast begins to suggest an inter-relational factor that may be of pivotal importance. I will pursue this point later in this chapter.

The social chaos that would ensue if brightness constancy was not a part of our perceptual make-up is worth thinking about: cars left in car parks would not be so immediately identifiable, room colours would be constantly shifting, so many actions whose simplicity or speed depends principally on brightness constancy would need to be relearned. Thankfully, most of us can take brightness constancy (and all of the remaining constancies) for granted. What is important, however, is what perceptual constancies reveal about perceptual processing. The 'hard data' we receive through our senses, and the 'meaning' we construct from them, make plain once again the inferential elements in perception. In addition, there may be a strong perceptual reliance upon inter-relational variables.

Like phenomenologists, the great majority of perceptual psychologists conclude that each of us experiences an *interpreted world* and not one directly accessible via our senses. In addition, when we begin to consider the wide range of variations within an individual's perceptions of the world, the phenomenological argument that each of us experiences a *uniquely* interpreted world becomes (alarmingly) obvious. To paraphrase a conclusion arrived at by the philosopher Immanuel Kant which has since become a perceptual truism: 'we see things not as *they* are, but as *we* are' (Kaufman, 1980a).

If the primary function of sensation is to react to stimuli, the primary function of perception allows us to impose a logic and order on the chaos of the thousands of sensations that bombard our senses. Even though our eyes detect lights and colours, and our ears react to tones of different loudness, pitch and timbre, we do not see or hear the world as a random array of light, dark, and colours, nor do we hear random tones of different loudness and pitch. Instead, perception allows us to make sense out of all these sensations.

Innate Biases in Perception: Wholeness and Organization

Is it the case that organisms may have developed perceptual processes that incorporate species-shared rules? There seems to be no logical or bio-logical objection to this possibility so long as it is understood that the rules still provide for wide degrees of flexibility.

All species may have developed in keeping with the rule we have labelled 'evolution', but the near-infinity of species-determined variables allowable within the confines of this rule demonstrates its vast interpre-tational possibilities. One such likely rule for our species, as I discussed in Chapter 1, is that our perceptual world is composed of objects, *things*. The 'blooming, buzzing, confusion' that William James supposed must be our earliest experience of the world has not been entirely borne out by exper-imental research (Rock, 1984) other than in those instances where an indi-vidual's perceptual processing has been severely damaged or restricted (Miller, 1978; Sacks, 1985; 1995).

It also appears to be the case that, in the act of experiencing the world, our species not only perceives 'things', but also organizes 'things' into forms that make up meaningful wholes (Koffka, 1935). In the course of organizing our perceptions into something meaningful, we have a pow-erful tendency to unify the various elements of our experience. For exam-ple, if we look at a tree, we don't see its various constituents – its trunk, branches, leaves and so on – and from these conclude that we are seeing a tree; we see the whole 'thing'. We unify the constituents into a mean-ingful whole which we label 'a tree'. Similarly, if we drink from a cup of tea, we do not note the wide variety of taste and touch sensations that the action brings forth; we unify them into a meaningful whole which informs us we are 'drinking tea'.

Indeed, so pervasive and taken-for-granted is this construction process that we become aware that it is a process only when it breaks down. Numerous scientific studies of various forms of agnosia (the inability to attach meaning to sensory impressions) provide compelling reminders of just how vital this unifying process is (Luria, 1969; Miller, 1978).

An intriguing, if somewhat extreme, case which demonstrates the fundamentality of this idea is reported by Oliver Sacks in his book *The Man who Mistook his Wife for a Hat* (1985) – an important text which presents a radical challenge to one of the most entrenched axioms of classical neurology.

In the case of Dr P, the man who mistook his wife for a hat, Sacks presents an unforgettable example of a man who has lost his ability to construct objects as 'whole things'. Dr P found himself increasingly inca-pable of seeing faces. His incapacity led him to make false judgements which, in turn, led to his adopting somewhat unusual behaviour. Genially Mr Magoo-like, when in the street he might pat the tops of water hydrants and parking meters, taking these to be the heads of children, or he would amiably address carved knobs on furniture, and be astounded when they did not reply.

Nevertheless, Dr P's musical powers, which were extensive, remained as dazzling as ever. His disability became a significant problem for him only when he developed diabetes. Aware that diabetes could affect his eyes, Dr P consulted an ophthalmologist, who, after conducting a series of tests, concluded that there was nothing the matter with Dr P's eyes, but that there *was* trouble with Dr P's visual cortex. Referred to a neurologist, Dr P went to see Dr Sacks.

In one test, Dr Sacks opened up a copy of the *National Geographic* magazine, and asked Dr P to describe some pictures in it. Dr P's responses were very curious. His eyes darted from one thing to another, picking up tiny features, such as any striking brightness, colour or shape that attracted his attention, but he failed to see the images as 'wholes'. He had no sense whatsoever of landscape or scenery.

Similarly, when presented with a glove, Dr P eventually posited that it was a continuous surface, infolded on itself, which appeared to have five 'out-pouchings' (a word invented by Dr P). Again, when asked whether, now that he'd given a description of the object, he could say what it was, Dr P queried whether it could be a container of some sort.

At the same time, when he was tested on platonic solids, he was perfectly capable of distinguishing cubes, duodecahedrons and more complex abstract shapes. These clearly presented no problems to him. Dr P's perceptual problems were with the *concrete world*, not with abstractions. It was this phenomenon which stood then-current neurological theory on its head.

Significantly, he had lost the emotional constructive element that gives deep meaning to one's world. When asked to describe the story of *Anna Karenina* for example, Dr P could remember incidents without difficulty, and had an undiminished grasp of the plot, but he completely omitted visual characteristics, visual narrative or scenes. He remembered the words of the characters but not their faces, and though, when asked, he could quote, with remarkable and almost verbatim accuracy, the original visual descriptions, these were quite empty for him, and lacked sensorial, imaginal or emotional meaning. It was a case of complete visual and internal agnosia.

The case of Dr P points to the fundamental and innate ability to interpret the world in a meaningful and holistic manner. So obvious is this ability that it becomes apparent only when we are confronted with evidence of its loss. Even so, Dr P's somewhat fanciful attempts to make sense of his world, in spite of his agnosia, further reveal how deep-seated is our need to extract meaning – regardless of how inadequate it may be.

Gestalt psychologists working during the first quarter of the twentieth century were the first to stress the features of wholeness and organization as being primary and irreducible aspects of human perception. These tendencies of perception, they argued, were universal and classifiable into several factors, principally: *similarity* (the tendency to perceive items of the same size, shape or quality as groups or patterns, rather than as dissimilar elements); *proximity* (the tendency to group together perceptually items that are physically close to each other); *continuity* (the tendency to avoid or deny perceptual breaks in the flow of a line, design, or pattern); and *closure* (the tendency to close or complete an incomplete pattern).

There is a substantial amount of experimental evidence in favour of the conclusion that many of our perceptual processes incorporate inherited rules or biases. There is no question here of any necessary allegiance to a Lamarckian-based system which posits the inheritance of particular experiences, or of ancestral knowledge and skills. Rather, what has been inherited is, as with functionally appropriate structures such as hands, likely to be the result of trial and error of natural selection which, over time, has become incorporated into the genetic code.

In addition to the perceptual tendencies summarized earlier, Wolfgang Kohler, one of the major figures in the Gestalt school of psychology, provided experimental evidence that animals learn to respond to *relationships* between stimuli, as well as to specific stimuli in themselves. For example, he taught a chicken to avoid a dark-grey square, and to approach a medium-grey square. When it was presented once again with the same medium-grey square, but this time together with another square of even lighter grey the chicken moved toward the lighter-grey square. It was evident that the chicken had learned to respond not to a specific stimulus, but to the *relationship of one stimulus being lighter than another* (Kohler, 1929).

The organization of sensations is a fundamental perceptual process. In general, there are three basic types of perceptual organization. The first, *form perception*, as I discussed earlier, refers to how stimuli are organized into meaningful shapes and patterns. A second type of perceptual organization deals with *depth and distance perception*. This relates to our ability to organize the world into three dimensions, in spite of the fact that our retina records only two-dimensional images. A pertinent issue, here, is the conundrum that was so central to even the earliest human artists of how to provoke the perception of depth in a two-dimensional drawing or painting. A third aspect of perceptual organization deals with *perceptual constancies*.

Perceptual constancies refer 'to our ability to perceive objects as relatively stable in terms of size, shape, and color despite changes in the sensory information that reaches our eyes' (Crider et al., 1986: 98). It might make most sense to argue that perceptual constancies are innate perceptual biases or illusions.

In his review of perceptual constancies, for example, Rock (1984: 36–43) concludes, on the basis of available experimental evidence, that *shape, spatial* and *lightness constancies* seem to be unlearned, or innate, perceptual processes. Rock also points out that there exists a fair degree of suggestive evidence that *form* perception (or from a phenomenological perspective, the invariant human structural given of experiencing the world from a 'thing-like' perspective) is innate. Direct evidence might be obtained from individuals who were born blind and later gained their sight (Rock, 1984: 140), but such data has not, as yet, been sufficiently researched.

The next-best type of evidence comes from studies with animals who have been deprived of normal vision in some way. Hubel and Wiesel's (1962) work on detector mechanisms appeared to suggest a means to study these possible effects. However, these data are also open to question since subsequent discoveries on detector mechanisms have shown that the animals' earliest environmental experiences influenced the kinds of detector mechanisms developed (Rock, 1984: 141).

Some fairly strong evidence that form perception is present at birth, at least in some animals, comes from Fantz's 1961 studies of the vision of newly hatched chicks, where it was found that three-day-old chicks showed clear preference for pecking at round-shaped objects on an innate basis. Human infants also appear to show preferences for particular shapes and colours (Rock, 1984: 143).

Zimmerman and Torrey obtained evidence that form perception is present in infant monkeys (Rock, 1984: 144). Such findings were supported by research carried out by Sackett (Rock, 1984: 145), who demonstrated that six-week-old infant monkeys reacted differently to pictures of other infant monkeys or to those of monkeys in a threatening stance. These various studies are intriguingly suggestive of similar tendencies in humans.

It is also likely that distance perception is present from the very beginning of human life. Studies of depth perception (such as those reported by Gibson and Walk (1960) on visual cliff phenomena) demonstrate that a capacity for depth perception in humans is likely to be innate. However, as Rock points out, this doesn't mean that learning plays no role in development of depth perception: 'we appear to be born with the axiomatic "assumption" that we are localized within a three-dimensional spatial world. … But we learn to use additional cues and learn to interpret given cues with greater precision after birth' (1984: 88–9).

On the other hand, *size perception* is probably a learned constancy. The issues here are somewhat complicated due to the fact that innate capacities need not be present at birth. The now-famous experiments carried out by T.G.R. Bower (Rock, 1984: 39–40) at Edinburgh University provide evidence that size constancy is present at birth. Unfortunately, experimental variations of Bower's work that have been carried out in Australia don't match his findings (Rock, 1984: 40).

The differing results may be due to *distance* variations that might influence infants' responses. Rock argues that even if Bower's conclusions were replicated, this doesn't rule out the possibility that size constancies may be the result of experience, since these constancies might develop very quickly in the first few weeks of life, as has been demonstrated by Heller's experiments on size constancy in rats (Rock, 1984: 41). Human infants may demonstrate innate size constancies under *dynamic* conditions (that is, when the infant subjects are motionless while attending to moving objects), but they seem to develop size constancy for *static* conditions (when the perceived objects are at rest) as a result of experience.

That there exists a number of important innate factors in human perception seems beyond doubt. However, it would be wrong to conclude, as did the Gestalt school, that the basis for all perceptual processing is innate. Experience, too, plays a major role in human perception.

Interpretative Variables in Perception: the Effects of Previous Experience

So prevalent is perceptual processing in our experience of the world that it becomes justifiable to ask whether any instances of pure sensation exist in human experience. No matter how unusual or novel a stimulus such as an odd noise may be, our common response is immediately to associate it or identify it with something that is already familiar to us. On the basis of the schemata built up from past experience, we infer its meaning and react to the perceived stimulus. If the previous experience recurs frequently, our interpretative schema becomes so fixed that our response becomes one of habit.

It is probable that the vast majority of our daily sensory experiences are perceived in an habitual manner, based on repeated previous experiences. In practice, many of our daily activities consist of responses to familiar cues or symbols. For instance, we smell coffee percolating and visualize breakfast being prepared; the young child hears the garage door open and concludes that mother has just come home and bedtime is near. In reacting to such cues we have, more accurately, trained ourselves to jump to conclusions, from partial yet familiar stimuli from the previous experience.

But does this imply that *only* previous experiences determine our perceptions of objects? Phenomenologists, while not denying the importance of past experience, consider it to be just one of several variables influencing perception and, even then, argue that it is more the currently remembered past, rather than an 'objective' past in itself that is the critical variable.

In general, we may say that whatever object each of us perceives at any given time depends on the nature of the actual stimulus, our previous experience, the background or setting in which the object exists, our feelings of the moment, and our general prejudices, desires, attitudes and goals. Such a conclusion is, of course, entirely in keeping with the phenomenological notion of intentionality.

Interpretative Variables in Perception: the Effects of Selection

When experience affects perception, it does not do so by molding the stimulus to conform to how things were seen in the past. It is not entirely a top-down process. Rather... *something* was first perceived bottom-up, on the basis of certain principles of organization and without recourse to experience. Once the initial perception occurred, if what was seen was similar in some respect to objects seen in the past, those memories were accessed and they played a role in the further processing of the stimulus input. A useful term to characterize effects of this kind is *enrichment*. The perception is enriched by, though not entirely determined by, memories of earlier *perceptual* experience. (Rock, 1984: 132)

One interpretative variable in perception based upon past experience is our *expectation* of what to perceive. This phenomenon is often referred to as the *perceptual set*. One of the earliest and most vivid demonstrations of perceptual set is a picture originally published in *Puck* magazine in 1915 and reproduced in Figure 2. Whether we first perceive a young society woman or an old crone can be influenced by what we see before it. If we see a picture that is clearly a young woman before we see the ambiguous figure, we see the ambiguous figure as a young woman. If the same image is preceded by a picture of an old woman, we first perceive the ambiguous figure to be an old woman. Through our perceptual set, we perceive objects in a particular way on the basis of *previous* information.

Closely related to perceptual set, however, is the *perceptual context*. In the perceptual context, other stimuli that are *present at the same time* affect our perception of a stimulus. An example of this has been provided by Coren, Porac and Ward (1978) which I reproduce in Figure 3.

It is likely that you read the message in that figure as: 'My phone number is area code 604, 876–1569. Please call!' However, if you look more closely you will realize that the word 'is' and the number '15' are identical, as are

Figure 2   Old woman/young woman ambiguous figure (from an original drawing in W.E. Hill, 'My wife and my mother-in-law' *Puck* **16 (11), November 1915)**

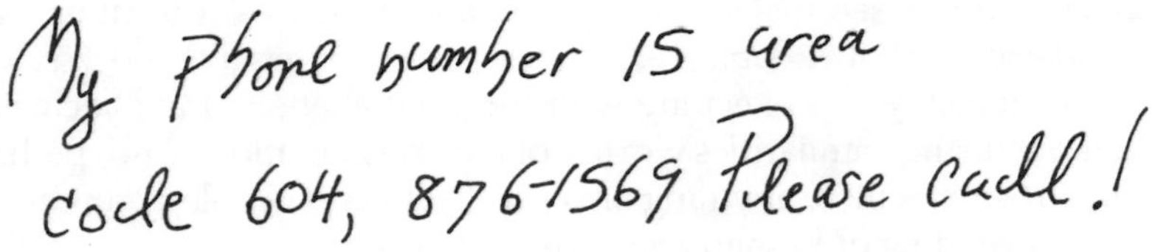

My phone number is area code 604, 876-1569 Please call!

Figure 3 **An example of perceptual context (Stanley Coren, Lawrence M. Ward, James T. Enns 1978. This material is used by permission of John Wiley & Sons, Inc.)**

the letters 'h' in 'phone' and 'b' in 'number', and 'd' in 'code' and 'l' in 'call'. Your different interpretations of these identical stimuli are due to the context or inter-relations within which you read them.

Another factor that can affect our perceptions is our current *motivational state*. One of the first evaluations of the effects of motivation on perception was carried out by R.N. Sanford (1935), who studied the effect of hunger on the perception of ambiguous figures. Sanford presented certain figures to ten children, both before and after they had eaten. In each case he asked the children what the figures looked like. The children responded that the figures looked like food twice as often *before* they had eaten as after.

Both these interpretative factors allow us to construct our perception of objects through our *selective attention* to certain stimuli over others. One of the most famous studies of selective attention is the so-called 'cocktail party phenomenon' (Crider et al., 1986: 153), which many people have experienced. Imagine that, while engaging in social chit-chat at a party, you happen to overhear a much more interesting conversation originating from another part of the room. As you politely try to keep up with your own discussion, you find your attention returning again and again to the other conversation. Unable to follow both conversations at the same time, your attention shifts back and forth between the two until you somehow manage to rid yourself of your partner or, as is more common, your conversation comes to an embarrassing stop.

This phenomenon has been studied under experimentally controlled conditions (Moray, 1959). Typically, participants wear headphones that play a different message into each ear and are told to attend only to the information coming from one of the speakers and, in order to ensure that they are following instructions, to repeat, or shadow, the attended information as they hear it. Through extensions of such studies, it has also been found that the shadowing abilities of participants become seriously impaired when the information coming from the unattended speaker deals with sexually explicit messages or mentions the participants' names (Nielsen and Sarason, 1981).

Phenomenological Theory and Object Perception

On the basis of this, admittedly brief, overview of some of the major concerns and conclusions arrived at by experimentally oriented studies on object perception, we can see that human perception, based as it is upon both innate and experiential variables, is primarily an interpretative process. This conclusion, of course, is in keeping with the phenomenological conclusion. Are there are further similarities worthy of our consideration? And, perhaps more importantly, is there anything of value that phenomenology might add to the understanding of human perceptual processing?

In considering the general issues involved, phenomenologists initially point out that all acts of perception have a particular orientation or *directional focus*. If I say that I am perceiving any particular object, what I imply is that I am directing my attention on to something.

As I stated earlier, it is important to recognize that the number of stimuli to which the brain responds at any moment in time is vast in relation to the selected stimuli that enter our conscious awareness. Neurophysiological studies have pointed out that one of the main functions of the brain is to 'filter', or select, incoming stimuli so that only a fraction of them become the focus of our attention (Bergson, 1907/1911).

We can gain a hint of how pervasive this filtering process actually is by simply recording and playing back a monologue or a conversation. While recording the event, we are only conscious of the sounds that are of significance to us, such as the voice or voices that hold our attention. Other sounds remain unnoticed unless there is something about them – their volume perhaps, or their repetitiveness – that intrudes upon our attention. When we play back the tape, however, we are likely to hear any number of irrelevant sounds of which we had previously remained ignorant. Almost magically, we can now clearly make out a whole cacophony of sounds remarkably similar to those of cars honking in the street, people shouting from other rooms, fingers scratching at skin or clothing, breathing, wheezing – all manner of noises captured and preserved as carefully as those to which we'd attended!

Of course, what has occurred is that the microphone picked up the sounds and taped them on the basis of 'filtering' mechanisms that are far less complex than those employed by our brains. The microphone's filtering is limited to factors relating to sound levels; that is the only 'meaning' that the different sounds have to it. But the human brain filters sounds on the basis of a wide number of variables – of which sound level is but one – in order to select out those variables that require our attention.

Figure/Ground Invariance

In arguing for, and analysing, this act of orientation, phenomenologists soon realized that a second basic invariant of perception could be considered. Through the process of attending to stimuli, we are confronted with the perceptual invariant commonly labelled as the *figure/ground phenomenon*.

In all acts of perception there is a focusing upon the object of our attention (the figure) and the receding away from our awareness of all the momentarily extraneous stimuli (the ground). As with the directionality of our attention, the figure/ground phenomenon is an essential component of our ability to employ selective attention. If, for example, I focus my attention upon my desk, I can only do this if I make the desk my figure, and make everything else in my vision its background. If I don't see the distinction between the two, I can't actually arrive at any object-based perceptual conclusions.

We can only perceive a world full of 'things' *because* we employ a figure/ground distinction. Otherwise, our ability to perceive boundaries and limitations, starting and ending points, even gaps between things, would not be possible. The mind organizes patterns of sensation into particular figure/ground differentiations. This view was initially hypothesized in 1921 by Edgar Rubin (Rock, 1984: 113–15) and is fundamental to all perception. We typically tend to perceive as *figure* those regions that are *surrounded, smaller, symmetrical, and vertical or horizontal.*

The figure/ground relation seems to be an innately based, fundamental invariant in the human perception of objects, as is borne out by studies with individuals who are born congenitally blind and who, subsequent to medical operations, become capable of vision only later in their lives (Rock, 1984). Although the figure/ground relation is initially independent of experience, experience enhances and clarifies this relation so that its variability increases as a result of perceptual learning. Nevertheless, *any* act of orientation *depends upon* a figure/ground perspective.

In most cases, we assume the perspective that has been adopted to remain static. That is, there will be no spontaneous figure/ground shift that occurs independent of a shift in our perceptual set of expectations. The great interest on the part of perceptual psychologists in ambiguous or reversible figures is largely because such images *do* allow for a seemingly spontaneous figure/ground shift. Studies of ambiguous images such as those illustrated earlier in this chapter provide researchers with keys towards an understanding of the shifting process between figure and ground and of the many general features of human perceptual processes.

As a result of varying elements of the figure/ground of ambiguous images, we can construct radically different perceptual images to the ones we may have initially perceived. Indeed, the very *meaning* of the images alters as a result of a shift in our figure/ground perspective.

It is not easy to state what principle of organization is at work here. The most commonly accepted theory of reversal is Kohler's *satiation or fatigue theory* (Kohler, 1929), which argues that each perceptual organization is determined by a separate neural event in the brain. If one ongoing neural event becomes satiated, the brain will resist its further occurrence. When resistance fully blocks that neural event, there is a switch to another neural event. Some evidence supports this theory (Hochberg, 1970) and reversals are said to take place spontaneously after about 15 seconds of viewing.

Rock (1984), however, remains sceptical about this argument. His own work at Rutgers University shows that reversals *don't* occur if participants remain unaware that the figure is ambiguous. Most studies tell participants in advance that there are two images to be found, thereby incorporating an important, if rarely considered, 'demand character' into the experiment, since participants will have been 'set' to assume that a reversal will occur.

However, Rock's analysis demonstrated that when these 'demand character' instructions were not given in a traditional experiment employing the vase/faces figure (see Figure 1), high-school participants failed to report reversals after over a minute, if at all, and that those who did report reversals did so only once or only a few times during the whole of the experimental period (Rock, 1984: 122). When traditional instructions were given at the start of the control study, however, reversals occurred as they were 'supposed to'. As Rock concluded:

> Merely thinking about the alternative not being perceived at any given moment may suffice to lead to perceptual reorganization in which it *is* perceived. In short, the explanation of reversal in the case of informed observers may have more to do with a shifting memory reference than with neural fatigue. (1984: 123)

Ihde's Phenomenological Study of the Hallway/Pyramid Illusion

One particularly illuminating phenomenological argument which focuses on ambiguous images has been presented by Ihde in his book *Experimental Phenomenology* (1986a). I will attempt to summarize some of the intriguing aspects of his analysis.

Consider the following example. Suppose a group of observers are shown (for the first time in each observer's life) the 'hallway/pyramid illusion' as represented in Figure 4. When each member of the group is asked: 'what do you see?', the response is divided. One group, Group H, says that what it sees is a hallway. The other group, Group P, asserts that what it sees is a cut-off pyramid. Let us suppose that both of the two groups remain obstinate in their belief so that each sees *only* either the pyramid or the hallway. Within this initial framework for analysis, we may say that the noema of each group is fixed, or sedimented.

In addition, although the noema perceived by each group is different, each group can argue that its perceptual conclusion is valid since each claim is open to repeated experiential verification. Ihde labels this ability to return again and again to one's previous perception in order to fulfil one's previous claim as *apodicticity*. As such, at this first stage of investigation, each group maintains its sedimented position apodictically.

Now, let us move on to the second level of investigation. Let us say that certain members from each of our first two groups somehow realize that *both* perceptual claims are valid. These individuals have ascended to

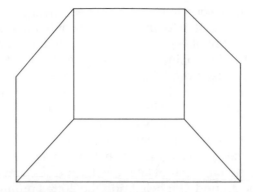

Figure 4   The hallway/pyramid illusion (Reprinted by permission from
Experimental Phenomenology: An Introduction by Don Ihde, The State
University of New York Press. © 1986 State University of New York. All
rights reserved.)

the second level of investigation and can be seen to belong to a new
group – Group A (for ascendance).

Members of Group A are in an ascended position over those in Groups
H and P insofar as their ability to see both claims is more comprehensive
or open and, in this sense, superior to the ability to see only one claim. In
addition, Group A members can still employ apodicticity for each perceptual claim; they do not lose this ability. However, in being able to return
to both claims apodictically, the superiority, or exclusive 'truth', of one
claim over the other begins to fade.

Since Group A's noema now contains two possibilities, phenomenologists argue that Group A's view is more *adequate* than that of the first two
groups. Moreover, Group A's apodicticity is irreversible. No member in
Group A can return to his or her initial, naïve, sedimented claim. In being
able to return to both claims, a viewpoint that argues for the superiority
of one claim over the other cannot be maintained; the apodictic significance is now permanently altered.

In order to arrive at this second level of analysis, members of Group A
have employed (knowingly or not) the phenomenological method in that
they have bracketed their initial biases and assumptions, focused upon
their immediate impressions and considered them descriptively, and
avoided any immediate hierarchical considerations with regard to the
interpreted sensory data.

This suggests that members of Group A have taken an active role in
arriving at their perceptual conclusions. This view runs counter to the
assumptions of many perceptual researchers who argue that the
reversibility of the images is spontaneous and requires no active involvement on the part of the perceiver. As I have already noted, Rock's experiments (1984) lead us to question this claim.

I will return to this disagreement later in the discussion. For the
moment, let us consider what might result were we *deliberately* to pursue

an active role in a consciously determined manner in order to test Husserl's contention that, in doing so, we not only increase the adequacy of our perspective, but also gain a greater richness in our perception. As Ihde demonstrates, in looking at the image actively one can claim that a *third* image emerges. Now, he argues, not only can we perceive both a hallway and a pyramid, but also a headless robot on crutches (Ihde, 1986a).

In order to perceive this third image, return to Figure 4. Now, 'flatten' the image so that it is perceived as being two-dimensional rather than three-dimensional. Imagine that the centre square is the robot's torso, that the upper diagonal lines are its arms, and that the lower diagonal lines are its legs. The two remaining vertical lines are its crutches, and the bottom horizontal line is the ground. If it helps, add the dotted outline of a head and neck just above the centre square until you have the image of a robot on crutches and then lop off its head in order to return to the reversible figure.

This third alternative, once its appearance has been noted, fulfils the same criteria as do our first two claims. The headless robot claim is apodictic and irreversible in that anyone who has surmised the existence of the headless robot can never go back to a previous claim that only the hallway and pyramid exist. In addition, as I argued earlier, this third claim also increases the relative adequacy or openness of our perceptual stance.

'But,' I can imagine some of my readers saying, 'there seems to be something wrong here! Perceptual psychologists using this illusion for their tests have never reported any participants who've claimed to perceive a headless robot when presented with the image. While the first two claims seem natural – even normal – the third is something that appears to be far less so. There is clearly some trickery or irregularity here. Could it be the case that in the first two variations normal perceptual effects are being noted, while the third is the result of something else?'

This reaction is not unusual. Nearly all of my students react in this manner when the headless robot is introduced to them for the first time. And yet, is there any basis for this reaction? *Is* the headless robot image any less valid than the previous two? At first, this would seem to be the case.

'The hallway/pyramid figures are obvious,' my students report. 'We see them spontaneously, whereas the headless robot is unusual, we had to be *taught* to see it.' What my students reveal, however inadvertently, is what phenomenologists refer to as a *sedimented* outlook. Their initial perceptions are contained within their beliefs and (psychological) background. They *know* that this particular ambiguous figure reveals two – and only two – possibilities. Even if they'd never seen this ambiguous figure before, its very label, 'the hallway/pyramid illusion', will limit or sediment their expectations – and their perceptual openness. After all, the image is not referred to as the hallway/pyramid/headless robot illusion.

Let us consider their contention that there is no evidence of anyone ever having perceived the headless robot spontaneously. Well, certainly, someone (perhaps Ihde himself) *must* have seen the headless robot spontaneously at some point in the past in order for it to be part of our current discussion. So, at the very least, its noematic perception is as possible as (if seemingly less likely than) the previous two interpretations of the image.

As such, there are really only two key points of contention. First, the headless-robot image is novel and seems unusual when compared to either the hallway or the pyramid images. Second, in order to see the headless robot, we had to be taught to see it, whereas the hallway/pyramid images seem to appear spontaneously.

Let us turn our attention to the first point. My students' reaction to the headless robot's novelty is not unexpected. The more sedimented your outlook is towards something, the stronger and more negative is your likely reaction to arguments which suggest alternatives or which extend the boundaries of one's perceptual possibilities. How many movements within the arts, how many scientific theories and hypotheses have there been, whose novelty and unusual approaches to the issues at hand provoked similar – if not more aggressive – reactions by both experts and lay-persons? It is easy to forget, for example, that most Impressionist paintings – which are today so admired and considered by many to be superlative representatives of Western art – were originally derided as being puerile rubbish that attacked the eyes and whose claim to artistic value was an insult to the history of Fine Art (Hughes, 1980).

Novelty implies temporality. With the passage of time and, possibly, with the lessening of the anxiety that externally imposed novelties induce, the novelty may become accepted, even highly valued, and itself become part of a new sedimented framework. Novelty which results from one's own insights or active search is more likely to produce exhilaration than anxiety. In this case, the novelty is likely to be more quickly accepted and treated as having significance equal to if not greater than any pre-insight standpoints.

Even in the case of the headless robot, once having been made aware of it, my students, like myself, can no longer see the hallway/pyramid images without also seeing the headless robot. Indeed, now our perception of the robot comes as easily, as spontaneously, as do the two earlier perceptions, such that the tendency to ascribe inherently different origins to its appearance seems not only unnecessary, but wrong.

As to the question why there should be so few (if any) reports of the headless robot by participants in perceptual experiments, it is important, as Ihde reminds us, that in typical psychological experiments on perception,

> Response times are usually limited, and the experiment is deliberately designed to eliminate reflection, critique or extensive observation. This raises the question of what such an experiment reveals. ... It is possible that an instantaneous glance shows us something basic about perception, isolated from so-called higher, or lower level conscious functions. It is equally possible than an instantaneous glance shows only what is most sedimented in the Noetic context, the context within which perception occurs. (1986a: 74)

The open-mindedness which allows us to perceive the headless robot as well as the hallway and pyramid results from the same sequence of investigation that allowed us to step aside from our initially sedimented view.

Phenomenologically, the greater the number of apodictic possibilities, the more adequate is our perception. If so, does that suggest that we haven't exhausted the range of perceptual possibilities inherent in the image? So it seems. Given the impetus, my students have been able to come up with an ever-increasing number of apodictic alternatives; where there was once the possibility of only one act of reversibility, the image has now opened itself to multiple reversals. (A personal 'practical' aspect of this increased adequacy is my ability to draw the hallway/pyramid figure relatively much more accurately now that I can also imagine it as a headless robot.)

Still, the persistent critic might argue, all well and good, but having now demonstrated a virtually limitless range of uncommon possibilities, so what?

Putting aside the increased adequacy that ever increasing open-mindedness allows, it also seems clear that the process seems central to what is usually referred to as 'creativity'. As Koestler so capably demonstrated in his text *The Act of Creation* (1964/1975), it is precisely this ability to see what is not usually seen, to form unusual or novel connections between seemingly disparate events, that is the basis to all acts of creation, be they artistic or scientific.

Sedimented beliefs may provide (illusory) security and a (seeming) order to our world-views, but it is increasingly adequate open-mindedness that allows for personal and cultural advancement.

If we consider the second common criticism, that of spontaneous reversibility *vs* 'learned' reversibility, we can see that the assumptions being made here are open to debate. The basic contention of perceptual researchers is that, with an increased response time, participants report that an ambiguous figure will spontaneously reverse itself. Standard accounts of this phenomenon seem satisfied to imply that the phenomenon is in some way a result of passive staring and, therefore no mental activity is required to experience the perceptual shift. Ihde, on the other hand, argues that it is more likely that, rather than the stimuli undergoing some mysterious spontaneous reversal, what has occurred is that the initial, sedimented noetic context with which we perceive the picture has now, through time, been able to diversify, to spread, 'to open itself' to other possibilities.

The experiments carried out by Rock (1984), as discussed earlier, take on particular importance with regard to this debate. Recall that Rock's data provide strong evidence in favour of the conclusion that reversibility only occurs for many observers if they are aware from the start that the figure is ambiguous or reversible. If they see no potential ambiguity in the image, they can sit passively and stare at it for extended periods of time and experience no reversibility.

Such evidence places serious doubt on the assumption of a 'natural and spontaneous' process of reversibility. Instead, it suggests a conclusion that is much more in keeping with phenomenological prediction. What it suggests is that reversibility occurs because, in some way, we expect it to, and, as a result, we actively engage in a search for the alternative possibility.

In other words, it is likely that reversibility is a 'learned' process. Through some means or other, those of us who can perceive the image reversal have been taught to do so. On consideration, this conclusion seems plausible. On looking at the hallway/pyramid image once more, we realize that it looks neither like a realistic hallway nor a realistic pyramid. Indeed, as with our headless robot, we must have been taught (in some way or other) to perceive the pyramid image, for example, by being asked to imagine a traditional pyramid and then lop its top off. Some strategy must have been employed at some time in our past to 'set' our perception to 'receive' these two images.

The discovery of a multitude of noetic possibilities in the hallway/pyramid illusion reveals the strength of the phenomenological method. Upon realizing that the noema can be viewed as an open range of possibilities that can be actively noetically interpreted, we see that we have been engaged in a special kind of viewing activity – that which searches for what is not immediately apparent. Regardless of its novelty, any constructed image which is apodictic cannot be dismissed – its 'reality' is no more nor less than the 'reality' of any other apodictic image. Moreover, in the acceptance of increasing apodictic possibilities, our previously sedimented interpretation of the stimuli becomes increasingly de-sedimented and therefore more adequate.

In order for any active viewer to be able to carry out this particular kind of object viewing, we have seen that a suspension of sedimented beliefs via the phenomenological method is required. In suspending such beliefs, according to Husserl, we have 'switched' from a (seemingly) 'natural' attitude to the phenomenological attitude.

Phenomenological Implications for Empirical Research on Object Perception

I have shown that phenomenologically derived findings on object perception vary from those arrived at by more standard psychological investigation. Recall that an ambiguous image like the hallway/pyramid illusion initially appears to observers in one of two variations which, typically, is where standard psychological studies, in their naïvety, tend to remain. Should a possible third variation be pointed out, it is usually either dismissed or viewed as being less valid than the expected two. For example, one study that focused on another example of a reversible image (the Necker cube), reported that, although some observers, rather than perceive a three-dimensional image, claimed to perceive a flat, two-dimensional image, this experience was dismissed by researchers as being a result of fatigue (Morris, 1971).

In contrast to this conclusion, phenomenological investigation demonstrates that, once our sedimented outlook is 'opened up', numerous perceptual possibilities become available which can be repeatedly returned to for experiential verification. Far from being insignificant and unworthy of serious analysis, this polymorphous variability provides us with important empirical and epistemological clues to a more adequate understanding of object perception.

We begin to realize, for example, that once it becomes evident that ambiguous images are open to multiple perceptual variations, the *order of appearance* of one image over the others is not dependent upon a perceptual structure but, rather, is the result of sedimented biases derived from a combination of unique experiential and socio-cultural biases. Once polymorphy is accepted, *any* variation derived from the image can be the first to appear. This conclusion is rarely considered in most psychological theories and (not surprisingly) reveals a reluctance on the part of most researchers in this area to give up sedimented assumptions that are linked to any number of theoretical commitments.

Equally, arguments that suggest only a limited number of variations (usually one or two) are *natural* perceptions while the others reveal only the workings of an over-imaginative mind fail to stand up to logical analysis since, with continued verification, the supposedly odd variations lose their oddity and become more 'natural'. Once again, such criticisms reveal the strength of sedimentation rather than (as is often claimed) provide evidence of a key characteristic of object perception. If central perceptual structures are ever to be discovered, it is more likely that they will come from clues derived from the applied variations of the phenomenological method than from the sedimented perspectives of empirical studies.

In applying this method, it becomes clear that the number of perceptual possibilities are not limited to 'natural' tendencies, but to 'the topographical possibilities of the thing itself, as an open noema' (Ihde, 1986a and b: 107).

However, the phenomenological method as applied to object perception not only transforms our experience, it provides us with a clearer understanding of how perceptual experience occurs. Regardless of how vast and complex the field of perceptual possibilities may be, it is apparent that our experience remains structured. Not all conceivable possibilities emerge, only those that 'fit' within the structural noematic boundaries of the image.

So far in our discussion, like most experimental psychologists engaged in perceptual research, we have depended upon unreal, laboratory-based studies to arrive at our conclusions about object perception. But are such conclusions valid for real-life experiences?

Everyday experiences of object perception are, of course, much more complex and imbued with theoretical difficulties. Far from being initially neutral, the objects we perceive in ordinary activities are charged with emotional significance. Yet here too, as in experimental studies, the meanings we give to objects, or the manner in which we perceive them, reveal a sedimentation based upon the mental frameworks of beliefs and habits generated from selective instances of past experience.

For example, in my earliest interactions quite a few years ago with the object that is my computer, I invariably became increasingly anxious when I approached it; while I marvelled at the advances in technology that it represented, I also shuddered with dread at the new and unique fears that my erroneous interactions with it might produce. This stance both added to, and altered, my perception of the object, bound it to my existence in ways far more significant than the receipt of ownership I possessed. Today, my interactions retain a residue of those early stances but as a whole my relationship to my computer has altered significantly. For one thing, having a computer has become increasingly a 'natural' part of my life and to contemplate no longer owning one creates a combination of panic and wistful longing for a return to an earlier, simpler, if hazily remembered, alternative.

Interestingly, experimental work carried out by Langer and Piper (Grant, 1988) confirms some of the points I've made in this discussion. Their research was concerned with demonstrating how familiarity with the functions of a particular object bred 'mindlessness' or an unthinking approach to its categories.

The two experimenters introduced an array of both familiar and unfamiliar objects to students either on an 'unconditional' basis (that is, 'This is a–') or on a 'conditional' basis (that is, 'This *could be* a–'). What they discovered was that students could find novel uses for both familiar and unfamiliar objects only when the objects had been presented 'conditionally'. The effects of 'unconditional' labelling hindered any creative thinking.

As Langer and Piper point out, it is unfortunately this latter ('unconditional') mode of object presentation that typifies the way we are taught to think about objects both by our parents and by our teachers. Whatever its merits, this mode does not 'cultivate the cognitive flexibility needed to deal with a world that is forever in flux' (Grant, 1988: 16).

The lessons of phenomenology force us to examine and perhaps reconsider our sedimented outlooks towards the real, everyday objects we encounter. We realize that our biases to these are far more fixed, far more difficult to apply the phenomenological method to, than when playing with the possibilities of simpler, more neutral, experimental examples. This insight holds the key to the origins of existential phenomenology. As we will see in Chapter 6, this branch of phenomenology takes as a basic invariant the recognition that all acts, even those as simple as my viewing my computer, or labelling objects, bear direct relationship to all viewers' very existence, and implicate them in their experience.

For the moment, it is enough to point out once again how real-life 'breaks' in sedimented perspectives allow us to be creative, to make discoveries both startling and mundane. In playing with the possible reversals of figure/ground, in realigning dominant and recessive features, in exploring new possible connections, we might conceivably produce revolutionary paradigm shifts. For example, in focusing his attention on light rather than upon objects, Monet produced the series of impressionistic masterpieces centred upon Rouen Cathedral. Similarly, in linking together elements as disparate as Charcot's demonstrations of hypnosis, the strange case of Anna O and the behaviour of hysterics, the young Freud formulated his developing theory of the unconscious mind (Gay, 1988).

Commonly, the more radical the shift, the more vociferously antagonistic is the social (and often personal) resistance to it. As in the typical reaction to being shown the figure of the 'headless robot' for the first time, we convince ourselves that alternative perspectives are somehow wrong or less justified than are our sedimented ones. Cultural relativities – and the clashes between cultures that arise out of such relativities – reveal the resistance to change held within sedimented viewpoints. Phenomenology provides us with the basis for lessening the hold of 'fixedness' on our perceptual frameworks. In doing so, it allows us to approach novel and unusual viewpoints and perspectives with more tolerance and flexibility.

The phenomenological investigation of object perception leads us to the conclusion that the objects we perceive, although certainly 'fixed' by a number of innate, species-specific structural invariants of perceptual processing, retain a plethora of interpretational possibilities. In shifting either or both the noematic and noetic variables in our experience, we 'reconstruct' it in any number of ways. Our willingness to do so expands our experience, opens us to the experiences of others and allows us to lessen the power of personal and cultural sedimented perspectives. In doing so, we realize our intimate personal involvement in our perceptions and are given the means to explore and understand more clearly how each of us comes to select hierarchically certain possibilities over others.

Such discoveries have major implications for our notions regarding 'self' and 'others', and for our relation to our world. The naïve and simplistic boundaries we devise in order to distinguish such notions no longer hold true. The assumed separation between experimenter and participant or between the data being analysed and the person who analyses them (separations which are commonly assumed by most empirically oriented psychologists) become questionable.

In recent years, advancements in brain science and research have added substantially to our understanding of perception. The already classic work of Semir Zeki (1993; 2000) on visual perception has demonstrated that our ability to access visual information requires numerous complex processes that put to rest once and for all the assumption of direct access to, and simple reflection of objects 'as they are out there'. Donald Hoffman's (2000) work on 'visual intelligence' confirms and extends Zeki's conclusions in arguing that the brain's ability to create visual perceptions is reliant upon a series of invariant 'rules' that provoke our perceptual experience of motion, depth, colour and shape. Such research, and more, strongly corroborates phenomenological conclusions regarding the perception of objects.

The words to a relatively recent anthem tell us that 'we are the world'; broadly speaking, phenomenology's emphasis on the inter-relational interpretations that give rise to our perceptions of the object world reiterates this statement.

4

The Perception of Others

Who are you?

The Caterpillar to Alice

It is useful to begin this discussion on the phenomenology of the perception of others (or 'person perception' as it is also commonly called) with a brief exercise. Take a blank sheet of paper and write down the numbers one through ten in a column along the left-hand margin of your sheet. Once you have done so, look at the photograph in Figure 5 and, while looking at it, without thinking too hard or too long about your impressions, simply write down the first ten things that come to mind about the person depicted in it.

Now, having completed the task, what overall impression would you say you have formed of this man? Would you say that his lifestyle is conventional or unconventional? Would you expect him to enjoy classical music or rock? What (if any) would you say this man's profession was? Would you think he was congenial? Optimistic? Surly? Cynical? Discontented?

When I asked several of my students to carry out this exercise, the range of responses was quite dramatic. Various students saw the man in the picture as being happy, content, a threat to society, unkempt, free, rebellious, dirty, scary, hairy, poor, relaxed, a liberal, originating from a working-class background, a musician, a busker, a slob, a person who is unattached to material things, an intellectual, cool, cute, attractive, a criminal, a spiritually awakened being and so on.

It is important to remember that, as in the exercise you just carried out, all these impressions were formed simply on the basis of the man's physical appearance and facial expression as represented by the photograph. Nowhere in that photograph are we given the information that would allow us to reach many of the conclusions that I've just outlined. Indeed, we can say with a fair degree of certainty that these various (and often contradictory) impressions were not formed on the basis of what was received directly from the senses. Rather, the impressions were the result of perceptual inferences dependent on a number of variables originating primarily from the observers rather than from the photograph.

What such an exercise very clearly points out is that in the area of person perception we are not content with simply seeing and noting the physical characteristics of others. Instead, we go beyond these obvious

Figure 5   (© Martin Smith)

features and infer their underlying motives, interests, personality traits, psychological state, fears, social status, thoughts and so on.

As with object perception, we attempt to form a unified impression of others. In our attempts to organize our impressions of others into meaningful and congruent wholes, we combine speculation and inference with direct data. More important than whether the impression that emerges is accurate or truthful, is our concern that it be unified and consistent.

Just as my students (and, most likely, you yourself) built up a coherent – if unsubstantiated – impression of the man in the photograph, so is the same process re-enacted in our everyday interactions with others. When we meet someone, we invariably feel the need to find out the kind of person with whom we are dealing; the formation of an organized, congruous impression helps us know what to expect from a person, and how to act in that person's presence.

Person perception involves numerous cues that dictate the impressions each of us forms of others and that, combined together, provide us with a total and consistent picture of the other person. Although the conclusions reached through such cues and our resulting behaviour are clearly of major significance, for the most part people remain largely ignorant of them and their fundamental role in determining social interactions.

A Summary of Psychological Research on the Perception of Others

The various means by which people form their impressions of others are a main focus of interest to researchers who engage in social psychological studies of person perception. Over the years, such studies have singled out a number of variables that play a key role in determining our impressions. Before we can engage in a phenomenologically oriented analysis of person perception, it is important to summarize briefly the major findings obtained by such research.

The Effects of Physical Appearance

As illustrated through the example of the photograph, a major determinant of our impression of others is formed from their *physical appearance*. This, not particularly surprising, conclusion is supported by a number of experimental studies (Middlebrook, 1980: 116–21). The typical procedure of these studies involves the presentation of photographs containing images of individuals whose physical appearance is varied. Participants are then asked to rate the images on the basis of a number of traits such as attractiveness, intelligence and so forth. In this way, numerous aspects of physical appearance have been discovered to be remarkably consistent in their ability to influence our impressions.

For example, whether or not the person in the picture wears glasses leads to variations of judgement with regard to the person's intelligence, reliability and industriousness (Manz and Lueck, 1968). As absurd as it may initially sound, people do seem to view others through the influences of a variety of cultural stereotypes, so that the equation between the wearing of glasses and intelligence, for example, seems to bear some subjective (though, alas, no empirical) validity, at least among Western subjects.

Equally, the clothes that individuals are seen to be wearing can have significant effects on others' impressions of them. In one experimental study, for example, participants reached major conclusions concerning a perceived person's personality, occupation, moral order, educational level and personal interests on the basis of clothing alone (Gibbins, 1969).

A third significant physical characteristic influencing our perception of others is the degree of attractiveness perceived in the individual. Studies such as those conducted by Dion (1972; 1977) demonstrate how we tend to assume the best about those we have deemed to be beautiful and the worst about those whom we have categorized as being unattractive.

Such conclusions are not limited to our perceptions of adults. Even nursery-school children considered to be physically unattractive are less liked by their classmates and are judged by their teachers as being more likely to misbehave (Dion, 1977). A related finding has gone so far as to demonstrate that an unacceptable act carried out by an attractive child is typically judged as being less naughty than the same act carried out by an unattractive child (Dion, 1972). And, similarly, Clifford and Walster (1973) demonstrated that teachers, too, are not impervious to such a variable: even when two children obtained the same grades on their monthly report cards, teachers assumed that the more attractive child was still more intelligent and predicted a greater likelihood of that child's going on to university!

When one adds the strong tendency towards self-fulfilling prophecies, the unfair power of the variable takes on unpleasant implications. One study, for example, reported that attractive defendants in criminal trials were likely to be seen as being less guilty and sentenced more leniently than were unattractive defendants (Sigall and Ostrove, 1975).

Numerous other variables in physical appearance such as the amount of body hair on males (Verinis and Roll, 1970) and women's hair colour (Lawson, 1971) have been shown to influence participants' judgements on variables such as the degree of virility and potency in a male and the level of warmth, intelligence and dependability in women.

Similarly, physical disabilities tend to lead individuals to generalize further deficits in the handicapped such that, for example, people will frequently shout instructions to a blind person (Wright, 1960) and will tend to assume that disabled individuals 'compensate' for their disabilities by striving especially hard in tasks which remain unaffected by their handicap (Ray, 1946).

Body weight is yet another physical variable that has been shown to influence our perception of others. In spite of the fact that obesity is largely dependent on both genetic and biological factors and active learning (regardless as to the worth or correctness of what is taught), obese adolescent girls were judged, in one study, as being undisciplined and self-indulgent (DeJong, 1977).

Obviously, the more information we can glean about someone, the less will be the influence of variables relating to physical appearance. Nevertheless, physical appearance remains a potent factor throughout our perception of others. As studies such as the ones mentioned here easily demonstrate, when we have limited information available, or when we are unduly influenced by first impressions, our biases with regard to physical appearance allow us to arrive at subjective judgements about others which are often as influential as they are illogical.

The Effects of Facial Expressions, Names and Possessions

Along with the many studies carried out on the effects of physical appearance are related ones dealing with *facial expressions*. Such research has yielded some evidence to suggest that certain emotions (namely anger, disgust, surprise, fear and happiness) may well form a 'common language of facial expression' (Middlebrook, 1980: 129).

Ekman and Friesen (1971), for example, showed photographs of Caucasian individuals to New Guinea tribesmen while reading stories with a specific emotional content to them. When asked to pick the photograph that most closely fitted the emotion of the story being narrated, the choices of the tribesmen correlated very closely to the photographs chosen by a control sample of American college students.

Nevertheless, nearly all studies in this area do not fail to acknowledge the great importance of cultural variations (Middlebrook, 1980: 129). So, for example, should you ever find yourself in Tibet, it would be useful for you to be aware that a Tibetan sticking his tongue out in your direction is not out to make trouble (or 'whoopee', come to that), but is merely greeting you as a friend (Ekman, 1975).

As well as facial expressions, social psychologists have noted several other major factors such as one's name (Marcus, 1976) and one's possessions or brand choices (Woodside, 1972) as further significant perceptual determinants.

Surprising as it may sound, there exists experimental evidence that demonstrates that males with culturally judged unusual names are more likely to suffer from neuroses and psychoses than are individuals with more usual-sounding names (Middlebrook, 1980: 122). There is also evidence to suggest that a person's level of popularity (especially so among children) is at least partly dependent on the desirability of one's name (Middlebrook, 1980: 122). And, to take the argument to an extreme, even the brand of beer that you drink can influence how favourably or unfavourably others might look upon you (Woodside, 1972)!

The Effects of Non-Verbal Behaviour and Voice-Related Variables

Studies have also demonstrated the influences of *non-verbal behaviour* upon our perception of others. The frequency of eye contact (Kleinke et al., 1975), a person's gestures (Neirenberg and Calero, 1971), posture (Mehrabian, 1968) and the extent of personal space that another person allows you (Davenport et al., 1971) are all variables which have been found, under experimental conditions, to affect our perception of others. In many every-day circumstances, it is likely that we employ such variables either to supplement or, in some cases, to override verbal statements.

In situations such as when we speak to strangers on telephones or when we hear announcers' voices on radios, we have the tendency to 'flesh them out' and, in so doing, construct all manner of (usually imaginary) physical and psychological characteristics. Experimental research backs up everyday experience. The speaker's *voice* – its pitch (Duncan, 1974), accent (Ryan and Carranza, 1975), depth (Allport and Cantrill, 1934) and loudness (Duncan and Niederehe, 1974) – has been shown to be a major factor affecting our perception of the speaker, regardless of the meaning of the words being spoken.

The Effects of Dispositional and Biasing Factors

Our *explanations* for others' words and deeds provide further variables that may determine our perception of others. For example, Tesser and his associates (Tesser et al., 1968) demonstrated that a friend's helpfulness may be attributed either to his or her generosity and concern for you, or to an attempt to get something he or she wants from you. The resulting emotions – pleasure and gratefulness in the first instance, resentment and hurt in the latter – may lead to quite different subsequent interactions. Equally, the consistency of a person's actions (Kelley and Stahelski, 1970) and the consensus of your perceptions with those of others (Wells and Harvey, 1971) have been shown to be determining features in our perception of others.

A whole gamut of variables dealing with *biasing factors* have also been examined by social psychologists for the purposes of seeing how such factors might influence person perception.

The *fundamental attribution error,* that is our tendency to underestimate the importance of situational factors and to overestimate the perceived person's dispositional factors (Yandell and Insko, 1977), motivational biases arising from stereotypical preconceptions such as gender bias (Deaux and Emswiller, 1974), and actor–observer differences which arise out of our contrasting views of self and others in that we tend to see the behaviour of others as being a reflection of their character while our own is usually judged as being a reflection of our situation (Jones and Nisbett, 1972), all provide further evidence of the often unsuspected variables which help to shape our perceptions.

The Effects of Social Context and Setting

In addition, there exists a great deal of evidence relating our perception of others to the *social context or setting* where our perceptions are constructed.

In one study, a number of therapists (who are generally acknowledged as having substantial expertise in observing and interpreting the personality and behaviour of others) were asked to view a videotaped interview session. Although all saw the same tape, some had been told that they would be watching a job interview while others were told that they were viewing a clinical interview. Their subsequent assessment of the interviewee's mental status differed markedly in that the therapists who thought they had been watching a clinical interview judged the person more harshly than their colleagues who thought they had just watched a job interview (Langer and Abelson, 1974).

Such studies point to the conclusion that if we are set to see a particular behaviour in someone else, we may act in any number of subtle ways to influence the enactment of expected behaviour in order to meet our presuppositions.

A study that demonstrates this conclusion was carried out by Snyder and Swann (1978). When their participants interacted with people whom they expected to be hostile, those people actually began to behave in a hostile manner, whereas those subjects who had expected to interact with friendly people developed a cordial and co-operative relationship with them. This subtle (if influential) enactment of the perceivers' self-fulfilling prophecies points us directly to the perceiver – rather than the perceived – as significant agent for the perception of others.

Effects due to Projectional Variables

More generally, the *halo effect*, that is, the tendency to judge a person as being all good or all bad simply on the basis of one positive or negative characteristic (Thorndike, 1920), has been noted as being a particularly powerful influence on our perceptions precisely because it operates at a level below our consciousness. For example, Nisbett and Wilson (1977) demonstrated that student participants' overall reactions to a professor were likely to have been determined by a single personality factor. A professor's mannerisms were generally liked by those students who saw him as being warm or friendly. However, those same mannerisms were strongly disliked and judged as being irritating by those students who saw the professor as being cold and aloof.

One final biasing factor that has been studied is concerned with *implicit personality theories* that each of us develops and acts upon. Such theories are concerned with linking personality traits together in order to predict the presence of other characteristics.

As Schneider (1973) has shown, the basic function of such theories is to sort out the various strands of data that we have at our disposal about someone and reshape them into a meaningful – though not necessarily accurate – whole. This often stereotypical tendency tends to remain quite stable in helping us to formulate our perceptions of others (Passini and Norman, 1966).

Nevertheless, evidence strongly suggests that our evaluations of others are largely determined by the values and standards we set for ourselves. In one study, for example, those participants who labelled themselves as 'achievement oriented' had a strong tendency to focus on achievement as a major factor in their evaluation of others (Cantor, 1976).

Once again, the implication that much of one's perception of others is confused with the perceiver's own personal biases, aspirations, anxieties and so forth seems beyond argument. Rather than objective analysis, our perceptions of others seem to involve, among other variables, distorting tendencies of projection.

The Effects of Central Traits

Solomon Asch (1952), one of the major theoreticians of modern social psychology, attempted to explain our tendency to create holistic impressions of others on the basis of what he has termed *central traits*. His research demonstrated that such central traits as 'warmth' and 'coldness' exert a greater influence on our overall image than do various other traits.

What factors determine whether a trait is central or not is an unresolved issue in social psychology; whether traits like 'warmth' and 'coldness' causally determine our overall image (Asch, 1952) or whether they simply correlate with numerous other traits remains debatable.

The Effects of First Impressions

Asch also pointed to the influence of *first impressions* on our interpretations of subsequent traits (Asch, 1952). Various researchers (such as Luchins, 1957) have obtained evidence to support the disproportionate importance given to first impressions.

Why first impressions should have such an influence on our perceptions remains unclear. A phenomenologist might suggest that they are certain to be important if one's approach to others does not follow the phenomenological method and, as a result, fails to bracket, describe and horizontalize immediate interpretational assumptions. This would suggest that the power of first impressions is not an invariant, but rather a tendency that may be controlled, at least to some degree. After all, conflicting data demonstrate that not everyone is so easily swayed by first impressions; individual variations may be due to attitudinal approaches that rely wholly or partly, implicitly or explicitly, on the various 'steps' of the phenomenological method.

Effects of Interactive Variables

A major criticism of a great number of studies on person perception is that such studies are unrealistic, insofar as they are essentially *static* (Middlebrook, 1980: 147). Such criticisms point out the obvious: in real life, perceptions are *interactive*; in our inter-relations with someone, we are aware that just as we perceive that person, so, in turn, are we being perceived.

As such, our perceptions may be modified on the basis of the other person's reactions to us, and vice versa. Unfortunately for researchers in the field of person perception, the intrusion of these inter-relational factors in perception greatly complicates the issues and raises key questions on the limitations of 'static' theories and hypotheses. Such factors as image seeking

(Goffman, 1967), reactive mechanisms (Merton, 1957), our assumptions as to how others see us (Hawley, 1971) and reciprocal perspectives (Laing et al., 1966), although likely to have major effects on the perception of others, are difficult to manipulate under the controlled conditions set by experimentally oriented research. As a consequence, in many studies, the issues are simply ignored.

Phenomenology and the Perception of Others

This brief overview of some of the major research findings on person perception demonstrates the great extent of inter-relational involvement in our perception of others. Our perceptions depend on a variety of physical cues, perceiver/perceived-based biases, attitudes, motivations, interactional factors and so forth. Together, they lead us towards a basic, if inescapable, conclusion that, far from being objective, our perceptions of others typically contain variables that more correctly define and describe psychological factors in the makeup of the perceiver rather than point out accurate, universally shared 'facts' about the perceived.

All of these findings, of course, strongly back up many of the central claims of phenomenology.

As with the perception of objects, our perception of others is not the simple response to actual 'stimuli' that activate our sensory awareness of the existence of others. Rather, as research indicates, our perceptions are principally formed from a wide variety of inter-relational factors determined by cultural, individually learned and, quite possibly, biologically derived variables. In essence, our perception of others results from *interpretational variables* that arise from both the noematic and noetic constituents of intentionality.

That there *are* others 'out there' (whatever they might actually be 'in themselves') is not disputed by phenomenologists; what *is* being stressed as requiring serious consideration, however, is what, how much and in what manner each of us *adds* to what is 'out there' in the process of person perception. Clearly, as we have seen, non-phenomenological research has already exposed a large number of these interpretational variables.

Nevertheless, the vast majority of social psychologists, trained in empirically derived systems of research and heavily influenced by either cognitive or behavioural models of the person, are likely to have little, if any, knowledge of phenomenology. In order for them to be tempted to consider the phenomenological implications inherent in their field of study, they must be convinced that such implications will add to and clarify central concerns. What, then, can phenomenological theory add to an understanding of person perception?

Firstly, existing research in the area of person perception demonstrates very clearly that a great deal of interpretation on the part of the perceiver *does* take place. What such studies fail to explain to any significant degree is both how and why such constructions occur at a psychological level.

It is true that there is a fair degree of knowledge at the neurobiological level with regard to the mechanics of perception; but such knowledge tells us little of how each of us arrives at a particular experience of our world. The gap between neurobiology and psychology remains – in spite of the many and varied attempts to reduce psychological knowledge to that of biology.

Whether this gap may ever be closed remains debatable. As such, the current situation demands an approach that neither dismisses nor assumes this possibility. In its neutrality, in its search for the invariants of experience that, obviously, must contain biological features (though not necessarily *only* these), phenomenology represents a highly desirable option which can no longer remain unconsidered. In the area of person perception, phenomenology is able to supply us with a theoretical basis that opens itself to both neurological and psychological investigation and which allows for the derivation and testing of new hypotheses.

For example, research on how each of us constructs our perception of others immediately benefits from the phenomenological observation that the perceiver's selectively remembered past experience of others plays a major role in any current perception of another. Someone might well remind us, physically or behaviourally, of others or another in our past. Our view of this person will be influenced by such memories and, in turn, lead to biases of perception, be they positive or negative, that have direct bearing on our attitude and behaviour towards the person. Phenomenologists such as Maurice Merleau-Ponty (1962; 1964) have pointed to the (likely invariant) tendency we have as human beings to categorize new experiences in terms of their 'fitness' to selectively remembered past ones in order to give the new experience a 'meaning' which rationalizes our current behaviour and attitudes towards it. Such a process clearly allows for learning to take place. Indeed, Piaget's notion of the development of more and more adequate 'schemes' deriving from the inter-linked processes of *accommodation* and *assimilation* contains an abundance of similarities with this phenomenologically derived perspective. Similarly, the hidden (that is, unconscious) variables considered by psychoanalysts to play determining roles in our conscious interactions with, and perceptions of, others are said to be derived from our earliest experiences.

With regard to the perception of others, we should, therefore, expect to find that a person whom we meet (that is, interpret) for the first time obviously undergoes this 'fitting' process. It is likely that the strength of our 'first impressions' (as demonstrated by Asch and others) is at least partly derived from this same process. If so, it becomes more understandable why first impressions are and remain such strong determinants in person perception.

Nevertheless, as was pointed out earlier, the fact that the strength of first impressions *varies* between individuals, or even within the same individual at different points in time, demonstrates that a naïve reliance on the explanatory power of 'past experience' further obfuscates our understanding.

Here again phenomenological theory provides us with potential resolutions that demand further research. For, as well as the effects of selectively remembered past experience, phenomenologists also point to the importance of the perceiver's *current affective state* in the perception of others. The psychological set or state that we are in at any given moment in time may well determine additional biases in our perception or, possibly, even determine which aspects of our past experience will take a major role in the process of construction being initiated.

Our willingness to be more open or closed, more sympathetic or antagonistic to the statements, behaviour and appearance of another is largely dependent upon our current mood. Dominated (and limited) as we may well be by past experience, there remains, nevertheless, a fair degree of flexibility as to the noematic and noetic aspects of the associations being formed and in the subsequent interpretations given to them. This flexibility in perception has not been adequately considered by other psychological systems, that have tended to approach person perception from a fixed standpoint either in terms of the static nature of the designed experiment or in the assumption that our perceptions of others remain (other than under exceptional circumstances) largely unchanged over time.

On the other hand, if, as phenomenological theory argues, our current mood is a significant influence, and our current mood is subject to continuous intentionally derived change, then each time we see the same individual, our perception of that person likewise will alter in some (often – though not necessarily – subtle) ways.

Even when our attitudes seem to remain relatively fixed or much the same as those adopted in the past, it would be naïve to assume that this was due to the strength of past experience alone. Our current mood affects how we interpret the various elements that make up our past experiences.

Even the extreme fixedness of irrational beliefs over rational conclusions has been questioned by any number of therapeutic systems; among the most recent to explore this have been behaviourally derived cognitive approaches such as rational–emotive behaviour therapy (REBT). As REBT has shown (Ellis and Whiteley, 1979), at least some long maintained beliefs *can* be changed and, in that change, contribute to an alteration of attitude, behaviour and perception.

Once again, we see that, in adopting a phenomenological focus, we not only find confirmation of our conclusions from other approaches, we also are able to provide testable hypotheses to clarify the weaknesses and inconsistencies in such research and are better able to provide an adequate understanding of person perception.

If we theorize beliefs, attitudes and/or reactions to stimuli as being essentially fixed, unyielding to change other than by dramatic intervention, we can make no sense of data that point to such changes outside these hypothesized limits. It is only once we have grasped that, even within the limitations imposed by selectively remembered past experience, an interpretational flexibility, based upon current mood, still remains that we can make more sense of the data at our disposal.

But, as well as the influences of past experience and current mood, phenomenologists emphasize the importance of those variables related to our *future expectations* with regard to the person being perceived.

When we consciously perceive someone, that is, when we direct our attention towards someone, we reveal the workings of the selective mechanism that is the primary function of our brain. Out of the unlimited variables that bombard our sensory system and which are interpreted and analysed by our brain, only a minute number are selected to 'filter' into our conscious attention. This selection process is obviously not random; at its most basic, its purpose is to increase the likelihood of survival. But, in agreeing that the mechanism is purposive, then, at some level, each conscious perception must strive towards some desired outcome.

It is on the basis of this purposive element in perception that phenomenologists argue that in our perception of others such variables related to desired outcomes, or future expectations (be they focused upon the other's or our own behavioural possibilities), must be present and must, in some ways, influence our perceptions.

At some level in our perception of another we must, in a sense, each be asking ourselves: 'what do I want from this person?' Though this may seem obvious when our perception is directed towards significant others such as our friends and family, it is important to note that, when duly considered, we can also find its presence in our perceptions of passing strangers. Even if all we may want is to ensure that the perceived person simply doesn't bump into us, we still reveal this expectancy variable.

Let me provide an example that, I believe, contains some commonly shared elements: at times, when I travel to work on the London Underground, I find my attention wandering to my fellow passengers. Upon consideration, I can realize that each perceived person points out a subjectively based 'want'. I may, for instance, want one person's newspaper, another's clothes, hairstyle or physique. I might want that person in a sexual sense, or I might require my perceptions of that person in order to convince myself that my life might actually be far less dreary than I all too often assume it to be, or in order to be (somewhat masochistically) reminded of how dreary my life appears to me to be today. Whether my brain led me to perceive the individual in response to internal conflicts, boredom or the random movements of my eyes is open to argument; what remains, however, is that once the perceptual process has been initiated, the variable of 'future expectation' plays a role in influencing my perception.

As important as the variable may be to understanding person perception, studies of its influence are uncommon in the literature. What studies there are, unfortunately, usually contain the additional weakness of being static in construction. Interactive perception studies, as mentioned earlier, although clearly more 'naturalistic' in their attempts to study person perception, are notoriously difficult to assess and analyse.

That our perception of others can change in the course of a conversation is beyond doubt; what interests researchers is the discovery of those variables that may influence that change. Our future expectations of someone obviously can, and do, undergo change in the course of an interaction. Indeed, our future expectations may be a – or even *the* – central variable determining such changes. To my knowledge, interactive perception research focusing on this variable has never been carried out.

Phenomenologists argue that it is primarily through the above-stated variables of selectively remembered past experience, current mood and attitude, and future expectations that each of us constructs our perception of others. In addition, such variables are always present on all perceptual occasions and, though limited and subject to individual variation as to their openness to re-evaluation and alteration, they are by no means 'fixed' to the point of stasis.

This argument does not deny the influence of sensory data in our constructed perception of others. 'Others', like 'objects', exist independent of our constructions of them. However, like objects, what others *really are in themselves* remains unknown and likely unknowable.

Clearly, our perception of others is so tied up with inter-relational factors (both psychological and biological) that, in a perceptual sense, the very existence of perceived others is dependent upon the self-awareness of the perceiver. This is, of course, a reminder of the invariant feature of perception known as the figure/ground phenomenon. Others (the ground, or 'not I') can only exist in my perception so long as there exists a constructed limit or boundary to my self (the figure 'I'); if I saw everything as being 'self', there would, obviously, be no others, and vice-versa. Far from developing and maintaining a solipsistic position (as can be argued is an outcome of many humanistically derived theories: see Chapter 9 for my discussion of this topic), phenomenologists in general and, as we will see in Chapter 6, existential phenomenologists in particular, stress the definitional inter-relationship of self and other. That self and others can be argued to exist independently of one another in some ultimate pre-reflective sense of course remains a possibility. But our lived, reflective experience of self/otherness is a construction largely determined by intentionality. Indeed, phenomenology does not necessarily presuppose any ultimate pre-reflective separateness of self and other since the evidence of such, either way, is not ever likely to be discerned.

To repeat, our perceptions of others typically reveal more about our self as perceiver than provide us with objective data about the perceived other. No 'other' is, in any non-relational sense, ugly or attractive, full of wrath or love, male or female, sane or insane. All such perceptions are inter-relational and intimately involve the interactions between the perceiver and the perceived. As such, each perceiver constructs a unique 'other'. Equally, as I argued earlier, each perceiver constructs a unique 'other' *in each act of perception*. Within the limitations of human experience, our perception of others undergoes continuous (if at times unaccepted or unnoticed) flux and alteration.

This last point allows an insight of some psychotherapeutic benefit. As a simple example consider a typical problem encountered by marriage guidance counsellors: what was once a stable relationship is now on the brink of self-destruction for no discernible reason other than that one of the partners has expressed a desire to change some aspect of his or her life. Whether it be something of seemingly small significance to the other partner such as a new hobby, a change of dietary habits or the altering of one's political affiliations, or whether it be related to desired changes to the relationship itself, say the wish to form separate friendships or to give expression to unmet sexual desires, the very threat of novelty and change is enough to raise doubts as to the viability of continuing with the relationship.

I have had to deal repeatedly with such situations in my own practice. Typically, the partner at the receiving end of the desired (or instituted) change claims that the other is no longer the same person that he or she has known for years, and why can't he or she go on being the person they used to be? Sadly, incomprehensibly, rather than show willingness to 'reinterpret' one's partner in a mutually satisfactory manner, the more drastic option of jettisoning the relationship by maintaining one's sedimented perception of the other is enacted.

In his book *The Art of Loving*, Erich Fromm (1956) addresses this issue in a highly pertinent fashion. Put simply, his argument is that when most of us supposedly claim to love someone else, we are loving them in a possessive manner, much in the same way as we might love an owned object. In other words, we are not really loving the being who is the other person, we are loving what we want them to *do for us* almost as if they were objects under our definitional and behavioural control. And so, when the other makes a claim at his or her independence by expressing a desire for novelty or change, this is experienced as threatening. It is as if the aggrieved partner is saying: 'I didn't sanction this, this isn't part of what I see for you, how *dare* you act in such a way that raises questions as to my control over you? Rather than question my assumptions – and hence my power – I'll discard you. Better to lose my partner than to lose the sense of self-importance I've taken to be as basis to all my interactions.'

Phenomenologically interpreted, such instances arise when one assumes self to be hierarchically placed above (or below) other, or, to put it another way, when one loves one's self more (or less) than one loves others. Why such a situation should emerge in the first place remains an open question.

Existential phenomenologists, as we shall see, argue that the realization that there is no known 'fixedness' in others, nor even in our perception of others, leads us (both through this conclusion itself and in its even more seemingly dreadful implications) to experience an overwhelming anxiety. Faced with such, we deny our very awareness of our conclusion and seek to reassert our previous position.

It is as if, having seen the image of the headless robot in the hallway/ pyramid figure discussed in Chapter 3, we seek to deny our apodictic re-viewing of it. The resulting stress created in the maintenance of this position has been categorized by other psychological approaches as symptomatic of 'neurotic' or 'psychotic' disturbance. As I'll argue in Chapter 8, phenomenologically influenced theorists such as R.D. Laing approach it from the stance of 'ontological insecurity' – the fragmentation of self.

To summarize the phenomenological argument concerning the perception of others, we can say that, in our everyday interactions with others, though it may appear initially, and naïvely, sensible for us to assume that we all perceive the same characteristics in others, both experimental data and our experiential analyses lead us to question this supposedly sensible conclusion.

Phenomenologists argue that, at heart, we perceive different appearances of reality, different phenomena. True, through any number of cultural, psychological and perhaps even biological variables, we learn to apply, if loosely, similar labels to the objects of our world through our language. So, certainly, there must be some common constructive processes or predispositions in humans that allow us to share, to some extent, the phenomenal world that each of us creates.

Nevertheless, our worlds remain separate and distinct. We can only know each other's worlds through interaction of some variety; even then, however, our knowledge and perception of each other's experience of the world will remain far from complete. Nor can there be any hope of this situation ever changing. For, if, by some near-miraculous event, I could become you, experience the world exactly as you do, even then, in that act, 'I' would no longer retain what personal psychological variables I possess and employ since those variables would not be a part of you! I/you would experience the world from your perspective which could not be fully communicated to anyone else, my self (as was) included.

At best, our communications and interactions with one another allow us to produce approximations of each other's experience of the world. While it is certainly the case, as I have attempted to demonstrate, that we can greatly improve the adequacy of our approximations, nevertheless approximations they remain. Our perception of others, once assumed to be fixed and certain – a shared and shareable perception – can now only be seen as a probability that remains dependent upon the quantity and quality of experiential information that has been communicated at any point in time.

In ending my discussion of the perception of others, I want to provide one final, and disturbing, case example to demonstrate how the development of different mental frameworks may lead to major differences in the perception of others. The incident was originally reported by Dr Oliver Sacks, in his book *The Man who Mistook his Wife for a Hat* (1985).

One day, while on his hospital round, Dr Sacks heard a roar of laughter emanating from the aphasia (speech disorder) ward. Curious, Dr Sacks looked into the ward and saw that the patients were watching a televised speech being given by the then President of the United States, Ronald Reagan. The speech was typical in its practised rhetoric, histrionics and appeals to patriotism and gut-level emotions. The patients loved it so much that they were convulsed with laughter. Jarred by their unexpected reaction, Dr Sacks soon realized that, although their aphasia left them incapable of making sense of the meaning of 'The Great Communicator's' words, the patients were taking their cues from the various tones and cadences of his voice and from the inadvertent gestures he made with his body. But, in their inability to understand his words, the patients (unlike the average listener) were able to avoid being beguiled by them. To them, the speech was grotesque, full of falsehood and incongruities, so patently a joke, that the only sensible reaction was laughter.

Here, in the example of the President's speech, we are confronted with the power of the various distortions, biases and misjudgements characteristic of our perception of others. In freely and unthinkingly allowing such to dominate our decisions and judgements of others, we open ourselves to misunderstanding and the carrying out of behaviour which often leads to unpleasant consequences. Worse than this, however, we also leave ourselves open to manipulation by (among others) those who, in making use of these distortions, might well become our political and religious leaders.

It seems that our perceptions of others are intricately and intimately bound up with our perceptions of ourselves. Perhaps, the better we come to know ourselves over time, the more able we become in 'bracketing' the self, as much as is humanly possible, from our perception of others. It is possible that, as infants, our perceptions of others were subject to fewer distortions and biases if only because both the range of experience and the development of a clear and distinct sense of self in early infancy were limited. However, the attempt on the part of adults to bracket out as much of their 'self' as possible from their perception of others would not necessarily return them to an 'infant's' view of the world. Precisely because adults *have had* a far greater number of experiences, *are* aware of themselves as beings distinct from others, and have *expectations* of others that, though quite possibly originating in their attempts to deal with infantile psychobiological demands, nevertheless are open to whole complexes of (symbolic) expression, suggests that their perception of others would have real and significant differences to that of the infant.

But, how well do we know ourselves? On that somewhat leading question, let us turn to the topic of self-perception.

5

The Perception of Self

The fact is that I think I am a verb instead of a personal pronoun. A verb is anything that signifies to be; to do; to suffer. I signify all three.

General (later President) Ulysses S. Grant

As we have already seen, both the perception of objects and the perception of others are interpretationally derived constructions that, based upon shifting combinations of variables, remain both unique and 'plastic'.

These conclusions lead us to a somewhat disturbing question: if the interpretational process discussed earlier is applicable to our construction of perceived objects and others, will the same process also hold with regard to any perceptions we might hold about our *self*? If so, this would suggest that the commonly held view that the self remains unitary, relatively stable, and 'fixed' over time is an illusion. Phenomenologically speaking, it would be more accurate to argue that we typically engage in a great deal of *selves-perception*.

Psychological Studies of 'the Self'

As a species, we are terribly interested in our selves and our place in the world. On the one hand, we strive for a sense of our own uniqueness, wanting to be singled out for recognition, status and love. On the other hand, however, our sense of distinctiveness may also give rise to feelings of isolation and loneliness. Thus, our self-awareness reveals opposing aspects that are often a major source of conflict as to our inter-relations with others and the world in general.

Just as such concerns have been the likely genesis to our greatest cultural achievements, they have also instilled a commonly assumed, rarely questioned bias dealing with the very nature of 'the self'. In the Western world, it is not unusual for individuals to claim, under certain conditions, that they have changed (or been changed). Alternatively, many people worry that they haven't changed sufficiently or at all, that they are 'still the same old person'.

Implicit in such claims lies the basic assumption that somewhere in each of us there resides a *core self*. The oft-asked question, 'who am I?', becomes sensible to ask only if we assume that there is a basic core self which, for any number of reasons, is inadequately accessible, or is failing to find its full and proper expression.

This assumption has dominated Western psychology and has formed the basis of virtually all studies on 'the self'. Indeed, the study of 'the self' has been a central concern of psychology from its earliest beginnings in philosophy right through to its modern-day scientifically derived approaches (Goffman 1959/1972; Middlebrook, 1980). An important summary of psychological research on 'the self' noted the existence of over 2000 titles on the subject (Gordon and Gergen, 1968). More recent interest on the self in relation to the questions and issues raised with regard to human consciousness has vastly increased the number of titles as well as provoked a return to phenomenologically focused research on this beguiling topic (Midgley, 1999; Strawson, 1997; Zahavi, 1998).

Psychologists interested in the basic nature and characteristics of 'the self' have typically attempted to measure the individual self concept scientifically, and to relate that concept to everyday behaviour. Yet, in spite of the large number of studies, the psychological understanding of 'the self', and its influence on behaviour, remains far from adequate.

In the early days of modern psychology, when its links with philosophy were still relatively strong and clear, 'the self' was an important theoretical concept. William James (1890), the most influential American psychologist of the late nineteenth and early twentieth centuries, extensively and insightfully attempted to analyse the *properties* of 'the self'. James's concern with 'the self' formed part of his broader concern with conscious experience in general, since, for him, it was the basic goal of psychology to both chart and examine its functions.

The psychological literature of the time focused on studies of conscious experience – including, of course, *self-consciousness*. Due to both the behaviourist and the psychoanalytic influences on psychology, such studies became, over time, increasingly less common; when they did begin to reappear around the latter half of this century, they tended to be written by adherents of the humanistic approaches in psychology and focused primarily upon issues of self-related growth, encounter and transcendence. Only relatively recently has the dominant (if still diffuse) trend in psychology – the cognitive approach – turned its attention to the broad issue of consciousness and, with it, began to refocus upon theories of 'the self'.

The 'Components' and 'Characteristics' Approaches to 'the Self'

Some contemporary psychologists still approach 'the self', as William James once did, by examining its *components*. Typically, however, there is little agreement as to what these components are or which can be ranked as the more significant. For instance, components such as the 'social self', the 'psychological self', the 'ideal self' and so forth all have their adherents and detractors (Middlebrook, 1980).

Due to the definitional limitations of the components approach, and to the growing recognition that people tend to think of their 'selves' not in such a segmented fashion but rather as 'a cohesive whole functioning as a single unit, and presenting a single image to those who view it at any given time' (Middlebrook, 1980: 50), several contemporary psychologists have refocused their attention away from the components of the self and on to its various *characteristics*.

Here, too, however, there have been unresolved difficulties both on the level of agreement as to which characteristics are central to a definition of 'the self' and, more importantly, with regard to inconsistencies *within* the defined characteristic. For example, if we consider a commonly held characteristic – that 'the self' is *the originator of its own behaviour* – we are presented with conflicting evidence as to the continuing belief in, or acceptance of, this characteristic in individuals (Middlebrook, 1980).

Under most circumstances people like to 'own' their behaviour; the decisions we make are commonly seen as originating from within. Over and over again, psychological studies have demonstrated that restraints on participants' perceived behavioural freedom are experienced as highly unpleasant and produce reassertive responses (Brehm, 1966). For example, in one task-oriented study based upon the assumption of this characteristic, housewives living in either Miami or Tampa, Florida, were asked to express their preferences for certain laundry products. Just prior to the start of the study, the Miami legislature had passed an anti-pollution ordinance which prohibited the sale or use of detergents which contained phosphates. In Tampa, however, this ordinance didn't exist. As had been predicted by the researchers, the Miami housewives, having had external decisions imposed upon them, expressed more positive attitudes towards the forbidden phosphate detergents than did the Tampa housewives (Mazis, 1975).

The results of such task-oriented studies lead to the conclusion that the greater the external pressure we feel being imposed upon us, the less attractive the forced activity becomes, the greater will be our emotional dissatisfaction, and the poorer will be our performance in the task (Middlebrook, 1980). In general, these studies suggest that when we feel we have lost our right to make our own decisions, or are not originating our behaviour, we seek to regain this 'power'.

On the other hand, several important studies carried out by social psychologists provide results that suggest the opposite conclusion to the one above. Research carried out by Zimbardo et al. (1969; 1972) and Milgram (1974), among others, demonstrates that many people are willing to *deny* their role in decision making, and do not feel themselves to be the originators of their behaviour, *when the results of such decisions are perceived as being unpleasant* or negatively disturbing of their currently-held self perception. Under these circumstances, individuals tend to invent excuses that serve to reinforce their denial of any decision making.

I will consider Milgram's and Zimbardo's studies more fully later in this chapter. For the moment, however, I merely wish to point out that such differing results lead us to question the constancy of this assumed characteristic of 'the self'.

These conflicting results go some way towards clarifying data obtained from studies dealing with the phenomenon known as *learned helplessness* (Seligman, 1974; 1975). Learned helplessness refers to the state certain individuals induce in themselves when feeling trapped in situations that provoke high levels of anxiety. Under such a condition, these individuals become convinced that no relationship exists between their behaviour and the unpleasant circumstance. Learned helplessness has been shown to weaken any motivation to alter or escape from the upsetting situation and to disrupt the individual's learning ability (Seligman, 1974). Under extremely stressful conditions, it can induce severe mental and/or physical illness and even death.

A study carried out in a nursing home in the Midwest of the United States demonstrates this all too well. The participants in the study were 55 women (all aged 65 years and above, with an average age of 82) who had all been recently admitted to the home. Seventeen of these women had applied to enter the home as a result of external family pressure and felt that they'd had no choice in the decision. Nearly all (16) died within ten weeks of their admission. On the other hand, of the 38 women who stated that they felt they had had a choice in the decision, only one had died during the same period. The trained staff in the home couldn't explain the differences on any medical grounds (Ferrare, 1962). However, it could be argued that the observed differences were due to differing stances taken with regard to the assumed characteristic of 'the self' as originator of one's behaviour.

Related research by Rotter (1966) theorized individual differences in beliefs concerning personal control on the basis of 'internal/external' dimensions. Certain individuals believe that there is a strong link between what they do and what happens to them (internals, or 'originators' of behaviour), while others deny or minimize this link and explain events on the basis of fate, luck or chance (externals, or non-originators of behaviour).

In addition, the disparity in our self-awareness brought about by such variables as our shifting focus upon either internal or external variables (Duval and Wicklund, 1972) points to the influence of far more complex mechanisms as determinants of self-awareness.

On the basis of the conflicting data, a phenomenological critic might reinterpret these diverse findings as being indicative not of an assumed 'characteristic' of 'the self' but, rather, as evidence for the powerful influence of held beliefs (which are, themselves, open to constant revision) in self-perception. In other words, a phenomenological perspective leads us, once more, to acknowledge the power of the interpretational element in determining our self-concept.

Rather than clarify or enlighten our understanding of 'the self', the components and characteristics approaches adopted by some social psychologists turn out to be far from precise and reveal various internal inconsistencies within each which deny the possibility of allowing anything other than superficial and broad generalizations.

Interactionist, Social Constructionist and Narrative Approaches to the Self

A far more satisfactory and useful approach to the study of 'the self' has been that employing an *interactionist model*. This view argues that our awareness of our self emerges as a result of a series of interactions that we undertake with others throughout our lives.

Virtually all contemporary theorists in this area agree that our self-percept results primarily from our attempts to compare and contrast ourselves to those who, in some way, matter to us. There have been various interactionist studies carried out which, though differing in their emphasis as to which interactive influences are the most significant, nevertheless have much in common with each other. There is general agreement that parents and family (Coopersmith, 1967; Wylie et al., 1979) and reference groups (Hyman, 1942; Mannheim, 1966) are central influences on the developing self-concept.

Interactionist approaches have been most productive when focusing on the motivations underlying social comparison. While a common motivation variable might be accuracy (Festinger, 1954), research has also indicated that attempts at self-aggrandizement (Jourard, 1964) – especially by those individuals whose self-esteem is particularly low (Jourard, 1964) – are equally important motivational variables.

More radically, social constructionist approaches have taken their lead from George Herbert Mead's assertion that a self only exists in relation to other selves. From this perspective, a self can no longer be claimed to 'reside' within an individual but rather is the resulting construct of that which emerges from the interactions *between* people. Such views challenge numerous deeply held contemporary Western assumptions surrounding the self and, as we will see, develop arguments that are closely allied to phenomenological perspectives (Gergen, 1991; 1999; Shotter and Gergen, 1989).

Likewise, various narrative approaches that have developed from social construction theories have argued that rather than view the self as a unified, coherent, relatively constant entity, it might be more adequate to reconfigure the self as a metaphorical 'glue' that links together moments and aspects of lived experience thereby constructing a (seemingly) coherent narrative. In this narrational sense, the self becomes not only the storyteller but, more significantly, the very means by which the 'storying' of experience becomes possible. Here too, as will be discussed later, narrative theories share many substantive ideas and concerns with phenomenological theories (Freedman and Combs, 1996; White, 1995).

Overall, however, it must be concluded that current studies on 'the self', while undoubtedly of substantial interest, remain somewhat fragmented. Perhaps, a phenomenological reconsideration may provoke more adequate analyses.

The Phenomenological Notion of 'Relationally-Dependent Selves'

If we initiate a phenomenological enquiry, we are immediately led to question a common (if rarely stated) assumption about 'the self'. This is the notion that there is a unitary core self which exists throughout each individual's life, and through which one can study components, characteristics, social determinants and so forth.

To the Western mind, this assumption seems to be so correct and obvious that any alternative argument appears to be distinctly dubious and unworthy of consideration. However, even within the area of social psychology, there are a number of theorists who have suggested that 'the self', far from being unitary, is, more accurately, a series of impermanent *relationally-dependent selves*, each of which appears and interacts with its environment according to the circumstances that have arisen and whose function is to interpret and respond to the current impact provoked by the presence of others or the world in general. (Harré and Secord, 1972; Sorokin, 1947).

Ken Gergen (1971) has summarized a series of experiments that support the argument for 'relationally-dependent selves'. In one such study (Gergen and Wishnov, 1965), participants were first required to rate their self-esteem. One month later, half of the participants were given the task of describing themselves to partners whose manner and appearance characterized them as being highly egotistical, while the remaining half carried out the same task with 'humble' partners who confessed to several of their own weaknesses.

The analysed data showed that the partners' character influenced the participants' self-ratings. Those participants who had been paired with the egotistical partner rated themselves highly favourably while those paired with the humble partner were more self-critical. In order to assess the authenticity of these ratings (especially as there was some disparity with their original self-assessments), the participants were then asked how honest and open they had been during the exchange. Over two-thirds of the participants replied that they had been completely honest, and denied any divergence from their earlier assessments.

In attempting to make sense of these results, the investigators hypothesized that 'habitual and unconscious modes of relation to others' (Middlebrook, 1980: 51) caused the changes in self-esteem assessment.

The evidence seemed to suggest that 'an individual is not a single self, but many selves, which change somewhat as the individual shifts from situation to situation. In short, we become what the situation demands' (Middlebrook, 1980: 51).

On the other hand, a critic of the 'relationally-dependent selves' argument might respond that, more plausibly, the participants had lied, and that they had done so not out of any conscious desire to fool the experimenters, but because they, like most individuals, had a tendency habitually to deceive themselves.

Is it possible that the notions of 'self-deception' and 'relationally-dependent selves might be reconciled?

The Phenomenology of Self-Deception

Psychoanalytic theory points out several mechanisms of distortion, denial and repression in everyday life (Freud, 1960/1980). In addition, there exist numerous experimental studies that provide evidence for unacknowledged self-deception (Middlebrook, 1980). Such studies have tended to confirm the conclusion that, under most circumstances, we base our conclusions not upon accurate self-analysis, but, rather, from the biased standpoint of self-created theories we have developed concerning ourselves and our behaviour.

Phenomenologists would not hesitate to agree with such a conclusion and would point out that this was an inevitable result of the failure to follow the phenomenological method. At the same time, phenomenologists would point out that the findings obtained from self-deception studies are highly reminiscent of those reported in studies of post-hypnotic suggestion.

While hypnotized, a participant may be given a suggestion to carry out an unusual action at the appearance of a specific stimulus (Marcuse, 1959/1971). Then, having been told to forget the instruction upon awakening, the participant emerges from the hypnotic state unaware of the instruction. At the appearance of the stimulus, however, the participant reacts in the instructed manner.

When participants are asked to explain why they acted in the way that they did, they typically attempt to come up with the most reasonable and rational-sounding explanation for what is, quite often, highly irrational behaviour and, more, will stick to this argument until they are made aware of the true reason for their behaviour. For example, having to explain why she suddenly jumped out of her seat shouting 'Fire! Fire!' when no evidence of any fire is available, a post-hypnotic participant is likely to explain that she suddenly felt hot, or that she'd smelled smoke, and that she'd arrived at the wrong – though far from irrational – conclusion that led to her behaviour.

Taken in tandem with self-deception studies, the behaviour of post-hypnotic participants points to the premise that there exists an invariant human tendency to create meaning from our experience. In both cases, participants seek to make sense of their utterances and behaviour. That the chosen 'meanings' were false didn't truly matter; they had still served the basic purpose of relieving the tension and anxiety generated by the lack of explanation (that is, the meaninglessness) of their behaviour.

My own view is that while I accept the phenomena being described, I remain concerned about terms such as 'self deception' since they remain all too suggestive of more traditional theories of self that require the assumption of a core, and real, self that can both be deceived and as well know that it is being (or has been) deceived. Instead, my preference is to consider the dilemma in terms of competing views of, or stances to, self awareness. This stance eliminates the necessity to explain how deceptive processes might occur while at the same time reconstruing the phenomena associated with deception as instances of competing constructs (or 'narratives') of self.

Whatever the stance taken however, it is evident that in everyday life, when we find ourselves carrying out actions (usually of a highly charged or emotional nature) that, under ordinary circumstances, we would have prevented ourselves from carrying out, our typical answer to this behaviour is to say something along the lines of 'I don't know what came over me' or 'I just blanked out'.

These explanations seem to be suggesting that 'the self' who is usually in control *somehow temporarily lost control*, or was denied such, by another force of either internal or external origins. Such explanations once more point to the tendency that we have of thinking in terms of a basic core self, which, under most circumstances, remains in charge of awareness and both categorizes and unifies experience over time. This theory is so basic to our everyday thinking about ourselves that we hesitate to 'bracket' it so that it may be more adequately evaluated.

But what might emerge were we to attempt to do so?

The Phenomenon of 'the Self'

Recall that, through the analysis of intentionality, as discussed in Chapter 2, Husserl was led to the phenomenological conclusion that the 'I' is the *result of*, and not the source or originator of conscious experience. Straightforward experience leads to (limited and biased) reflective experience; it is only while reflecting upon experience that any conscious sense of 'I' (or 'the self') emerges.

This argument leads us to view the 'I' as being an impermanent construct. Each act of intentionally derived reflection, of necessity produces a new and unique interpretation of 'I'. In that act of self-reflective construction, we rely on the relationship between the external stimulus and the perceptually selective variables of past experience, present mood and future expectation.

In other words, at each point of self-reflection, the *self-construct* that emerges is the result of the prior intentional act. But no one intentional act is entirely identical to any other since both the physical and perceptual variables will have altered at each instance of reflective awareness. As such, 'the self' that emerges at any given intentional moment is phenomenologically 'real', singular and relatively coherent insofar as it is able to construct, or 'story', a temporal narrative incorporating (selective) past experience, current mood and future expectations or goals. But, at the same time, this 'self' is also revealed as an impermanent construct that, at best, is a partial expression of an infinity of potential interpretationally constructed selves.

The processes that generate self-structures, remain currently little understood and are subject to widely divergent competing views by cognitive scientists and theorists in consciousness studies (Harré, 1998; Stevens, 1996; Yardley and Honess, 1987). Even so, however it may emerge, the specific form of consciousness that is *self-consciousness* stands out as yet another pivotal invariant in human experience. Phenomenologists certainly do not question this assumption. What they *do* question, however, is the notion that, once developed (at some indeterminate point in our existence), the 'self' remains fairly fixed and permanent over time. Instead, they suggest a competing view that presents 'the self' as a necessary if impermanent construct that emerges through a combination of intentionality and a human invariant structure to consciousness – self consciousness – through which each of us construes a particular form of meaning or narrative out of the plethora of stimuli that make up our current conscious experience.

Is there any suitable evidence to back up the phenomenological stance on the self-construct? I believe that there is. Three broad areas that might be usefully pursued are those of variations in proprioception, psychologically compelling situations and multiple personalities. I will briefly consider each separately.

Variations in Proprioception

Towards the end of the nineteenth century, Sherrington (1941) coined the term 'proprioception' in order to make plain the basic 'sense' through which each of us defines our relationship with our bodies. It is only through proprioception that we feel that our bodies are our property, that they in some way belong to us, and that they are therefore under our operation. This is such an automatic assumption on our part that any assumed alternative to this viewpoint seems inconceivable. And yet there exist numerous examples from medical literature that question this assumption.

In his book *The Body in Question*, which is itself based on a highly successful British television series, Jonathan Miller (1978) reports a number of such cases. Injuries suffered as a result of a stroke can sometimes wipe out recognition of either the whole body or, more commonly, of one side of the body, and thereby impair our sense of proprioception. To quote Dr Miller:

> If one half of the felt image is wiped out or injured, the patient ceases to recognize the affected part of his body. He finds it hard to locate sensations on that side, and although he feels the examiner's touch, he locates it as being on the undamaged side. He also loses his ability to make voluntary movements on the affected side, even if the limb is not actually paralysed. If you throw him a pair of gloves and ask him to put them on, he will glove one hand and leave the other bare, and yet he had use of the left hand in order to glove the right. The fact that he could see the ungloved hand, doesn't seem to help him, and there is no reason why it should: he can no longer reconcile what he sees with what he feels. That ungloved object lying on the left may look like a hand, but, since there is no felt image corresponding to it, why should he claim the unknown object is his?
>
> Naturally he is puzzled by the fact that this orphan limb is attached to him, but the loss of the felt image overwhelms that objection, and he may resort to elaborate fictions in order to explain the anomaly, fictions which are even more pronounced if the limb is also paralysed. He may claim, for example, that the nurses have stuck someone else's arm on while he wasn't looking; he may be outraged by the presence of a foreign limb in his bed, and ask to have it removed; he may insist that it belongs to the doctor, or that prankish medical students have introduced it from the dissecting room; one patient insisted that his twin brother was attached to his back. (1978: 15–17)

A more detailed, and dramatic, account of total proprioceptive loss is given by Oliver Sacks in his book *The Man who Mistook his Wife for a Hat* (1985).

Just prior to an operation to remove the gall bladder, Christina, a 27-year-old woman, was placed on a routine antibiotic. Later that same day, Christina found herself no longer able to stand up unless she fixed her attention upon her feet. She also became incapable of holding anything in her hands (which seemed to take on a life independent of her own), and was unable to sit up without slumping. In sum, she had begun to lose all control over her own body. Her face now expressionless and slack, her jaw fallen open, her words slurred, she reported, with a dispassionate voice, that she felt herself to be disembodied.

Subsequent tests on her parietal lobe functioning revealed that, though undamaged, the lobes were not responding to bodily messages; she'd effectively lost her proprioceptive sense.

Christina now had the task of learning to compensate for this loss through her use of her sense of vision. Over time, Christina learned to recover some of her control over her body; visually monitoring her behaviour, allowing the time for the compensatory mechanism to replace the lost original, her body movements gradually became more natural, and she was discharged.

Even so, Christina continued to feel disembodied; her sense of proprioception never returned. Her ability to control and bring a 'naturalness' and fluidity to her movements remained dependent upon her use of vision. Even when she saw her 'old' self in home-movies, the recognition remained emotionally neutral; she could no longer affectively identify herself with the person she saw.

Just as confounding as the total or partial loss of proprioceptive sensation is the reverse of this phenomenon, best known as the 'phantom limb' effect.

It is a common experience for individuals who have lost a leg or an arm as a result of accident or surgery to report that they still 'feel' sensations in that now missing limb (Miller, 1978). Even the knowledge and acceptance of the fact that the limb has been severed from their body neither reduce their experience of 'phantom pains' nor prevent them from continuing to have a proprioceptive 'image' of the limb. Nor is such an image stationary: 'the phantom limb may seem to move, it may curl its toes, grip things, or feel its phantom nails sticking into its phantom palm' (Miller, 1978: 20). Over time, the phantom limb seems to recede, like a telescope, until only its extremities – the fingers or toes – somewhat disturbingly continue to make their unseen presence felt. This phenomenon suggests that 'it is as if the brain has rehearsed the image of the limb so well that it insists on preserving the impression of something that is no longer there' (Miller, 1978: 21).

The odd effects of proprioceptive impairment lead to the conclusion that the relationship between 'the self' and its physical body is by no means as straightforward as one might have assumed; rather, the relationship reveals the naïvety of most theories of 'the self'. Once again, the phenomenological prediction of an interpretational process in the self-construct open to significant variation seems borne out by research. Our image of our bodily self, therefore, is not a reflection of what is truly there, in a physical sense, but is, more accurately, the reflection of what we *believe* to be there.

This view is further borne out from studies carried out on individuals who suffer from anorexia nervosa. When tested under experimental conditions, it has been found that such individuals, although as capable as non-sufferers of describing and physically outlining the dimensions of a body other than their own, consistently overestimate the dimensions of their own body, perceiving it as being far greater in size than outsiders do (Hilgard et al., 1987). As a result of these distorted perceptions, their avoidance of food for dietary purposes makes sense to the anorexic, if to no one else.

Of related interest are those incidents where our notion of 'self' seems to extend beyond the limits of our bodies. Specific persons or objects can often become so closely associated with one's self that anything which happens or is done to them is experienced as though it were happening to one's self. As an everyday example of this, consider your reaction when your car bumper hits the bumper of another car. Typically, people tighten their teeth, assume a 'scrunched-up' posture, make statements like 'Ouch! I really felt that!', and so on. Regardless of logic, both their behaviour and their experience is indistinguishable from that arising from direct injury to their own bodies (Middlebrook, 1980).

When such data are pieced together and analysed, we are forced to conclude that the boundaries of the self-construct are by no means defined or limited by the material extension of our bodies. We may reject parts of our bodies as not belonging to us, we may persist in 'owning' parts of our bodies that no longer exist, we may take objects or people that are clearly separate from our bodies and convince ourselves that they are inseparable from our sense of self, and we may have highly distorted perceptions of what our bodies look like. All these beliefs are *independent* of the actual physical boundaries and dimensions of our bodies.

The Phenomenology of Psychologically Compelling Situations

It is common for self-theorists to speak of psychologically compelling situations that may drastically alter an individual's self-concept. Sudden unexpected aversive changes in one's ordinary environment, such as finding oneself in the middle of a riot, or caught in an earthquake, or, alternatively, being suddenly imprisoned, kidnapped or brainwashed are said to be so psychologically confusing, or compelling, to certain individuals that they behave in a manner suggestive of a dramatic change in personality. It is as though, in psychologically compelling situations, such people cease being their usual, or normal, selves for a period of time.

One of the most important studies of this effect was carried out by Zimbardo and his associates in 1972 (Middlebrook, 1980: 66–8). In order that he might measure the psychological consequences of both imprisonment and the guardianship of prisoners, Zimbardo set up an experiment in which 21 North American male undergraduate students, previously tested to ensure their 'normality' via clinical interviews and personality questionnaires, were paid to become participants in a simulated prison study.

Half of the participants were randomly designated as prisoners, while the remaining half were assigned as guards. Although there were certain ethical limitations placed on the simulated prison environment constructed by the researchers, it included many significant similarities with real instances of imprisonment:

> The prisoners were unexpectedly picked up at their homes by a city policeman in a squad car, and taken to the station house where they were searched, handcuffed, fingerprinted, and booked, and then taken blindfolded to the simulated jail. There they were stripped, issued a uniform, given a number, and put into a six by nine foot barred cell with two other convicts. There were no windows in the cells, and the prisoners could be continuously observed by the guards. Toilet facilities without showers were in a nearby corridor. After ten o'clock at night, all toilet privileges were denied, so that the prisoners had to use buckets if they wished to relieve themselves. No clocks or any other personal effects were permitted. To perform routine activities such as writing a letter, or smoking a cigarette, the prisoners were required to get permission from the guards...

The setting was highly realistic for the guards, too. They were given billyclubs, whistles, handcuffs and the keys to the cells – all symbols of their power. They were told that they should maintain 'law and order' and that they would be responsible for any difficulties that might develop. Sixteen prison rules, including one that prisoners must address each other by their ID number only, were provided, and the guards were told to enforce these to the letter. (Middlebrook, 1980: 67)

Significant changes in the behaviour, thought processes and emotional reactions of the majority of the participants were noted within a week of the study's initiation. Many of the prisoners had already become 'servile, dehumanized robots who thought only of escape, of their individual survival, and of their mounting hatred of the guards' (Zimbardo et al., 1972: 3). Similarly, the guards began to abuse their power over the prisoners. They invented petty, meaningless and rarely consistent rules which they insisted the prisoners follow.

For instance, they required the prisoners to engage in tedious and useless work (such as moving cartons back and forth or picking thorns out of their blankets) for long periods of the day and night; they made the prisoners sing songs, or laugh, or refrain from smiling, on command; they encouraged the prisoners to curse and vilify each other publicly. Almost any indignity became acceptable as far as the guards were concerned. As one of them subsequently wrote:

I was surprised at myself, I made them call each other names and clean the toilets out with their bare hands. I practically considered the prisoners cattle. I kept thinking 'I have to watch out for them in case they try something'. (Zimbardo et al., 1972: 9)

What had originally been intended as a two-week experiment had to be stopped after only six days: four of the prisoners had had to be released because of strong signs of either severe emotional depression or acute anxiety attacks; one other prisoner was taken out of the study when he developed a psychosomatic rash over his entire body; some of the guards showed increasingly brutal behaviour.

In order to explain these disturbing findings, Zimbardo and his associates argued that the changes were due to the demands of the psychologically compelling situation; the persistent role-enactment temporarily created different beings.

An even more famous series of studies which, although not usually examined from the standpoint of 'psychologically compelling situations', nevertheless bears all the central characteristic features of such studies, was that carried out by Stanley Milgram (1974) on the issue of 'obedience to authority'.

In Milgram's core experiment (he carried out 15 related studies in all, some with procedural modifications) volunteer adult participants answering an advertisement were asked to be 'the teacher' in a task which purported to measure the effects of punishment on learning. The experimenter led each teacher to a large box of electronic equipment containing

30 switches marked in 15 volt intervals going up to a maximum of 450 volts. Above the switches were descriptions of the intensity of the shock each would deliver: these ranged from statements such as SLIGHT SHOCK to those warning DANGER – SEVERE SHOCK.

The teacher was instructed to read a series of questions, one at a time, to another participant (who, unknown to the teacher, was actually working in collusion with Milgram's experimental team) who was designated 'the learner' in the study. Each time the learner gave the wrong answer to the teacher's question, or, alternatively, failed to give any verbal response, he was to be punished with an electric shock by the teacher. The intensity of the shock was increased for any subsequent mistake by moving along the line of switches and continuing until the final (450 volt) shock was to be administered.

The teacher saw the learner being strapped into place and having various electrodes connected to parts of his body. Then he was led to his seat behind the shock switches and the experiment began. The experimenter stood beside the teacher throughout the experimental run; if the teacher refused to continue, he would remind the teacher what his instructions were and tell him to go on with the experiment.

Of the 40 participants tested in the first study, wherein the learner was in another room and remained unseen and unheard (save his pounding on walls as protest at the 300 volt level) 26 participants (65 per cent) obeyed instructions until the completion of the run. In a second experiment where 40 participants heard vocal protests from the learner, 25 (62.5 per cent) obeyed instructions until the completion of the run. In a third study where 40 participants remained in the same room and only a few feet away from the learner who gave obvious verbal and bodily cues to his increasing distress, 16 participants (40 per cent) obeyed instructions until the completion of the run. In a fourth variation, where participants were ordered physically to place the learner's hand on a shock plate, 12 out of 40 participants (30 per cent) obeyed instructions until the completion of the run. In a fifth study, where the learner began to express his concern over his heart condition and made loud, anguished, verbal protests, 26 out of 40 participants (65 per cent) obeyed instructions until the completion of the run. (Interestingly, only 7 of these participants expressed their willingness to sample the shock that they doled out.)

Since all the participants in the above studies had been males, a further study was carried out (following similar conditions to those of the second experiment) with female participants; of the 40 female subjects tested, 26 (65 per cent) obeyed instructions until the completion of the run.

Certain variations, however, provided quite different data. In one study (Experiment 7), the experimenter left the lab and monitored the study by telephone. Under this condition, only 9 out of 40 participants (22.5 per cent) obeyed instructions until completion of the run and participants tended to administer shocks of lower voltage than was required. Under another variation (Experiment 11), when participants were free to choose their own shock level, only 2 out of 40 (5 per cent) went beyond 150 volts. And in yet another (Experiment 12), where the learner insisted on being shocked but the experimenter forbade the action, all 20 of the participants (100 per cent) obeyed the experimenter. In an extension of this last study (Experiment 15), when there were 2 experimenters present and each gave contradictory orders to the participant, all the participants stopped giving shocks at an early point in the study and made attempts to guess which experimenter had the higher authority.

When interviewed after the completion of the experiment, participants often attempted to justify their conduct by blaming the learner for his own stupidity or by arguing that the learner knew the conditions of the study and therefore was responsible for the punishment, or that, commonly, they were simply obeying the experimenter's orders, and that he held ultimate responsibility. Many participants resorted to the explanation that they simply *had to* follow orders.

As Milgram suggests, participants saw their actions as having an external origin. 'Subjects in the experiment frequently said, "If it were up to me, I would not have administered shocks to the learner"' (Milgram, 1974: 146).

There are significant similarities in participant responses in both Zimbardo's and Milgram's studies. In both cases, the psychologically compelling situation seemed dramatic enough to alter the participants' ordinary behaviour such that, explicitly or implicitly, it no longer fitted in with their view of their 'ordinary' selves. But if, as is generally claimed, 'the self' maintains a relatively stable and permanent core of characteristic attitudes and behaviours, how *could* individuals act in the way that they did?

The explanation given by invocation of the term 'psychologically compelling situation' leaves us with more questions than it answers. Why is a situation psychologically compelling to one individual and not to another? Why are there marked variations in the behaviour of different individuals under these conditions? Indeed, in real-life cases, it is often difficult to find anything unusual or compelling in the immediate situation that has triggered off an extreme response such as an uncontrolled killing-spree.

It is the commonly held assumption that there exists a core self that leads us to search for compelling events as explanation for these disturbing results. That these are not easy to find should be enough to have us question the validity of this assumption.

If we approach the issue from the phenomenological standpoint, we realize that since the self-construct is the emergent interpretative structure that construes meaning from the chaos of experience, it is inherently impermanent over time while still appearing to be stable at any given point in time. As such, the behaviour of the Zimbardo or Milgram subjects does not reveal an aberrant self, nor an unusual strand in the core self of the individual, but rather points out the behaviour of a self-construct that emerged dependent upon the inter-relational set of conditions then present – just as the self-construct does all the time – regardless of the relative 'intensity' of the situation.

Studies of psychologically compelling situations reveal obvious changes in the self-construct, not because these changes are unusual, but because they are so extreme. Under everyday conditions, such changes are less discernible. In our obedience to inadequate theories about 'the self', we construct pseudo-explanations that support the theory but obscure what may well be a more adequate conclusion.

The Phenomenology of Multiple Personalities

The multiple personality refers to an avowedly pathological condition in which two or more personalities, or 'selves', appear to manifest themselves in one human being (Crabtree, 1985; Schreiber, 1973).

The 'classic' examples of multiple personalities are all relatively modern. The first such case to be publicly recorded, that of Mary Reynolds, was written in 1816 as a case of an alternating, or dual, personality thought to be related to a state of 'double consciousness' brought about by somnambulism (Crabtree, 1985).

However, it was the success of the book (and subsequent film) *The Three Faces of Eve*, that was based on an article that appeared in the *Journal of Abnormal Psychology* under the title 'A Case of Multiple Personality' written by C.H. Thigpen and H. Cleckley, that introduced most psychiatrists and lay-persons to the idea of the multiple personality (Crabtree, 1985).

Briefly, the subject of the study, Eve White, a shy, inhibited and unhappy woman in her early twenties exhibited dramatic behavioural changes from time to time which led to the establishment of an alternative personality – Eve Black – who dressed in sexy clothes, used 'bad language' frequently, drank liberal quantities of alcohol, and behaved in a generally uninhibited manner. The doctors and nurses who examined her even noted that she appeared to be more attractive, and that her posture and mannerisms changed markedly when she believed herself to be Eve Black.

More surprising, although Eve White had no notion of the existence or thoughts of Eve Black, Eve Black retained knowledge of Eve White's thoughts and problems. Eve White suffered from 'black outs' (pun intended) whereupon she would eventually awaken with no memory of what she'd done or where she'd been but suffering from the effects of Eve Black's 'wild' behaviour. The analysts treating Eve saw their task as that of 'fusing together' the two personalities.

That they fully succeeded (with the assistance of a third personality in Eve – 'Jane') is disputable; in 1977, Eve herself published her account of the story claiming the existence of 22 different personalities which required further extensive therapy before being 'merged' into the far more flexible and self-accepting 'new' Eve (Sizemore and Pittillo, 1977).

More recently, the cases of Sybil (Schreiber, 1973) and of Billy Milligan (Keyes, 1981), among others, have provided even more startling accounts of multiple personalities. In turn, such accounts have led to significant disputes either as to the authenticity of these accounts or as to the adequacy of hypothesis of multiple personality (or, as more recently reformulated, dissociative identity disorder). While it is beyond the scope of this text to detail the debates, nonetheless fascinating accounts of the important issues arising from them have been addressed by Ian Hacking (1995) and Stephen Braude (1991).

Acknowledging the above, if we retain only the 'core characteristics' of the phenomenon in question, we can discern that there exist distinct similarities in all of these reported cases, most notably the core personality's complete lack of awareness of the existence and thoughts of the others; the existence of an 'overseeing' personality who has knowledge (and some control) over all the various personalities; and the 'representational' role of each personality as the embodiment of attitudes or behaviours that are prohibited by the core personality.

The early life of people like Eve, Sybil and Billy appears to be a significant factor in the development of their multiple personalities. Such individuals tend to have been reared in particularly violent, severely punitive settings. The parents of multiple personality individuals often hold strict moral codes which they impose upon their children via forms of severe punishment. It is possible that the genesis of the multiple personality lies in the child's attempts to deal with, satisfy and defend against parental demands and behaviour which bring on intolerable anxiety and guilt (Schreiber, 1973).

Although by no means a common clinical phenomenon, multiple personalities can be seen as somewhat extreme case examples of the phenomenological position with regard to the self-construct. Typically, the patients' memories of their violent and severely punitive early upbringing, as evoked while in therapy, contain the shared insight that a decision of sorts was made with regard to feelings and desires that were both inexplicable and anxiety-provoking. Not being able to come to terms with such, the patients attempted to 'split' them off, dissociate from and deny them as part of their own complex of affects, and thereby severely limit their range of 'allowable' thoughts, feelings and behaviours.

In an attempt to deal with their unacceptable desires and feelings, and yet avoid the guilt each evoked, the extreme strategy of creating alternative personalities via acts of dissociation was put into operation.

Each of these personalities allowed the expression of the forbidden thoughts or desires and, at the same time, eliminated the guilt associated with each since it was now someone else – and more, someone of whom the patients did not even have any awareness – who expressed each of these desires to the point of making them his/her own and, under extreme conditions, becoming their living embodiment.

Phenomenologically, the other personalities reflected the various intentional self-constructs, *but* these emergent constructs did not fit the extremely limited range of owned or 'acceptable self-constructs' allowable to the patients. Faced, nevertheless, with the appearance of disowned or 'unacceptable selves', the patients were led to 'create' alternate dissociated or 'split' personalities that fitted these unallowable self-constructs while at the same time 'owning' those self-constructs that emerged that were deemed acceptable within the restricted range of allowable experiences. All the disowned personalities could be allowed to remain aware of the existence of each other since they were not restricted to the same limited range of allowable thoughts and behaviours permitted of the owned personality.

It was this flexibility that allowed the various therapists to assist their patients in 'merging' various alternative disowned personalities prior to attempting to reunite all of the personalities together. When the patient learned to accept previously forbidden thoughts or desires, and when the range of possibilities in being was allowed to be broadened, the alternative personalities were no longer required. In consciously accepting these multiple selves and allowing them expression without resorting to losses of memory, the patients became 'whole' once more.

As some experts in multiple personality (or dissociated identity disorder) have argued, is the above scenario so wildly different from the experience of those of us who do not claim to suffer from such dissociative disorders? Is it not the case that, when forced to acknowledge thoughts or actions that run counter to our theories about our self, we typically evoke external agencies – be they human, circumstantial, chemical or demonic – that, we claim, *compel* us to act in such ways? And do we not also, if necessary as a defence, claim and create memory lapses that both alleviate feelings of guilt and allow the maintenance of restricted views of our selves? The sole difference between 'ordinary' individuals and 'multiple personality' individuals seems to lie in the *frequency and consistency* of such claims.

From this perspective, one might argue that we are *all* 'multiple personalities' to some degree. We continually construct and reconstruct our selves. As long as the current constructed self falls within the range of possibilities that holds true to who we say or insist we are, we can acknowledge ownership. But when we think or act beyond this owned or sedimented range of possibilities, we construct meaningful – if dissociative – explanations to make sense of the thoughts or behaviours *and* either reduce or remove the anxieties that such thoughts or behaviours generate.

All of the above critiques suggest something similar to a phenomenological stance. Nonetheless, important divergences and alternate perspectives now require clarification.

Phenomenological theory takes the view that it is not the personality that 'splits' or dissociates. Rather, it argues that the dissociation that is experienced reflects the attempt to resolve a deep conflict that has arisen between a fixed or sedimented self-construct and those lived experiences that in some manner challenge the self-construct's values, beliefs, defining characteristics and, in general, its very 'truthfulness'. In other words, phenomenology would suggest that the dissociations that arise as instances of 'split personality' can be better understood as the consequences of dissonance between 'who I claim to be' and 'my lived experience of being'.

For instance, let us say that I believe myself to be someone who always tells the truth. What happens should I find myself telling a lie? Basically, I have two options: I could either alter my belief about my always telling the truth or I can convince myself that in some way or other the lie I have told is not a lie, or that it was not in fact I who lied, but rather that the lie emerged because I had been temporarily overwhelmed or possessed by forces (be they biochemical, situational, psychological or supernatural) that are the responsible agents for the lie.

While the former option of altering my belief about my ability to lie might seem to be the most rational one for me to take, it is of critical importance to recognize that in taking it I am forcing an alteration to *the whole* of my self-construct. I am no longer a person who never lies. I am now a person who often tells the truth but is capable, sometimes, of lying. Regardless of how I might view this shift, it is vital to be aware that it will impact in some way or other upon all facets and aspects of my views and values, beliefs and reflections about 'my self'. Further, it is obvious that I have no way of knowing, or predicting the extent or direction of such an overall impact. As such, the 'rational' step of my re-constructing my self-construct is steeped in uncertainty and risk as to the consequences of taking such a step. Under such circumstances, a more 'irrational', defensive step that seeks to maintain my self-construct as it is might be considered as a preferable option that might avoid or at least minimize the impact of the unknown and the uncertain.

If my deepest values, beliefs and feelings about 'my self' and who I believe 'my self' to be are not deeply shaken by this alteration in my self-construct, I will likely be more willing to take the risky step into uncertainty and alter the currently held self-construct. But if such a shift appears to attack something so fundamental about my beliefs and values concerning 'my self' then it becomes dangerous and disturbing to the maintenance of my current self-construct that I acknowledge or 'own' this alteration. Under such circumstances, my alternative is to 'disown' or dissociate my self-construct from the threatening or disturbing experience in any number of ways such as claiming 'possession' of one sort or another or suppressing the memory of the event. But, although this latter strategy permits the maintenance of the inadequate self-construct variable 'I always tell the truth', its cost is that of a necessary experiential 'split-ness' or dissociation from any event or memories of events that contradict this belief and thereby challenge my self-construct.

This phenomenological reconsideration of 'split personalities' retains much of the felt experience that those who suffer from or study such disorders have attempted to convey. At the same time, it challenges the view that an actual 'split' in personality or, more broadly, in consciousness actually does occur and suggests instead that the experience of splitness or dissociation emerges from the attempt to retain a deeply-held or sedimented stance toward one's self-construct under circumstances when that stance has been challenged by contradictory or dissonant life-events.

The Fiction of the Self

The separate issues of variations in proprioception, psychologically compelling situations and the cases of multiple personalities all suggest that deeply ingrained Western assumptions concerning 'the self' obscure and confuse, rather than clarify, our attempts to understand its origin and basis.

Although the areas discussed earlier do not, by any means, provide direct evidence in favour of the phenomenological position, I hope that my discussion has demonstrated the value of pursuing a phenomenological line of enquiry with these issues. Indeed, such pursuits pave the way for novel and enlightening approaches to both these and many other areas related to 'self' studies, such as that whole complex of 'self-related' phenomena dealing with mind-manipulation, brainwashing, conversion and possession. I hope to focus on these in a future text.

For the moment, however, I hope that my discussion – however limited – has stimulated readers enough to bracket at least temporarily their assumptions about the exclusivity of a singular and permanent self.

Part of the difficulty in presenting this phenomenological view of 'the self' lies in our very language. So sedimented is our stance and conviction as to the existence of a unitary core self that any alternative to this view is difficult to express in words without making such sound like patent nonsense. Nonetheless, many who come across it have found the phenomenological approach to questions of the self to be particularly engaging and challenging. Equally, many practising psychotherapists and counsellors have found it to provide both original and powerful means to address and consider the dilemmas presented to them by their clients. Readers particularly interested in the arguments I have summarized on this topic might wish to refer to my texts *Demystifying Therapy* (Spinelli, 1994) and *The Mirror and The Hammer* (Spinelli, 2001) for more detailed accounts of the self-construct.

Nevertheless, as problematic as our language may be, it is also the case that other cultural systems have developed languages that either minimize or avoid this problem. Many Eastern approaches, most notably some schools of Buddhism, support an alternative perspective that argues for the impermanent and transient nature of 'the self' (Benoit, 1955; Olson, 2000; Watts, 1957/1974). This does not mean, of course, that phenomenology and some branches of Eastern philosophies are one and the same thing; only that they have arrived at certain similar and specific conclusions about aspects of existence. A phenomenological perspective simply seeks to point out that although the self-construct, as a product of intentionality, undergoes continuous alteration throughout life, at each point of self-analysis or 'meaning production' it *appears to us* as having stability and permanence.

In considering the adoption of this phenomenologically derived view of 'the self', we confront a major dilemma. As the British philosopher Hume once wrote: 'I venture to affirm... that [we] are nothing but a bundle or collection of different sensations, succeeding one another with inconceivable rapidity, and in a perpetual flux and movement' (Sacks, 1985: 119). Personal identity, he argued, was a fiction. But how does such a fiction originate? The phenomenological 'I' undergoes constant reconstruction. In our reflections upon straightforward experiences, we require the 'I' to bring order and meaning to our perceived world. The constancy of the 'I' is an illusion; the 'I' that defined who I was when I began to write this book no longer exists, not because *it* has changed, but because the intentional variables that gave rise to that particular construction of 'I' have changed.

As I argued earlier, an invariant of human perception is that process known as the figure/ground phenomenon. This invariance leads us to the recognition that, in order for an individual to assign any descriptive features to the self (the figure), some acknowledgement of, comparison with and distinction from others (the ground) is required.

Stated more phenomenologically, the 'I' defines itself through its interactions with 'not I'. As such, the process of self-construction bears striking similarity to our perception of ambiguous figures. The shifting of the figure/ground in such figures produces quite different perceptual phenomena. Equally, the less sedimented we are in what we allow ourselves to perceive, the greater will be the number of valid interpretations of the ambiguous figure. The more flexible we are with our meaning-constructions, the more adequate will be our knowledge of that figure.

If we conceive of 'the self', or 'I', as yet another example of an ambiguous figure, we become readily aware of the fact that it, too, is open to a multitude of meaningful interpretations. Whatever limits may have been set on its definition are not inherent in the 'I' itself, but in the strictures of sedimentation. The more willing we are to bracket our sedimented beliefs and theories about our selves, the more adequate (if, nevertheless, still incomplete) will be our knowledge of who we are – and can be.

The Problem with Memory

In spite of the potential value to our understanding of 'the self' that the phenomenological approach offers, we are left with one crucial issue which, at first, seems to raise major logical obstacles to the argument. That issue is, of course, the role played by *memory* in the self-construct.

A critic of the phenomenological view I've put forward might well argue that our more established notion of 'the self' is tied up with one's remembered past. If I have no memory of who I have been, I can say very little about who I am today. This would suggest a continuation of self over time rather than, as is being proposed, a continual reinterpretation. If so, then there must indeed be a core self who remembers, who acts upon those memories, and who defines itself through them.

This is a valid criticism, requiring a suitable response. To give this, however, I must make a brief excursion into the problematic area of memory.

The study of memory, one of the earliest and most widely researched subject areas of modern experimental psychology, has remained popular to this day. Most contemporary theorists of memory are convinced that human memory consists of three central systems: sensory, short-term and long-term memory. Such theorists typically adopt an information-processing approach to the topic, and focus their studies on the encoding of information, its storage into the memory system, and its recall or retrieval (Gregory, 1981).

It is generally agreed by such theorists that although the brain's capacity to store memory is very large, the duration of most memories is very brief; it has been suggested, for instance, that memory can start to decay after only one-tenth of a second, and can completely disappear after one second (Crider et al., 1986). The basis for such conclusions rests on the substantial amount of data obtained in a wide variety of experimental studies which typically measure participants' ability to recall stimuli such as rows of letters (Sperling, 1960) or, more classically, nonsense syllables (Ebbinghaus, 1964).

Nevertheless, several critics have pointed out that the data obtained in these studies, though certainly revealing that human memory may encounter problems when it attempts to *recall* information, need not lead us to conclude (as many researchers have) that memory *storage* is temporary. For all we can say, the storage of memory is permanent and faultless, but our ability to get at the stored data may vary.

In addition, it seems evident that the pivotal function of memory is that of influencing our interpretations and subsequent behaviour in ways that increase the likelihood and enhance the felt value of our survival. If our ability to recall stored data corresponds to its meaningfulness or significance (a not surprising correlation) then it is little wonder that typical memory experiments, based as they are on insignificant or meaningless stimuli, should provide us with the kind of data that they do obtain.

Furthermore, as one of the great researchers on memory, Sir Frederick Bartlett (1932/1967), demonstrated, it is both false and misleading to conceive of memory as being primarily concerned with the *exact reproduction* of material. Once again, however, this is exactly what most studies on memory ask participants to achieve. As such, the results obtained by a great number of 'recall' studies may merely be demonstrating, again and again *ad nauseam*, the accuracy of Bartlett's hypothesis.

An alternative to this dominant view of memory storage was suggested by Bergson (1911), among others, in the early part of last century. Bergson argued that memory storage was permanent to the extent that each of us is potentially capable of remembering all that has happened in our life, regardless of its significance. It was Bergson who first pointed out that the primary function of the brain was to *filter* incoming stimuli so as to protect our consciousness from being overwhelmed by a constant barrage of information. Were the brain not capable of this feat, our lives would be both chaotic and unbearable.

The brain seems to order incoming data into hierarchies of importance. Just like the phenomenological notions of straightforward and reflective experience, most data entering the brain remain at levels below our consciousness – we remain unaware of them – with only a small fraction of all the incoming data becoming the focus of our awareness. Even so, there is no necessary reason to suppose, as do many psychological theories of memory, that the remaining data go unstored and 'disappear'. Since storage capacity appears to be no problem, it makes little evolutionary (if not logical) sense to suppose that the data will be 'thrown out'.

Is there, however, any evidence in favour of this alternative position? Certainly, one could point to any number of reported psychoanalytic case studies in which, either by hypnosis or by free associations, patients have recovered long-forgotten or suppressed memories that commonly claimed to originate from the patients' infancy and early childhood. However, it could be argued that these memories have remained meaningfully significant to the patients and, hence, they (as opposed to insignificant memories) have been retained in their storage system even if their retrieval has been difficult.

Is there, then, any evidence to suggest that we are capable of remembering *insignificant* memories on a long-term basis? One important experimental study that strongly suggests this possibility was carried out by Haber (1970). Haber presented a total of 2560 photographic slides showing a range of images to a group of volunteer participants. Each individual slide remained on screen for a total of ten seconds before being replaced by the next. Each session with participants lasted either two or four hours in all. After having seen each of the slides, the participants were shown 280 picture pairs, one of which had been seen in the slide show, the other being similar in nature but previously unseen. The participants were asked to state which of the picture pairs were familiar to them. Nearly all participants gave the correct response nine times out of ten. In addition, the length of the slide demonstration did not produce significantly different scoring results. Even when Haber showed the familiar pictures in reverse, scores declined only slightly.

Haber's study places the adherents of short-term memory theories in a quandary. Not only were the participants able to remember large numbers of briefly observed images over a fairly lengthy period of time, the images contained nothing of any obvious or intended personal significance to them. Even so, they were recognized accurately nearly all of the time.

In order to explain these odd results, Haber himself argued for the possibility that there is a distinction between linguistic memory and pictorial memory. Perhaps so; but recognition is not merely visual, it can be acoustic, olfactory and so on. Indeed, many contemporary researchers on memory find it both useful and valid to distinguish between memories that have been construed from different sensory inputs (Damasio, 2000; Edelman, 1992). Nonetheless, acknowledging the complexity of a system that can distinguish between all these inputs and store them, it seems questionable to me to insist that this same system somehow remains resistant to the storage of so called 'linguistic inputs'. Such an argument seems unnecessarily burdensome and unwieldy and requires that human memory be somehow reduced to a more primitive functional system in relation to other linguistically dependent cognitive processes available to our species. Similarly, we can turn to evidence supplied by research dealing with exceptional instances of the ability to recall rote memories. Studies reported by the great Russian psychologist, A.R. Luria (1969), for instance, provide, at times mind-boggling, evidence of some individuals' almost limitless ability to demonstrate near-perfect recall.

One of Luria's participants, for instance, could recall which suit Luria had worn at the time of his earliest experiments with him – experiments carried out some 30 years in the past! If this subject, like many others who have been studied, had memory-related problems, they had to do not with recall ability, but with forgetting. Anything which remained fixed and unchanged over time, such as word lists and suits, could be forgotten by him only if he carried out rituals of forgetting. Interestingly, however, more ambiguous, changing items, such as people's faces, were difficult for him to recognize or recall.

This suggests that the participant's memory dysfunctions were related to unusual limitations in his ability to understand, or give meaning to, his memories, not to problems of storage. This dysfunction may well be the explanation for the amazing feats of memory of which many so called *idiot savants* are capable. The ability to state accurately, for example, what day 10 February 1849 fell on relies on relatively simple levels of understanding which depend on a form of 'rote' memory rather than symbolic meanings.

Similarly, there is some suggestive evidence that eidetic imagery ('photographic memory') may be a precursor to, or early form of, human memory proper, since evidence for this ability seems strongest with subjects in the first few years of their lives but declines as the subjects become chronologically older (and, by implication, add to their intellectual abilities) (Haber, 1969).

The ordinary individual's problems with rote memory, therefore, may have nothing to do with the process of memory storage but, rather, derive from a growing reliance upon active interpretations of input rather than upon passive recall. Put in this light, the intriguing findings reported by Wilder Penfield in his book *Speech and Brain Mechanisms* (Penfield and Perot, 1963) become extremely significant.

Penfield's participants in the research were, in fact, patients of his who were undergoing brain surgery which, in most cases, was being carried out to eliminate the debilitating attacks, and subsequent suffering, of epilepsy. The patients' temporal lobes were electrically stimulated with micro-electrodes. Conscious throughout the operation, these patients would suddenly report that they had just experienced a multi-sensory 'flashback' of a single event from their past. All insisted that the experience was ineffable in its vividness and fullness of sensory data.

This experiential response seemed to be made up of 'a random reproduction of whatever composed the stream of consciousness during some interval of the patient's past life' (Penfield and Perot, 1963: 687). Yet, powerful as the experience of 'reliving' one's moments of past time was, the incidents recalled were rarely loaded with strong affective meaning or significance.

The localization of these memories was specific. Stimulation of a certain point of the temporal lobe always evoked exactly the same memory in a complete form; but it was only that one memory and no other. In many cases, these memories had a musical component to them: orchestras, choirs, piano pieces, even radio-show theme songs were heard over and over again, and always as exact reproductions of each other.

On the basis of these reports, Penfield concluded that

> the brain retained an almost perfect record of every lifetime's experience, that the total stream of consciousness was preserved in the brain, and, as such, could always be evoked or called forth, whether by the ordinary needs and circumstances of life, or the extraordinary circumstances of an epileptic or electrical stimulation. (Sacks, 1985: 130–1)

A recurrent criticism of Penfield's conclusions (principally by researchers committed to short-term memory, of course) has been that one can never be certain that these memories are true and not made-up fantasies. This is a valid point so long as there are no examples of instances which can be checked for their historical reliability. Close reading of Penfield's text, however, reveals a number of specific instances where patients' memories were anything but fantasy.

In one particularly disturbing example, a 12-year-old female patient saw herself frantically running away from a man who pursued her while carrying a bag full of writhing snakes and whose intentions, she perceived, were clearly murderous. Although this might initially read like a classic example of Freudian symbolism, the experience was found to have been a precise replay of an actual event which had occurred some five years earlier (Sacks, 1985).

Further independent evidence for Penfield's conclusions is recounted by Sacks (1985), who reports the case of a male patient who had previously killed his girlfriend while under the influence of a powerful narcotic (PCP). This man had no conscious memory of this experience, nor could it be evoked through hypnosis or sodium amytal. During his trial, in fact, doctors attested that the loss of memory was not due to repression, but, rather, was the result of organic amnesia brought on by the drug. In addition, although the murder held a number of macabre details, they were left concealed from both the culprit and the general public.

Four years after he began serving his sentence in a psychiatric hospital, the man became the victim of an accident and sustained a severe injury to both his frontal lobes. Emerging from a two-week coma, he began to regain a full memory of his criminal deed, and was able to describe the murder complete with all its suppressed details. His memory now fully recovered, the guilt he experienced became so unbearable that he attempted suicide on two separate occasions.

Put together, all these disparate, if related, findings place doubt on the often attested suggestion that much of our memory is of short-term duration. Instead, they lead us to conclude that *all* experiences from our past can be permanently stored and are, at least theoretically, capable of being remembered, regardless of the level of significance we have assigned them.

Memory and the Phenomenology of Self

Now, what has this somewhat lengthy digression into memory to do with 'the self'? At one obvious level, our awareness of self depends on memory. Through our memories, each of us constructs a history, a narrative, of who we are, or, more accurately, who we claim to be. But here is a phenomenological paradox: the very method by which we come to interpret ourselves (that is, memory) is itself an interpretative construct arrived at through intentionality.

The events in our lives require explanations, meaning, interpretation. But the noematic and noetic variables that allow such are under constant flux. We typically assume that memory is static; but why should it be so? Is it not more likely that at every moment in our experience of the world, our memory is reconstructed, altered and reshaped both by the sensory experiences that we encounter and by our interpretation of them?

Memory provides us with potential responses to a current event by provoking our awareness of meaningful resonance between the current event and previously experienced events. These meaningful resonances can be drawn from a complex 'pool' of stored memories – be they visual, auditory, 'body-based feeling tones', and so forth. At any given point in time, the memory that emerges from such resonance allows us to construct a particular version of, or particular focus on, our past and, in doing so serves to give substance or validity to the currently experienced self-construct. On reflection, the points being made should become quite obvious. If we draw upon incidents in our past that had great emotional significance to us, it may well be that the emotions engendered current to the time when the incident took place and the emotions produced as we currently remember the events may be radically different. In similar fashion it could be argued that the self-construct in each instance might be highly dissimilar even if in each case we experience that being described and defined through it as 'my self'.

For example, imagine that at the age of 15 you were jilted by your then boyfriend or girlfriend. You took that incident as being the most cata-strophic event in your life, and experienced any number of emotions linked to that event. You may have felt a despair the likes of which you have never felt again. If you reconsider that incident now, at a later age, years gone by, the memory of that incident may remain vivid, but the emotional experience of it that you have now is unlikely to have remained the same. Now, it might be a humorous anecdote that you tell your children as a way of preparing them for the traumas of life; it may fill you with a great relief that that particular relationship did not continue; it may bring about a realization of the naïvety of your thoughts at that time.

In each case, the manner by which that memory is understood and interpreted, the significance it now has to you, the status and meaning that you bestow upon it, has emerged via the resonance or modulation between your currently lived experience and the stored memory variables of previously lived experience. In each case, this resonance serves to pro-voke some sort of action or response on your part, even if the emotion-focused actions that it provoked then are radically different to those that it provokes now.

But note: this same resonance also permits us to define and redefine our self-construct. Whereas at the age of 15 you might have placed that inci-dent as the centrepiece of your narrative story, now, at a later age, it may simply be a brief footnote or addendum; it may even be considered to be so unimportant as not even to assume any great significance, or, alterna-tively, it may have taken on such pain-filled significance that it can only be evoked in some less threatening guise. Whatever the case, a process of interpretation, constant and continuous, leading to the construction of a (seemingly) constant, coherent, valid and recognized 'self' has taken place and will continue to take place.

Not long after I completed my first draft of this section sometime in 1988, I happened to have a conversation with my mother with regard to a diary she had kept over most of her life. Without any prompting on my part (a wonderful example of serendipity, in fact), she announced sud-denly that when she had occasion to reread her passages, she was struck by the uncanny sensation that the person who wrote those passages and the person who read them must be two very different people. To be sure, she acknowledged the 'raw data' – the noematic components – contained in those passages; she remembered, through them, *what* happened. But the noetic constituent, the manner by which she reviewed them, was, often, so very different to the noetic perspective supplied by her 'earlier' self (the writer of those passages) that it might almost (if it did not seem so absurd) convince her that different people (that is, different self-constructs) had inhabited the same body, and called themselves by the same name, at different points in time.

This conclusion, though simply stated, expresses much of the essence of the phenomenological stance on 'the self' insofar as it is concerned with the felt sense of continuity over time and experience through memory. That such a conclusion might seem to be fanciful or even absurd to us at first is, I believe, largely the result of cultural sedimentation. We remain unaware of the reconstitutive process during the daily run of events, and so conclude that no such process exists. It is only when we distance ourselves from this assumption, when we examine the changes in our lives, in our sense of our selves, in a more detached, more neutral manner, that we become aware of the fluidity of self consciousness. We are beings with an infinity of experientially derived pasts, at each moment believing there to be only one past.

The phenomenology of 'the self' suggests that, just as our development allows us to move from an egocentric view of the world to one that acknowledges alternative views which are ascribed to 'others', so too is it possible to come to regard 'the self', or 'I', that defines itself, to be a temporary construct, just one of an infinity of possibilities. As Richard Wollheim has stated: 'a person lives his life at a crossroads: at a point where a past that has affected him and a future that lies open meet in the present' (1984: 31).

6

Existential Phenomenology

How does it feel
To be on your own
With no direction home
Like a complete unknown...

Bob Dylan

As I originally noted in Chapter 1, phenomenology is generally divided into two distinct, though interrelated branches, commonly referred to as transcendental phenomenology and existential phenomenology or, as this latter branch is more popularly known, existentialism. Of the two, transcendental phenomenology has been largely influenced by, and derived from, the writings and ideas of Edmund Husserl; a number of its central ideas have served as the basis for the previous chapters on the perception of objects, others and 'the self'.

While it would be false to argue that Husserlian thought has played no role in the development of existential phenomenology, it is the case (as I hope will become increasingly evident throughout this discussion) that this second branch places different emphases on issues of inter-relational experience.

For existential phenomenologists, the key concern for investigation is existence as it is humanly experienced (Heidegger, 1962). While transcendental phenomenologists, from Husserl onwards, have focused on the issues of essence (that is, 'that which makes things what they are' (Misiak and Sexton, 1973: 72)), existential phenomenologists, on the other hand, have tended to argue that our focus on existence must take precedence over questions of essence since existence *precedes* essence in that 'man does not *possess* existence... he *is* his existence' (Misiak and Sexton, 1973: 72).

This emphasis is in keeping with the etymological basis of the Latin verb *existere*, namely 'to stand out, or to become, to emerge' (Misiak and Sexton, 1973: 72).

Obviously, such a complex realm of discourse as 'existence' demands some degree of subdivision in order for methodological investigation to be carried out. As such, existential phenomenology can also be characterized by its emphasis on several key 'themes' of human existence, such as: freedom and its limitations, temporality, engagement and encounter with the world and/or others, and meaning/meaninglessness.

What is common to these themes is that each has a major psychological impact on the way we elect to live out our lives. As such, there is some justification to the claims made by a number of its adherents that existential phenomenology is, first and foremost, a practical philosophy with clear-cut psychological, political and social implications. Indeed, it is probably due to the powerful works of fiction created by existential writers such as Samuel Beckett, Albert Camus, Simone de Beauvoir and, of course, Jean-Paul Sartre that existentialist thought gained (and retains) a fair degree of popularity.

For instance, both the 'beat' and 'angry young man' influences on the drama, literature, poetry and music of the West during the middle years of the twentieth century owe a great deal to existential notions (whether mis-understood or not) just as, every few years, an 'existential style' regularly resurfaces in the somewhat fragmented music and fashion industries.

As a philosophy, however, existential phenomenology initially made little impact outside Continental Europe. Both North American and British philosophers tended to dismiss key works as 'unreadable' and from a tra-dition in philosophy that was alien (and, implicitly, inferior) to the schools of logical positivism and linguistic analysis that were then dominant. Even Bertrand Russell, in his otherwise masterly *History of Western Philosophy* (1946/1961), failed to so much as mention, much less discuss, Heidegger's ideas.

The current situation has changed somewhat. Over the 15 years since the first edition of this book, there has been an obvious flowering of North American and British texts and conferences dedicated to the study of Heidegger's works in particular and to existential phenomenology in general. As we shall see in Chapter 8, the influence of existential phe-nomenology on psychology has grown steadily and is generally conceded to have had substantial impact on theories of personality and abnormal psychology and most significantly, upon psychotherapy.

The Roots of Existential Phenomenology

As is now generally acknowledged (Barrett, 1958; Cooper, 2003; Grossmann, 1984; van Deurzen-Smith, 1988; Warnock, 1970/1979), a number of ideas that have become the central themes of existential phenomenology are to be found most plainly in the writings of two major nineteenth-century philosophers: Sören Kierkegaard (1813–1855) and Friedrich Nietzsche (1844–1900). Both writers invoked an anti-rationalist stance and, in a sense, sought to 'convert' their readers to their ideas via a combination of emo-tional appeal, provocation and, perhaps most of all, through profoundly moving, unique and insightful writing styles which succeeded in turning their texts into major works of literature as well as of philosophy. Interested readers are referred, in particular, to Mary Warnock's invaluable and highly readable introductory text, *Existentialism* (1970/1979), for a detailed sum-mary of the influences of these two philosophers on the development of existentialism.

Briefly, what both authors attempt to demonstrate is that each of us possesses a far greater degree of freedom of thought and belief (and, by implication, of behaviour) than many of us think possible. Such freedom, when acknowledged, may be truly liberating, but it also forces man into a recognition of subjective responsibility. While Kierkegaard explores the anxiety and isolation that this recognition forces upon our thoughts and beliefs, Nietzsche marvels at the power with which it provides us. Both authors rail against the collective, socially imposed morality in Western culture and invoke an alternative vision of human beings as conscious self-generators of their beliefs and morality; for each author, it is less important *what* we believe than *the manner* in which we believe.

While there is no doubt that these arguments tap into the central concerns of existential phenomenology, I am personally reticent to include both authors as representatives of existential phenomenology. My reason for this is that, as I have understood their writings, neither author truly addresses or acknowledges what I take to be the *foundational* assumption running through all branches of phenomenology – *the inter-relational basis of all human reflections upon our existence*. While both Kierkegaard and Nietzsche concern themselves with subjectivity and individual freedom, choice and responsibility, what unifies phenomenological inquiry is the inter-relational grounding from which our relation to freedom, existence and all the remaining major themes explored by these, and other great thinkers emerges and is opened to elucidation.

Martin Heidegger: Beings in Relation

The development of existential phenomenology proper took place between the two World Wars in Continental Europe. More specifically, we can say that a series of important writings by the German philosopher Martin Heidegger (1889–1976) make up the formal origins of existential thought. Although never claiming to be an existentialist, Heidegger's contributions are pivotal in their examination of key existential notions and are acknowledged major sources in the development and rise of existential thought in France, most notably in the writings of Jean-Paul Sartre (1948; 1956/1991) and Maurice Merleau-Ponty (1962; 1964).

Heidegger worked as Husserl's principal assistant at the University of Freiburg during the early 1920s and eventually went on to succeed him as Professor of Philosophy, where he remained until the end of the Second World War. Following the war, he isolated himself in the Black Forest region of Germany in order to continue his writing and, as well, as part of the conditions imposed upon him by the Allied Forces as a consequence of his support of National Socialism during the 1930s which, though it became more muted as the atrocities perpetrated by the Nazis became more apparent, was not retracted insofar as Heidegger retained his Party membership until the end of the Second World War (Ott, 1994; Wolin, 1993). I will return briefly to this issue later in the present chapter.

Although now generally acknowledged to be a brilliant and original thinker, his writings (though widely available) remain difficult to read in English translation both because of the unwieldiness of their terminology and because of their stylistic uniqueness. As an associate of mine once put it: 'with Heidegger, you're forced to always have to literally read between the lines; it's there, in that "nothingness" of white space, that Heidegger's message comes across' (Rosen, 1984).

Such a stance may well be somewhat extreme, but it remains the case that the divergence of opinion among Heidegger's many interpreters leads one to wonder whether the injunction holds some truth. At any rate, what follows is yet another 'between the lines' interpretation of some of Heidegger's ideas which I believe to be most pertinent to psychology.

being and being

During his Inaugural Professorial Lecture at Freiburg University, Martin Heidegger asked the question: 'why are there beings at all, and why not rather nothing?' (Heidegger, 1993: 110). This question, which in many ways underpins all the questions we ask with regard to our selves, the universe, and the relation between them, became Heidegger's most pivotal concern and formed the centrepiece to his investigations on existence.

In addressing this question, Heidegger makes a distinction between 'beings' and 'Being' itself. Something is, because *Being is*. Whatever can be said to be – a person, a table, a building, or a cat, for instance, is more than just the sum of its features and characteristics. In its specific, even unique being, it stands out as an expression of Being in general. Each being points us toward the reality of Being – that in spite of all the likelihood that there should be nothing, Being emerged.

I utilize this distinction between 'being' in lower case and 'Being' in upper case, like others have done before me, as an attempt to clarify Heidegger's concerns and the distinction he wanted to make between particular beings (a plant, a cushion, a computer, a person) and what they all share – *that they are* – which is Being. Heidegger's primary focus was on the clarification of Being. His interest in 'beings' lay insofar as any 'being' pointed the way to Being. Or, to put it another way, the investigation of any being will to some degree disclose or reveal Being.

Existence

Heidegger argued that 'human beings' are unique 'beings' in that we alone of all the 'beings' that are, *are* in a particular way. What is it that is so particular about human being? It is, for Heidegger, that human beings alone can contemplate Being. We are, whether we are aware of it or not, always concerned with questions of Being and not just with questions regarding specific beings – even if our questions are couched in views and attitudes and fears regarding our own, or some other, particular being. In this sense, Heidegger argued, human beings can be distinguished from all other beings in that they not only 'are', but they also *exist*.

To exist is to 'stand out' from the ground of being shared by all beings in such a way as to be aware 'that I am'. This knowledge 'that I am' connects me not only to my sense of my own specific being in that I can describe my appearance or communicate characteristic features and qualities of my being. It also connects me to the knowledge that in my very attempt to address 'who and what I am' I am also revealing the 'that-ness' or 'is-ness' or Being which both underpins and structures my attempts to address and describe 'my particular being'.

Existence then, for Heidegger, addresses our awareness of the fact *that we are* and that, therefore, each being that is, is an expression or manifestation of Being.

This may initially seem like a befuddlingly abstract concern for Heidegger to present to us and, equally, it is likely that we might find it confusing to make the distinction between 'being' and 'Being'. We might also ask: 'even if such a distinction is possible for me to make, so what? What significance does it have?' These are good questions to ask and I am not myself entirely clear that Heidegger answers them satisfactorily. But, let us see where they take him, and, possibly, us as well.

Dasein

Rather than speak of human beings, Heidegger prefers the term '*dasein*'. He employs it to designate the uniqueness of human beings in that we, unlike all other beings, 'are' in a particular way in that we 'exist'. To exist is to be able to both consider and to illuminate 'Being'. *Dasein* has been translated into English as 'being there' or 'the there of being' (Cohn, 2002). This implies some sort of location and in a sense it can be seen as this in that *dasein* points in the direction of Being and, at the same time, it locates *dasein* in a particular relationship to Being. All beings are expressions of Being, but *dasein alone, of all beings, accesses and seeks to discern Being*.

Heidegger argued that although Being itself remains directly indescribable, nonetheless our investigations of *dasein's existence* can discern recurring characteristics or features of existence. These universally shared 'givens', (or *existentials*, as will be discussed later) are present in all *dasein* and through them *dasein* points itself in the direction of Being.

Being-in-the-world

There is, as well, a further implication to Heidegger's use of the term *dasein* which is more clearly brought out in its more common English translation as *being-in-the-world*. Like Husserl, Heidegger assumes that all of our investigations and reflections regarding human existence arise out of the indissoluble inter-relationship between 'a being' and 'the world'. The term *being-in-the-world* seeks to express typographically this foundational inter-relationship through the hyphens that connect the separate words together such that they become one interconnected whole. For Heidegger, *dasein's* status as a being-in-the-world permits the investigation of the equally inseparable inter-relationship between being and Being. In brief, Heidegger argues that '[h]uman existence... is tied inseparably to the world' (Misiak and Sexton, 1973: 75).

Heidegger took great pains to insist that like Being, *dasein* cannot ever be fully contained, captured, defined or objectified. In this, he echoes Husserl's emphasis on the indissoluble inter-relationship between the investigator and the focus of investigation. Rather than be able to separate one from the other, Husserl's analyses led him to the foundational rule of phenomenology – intentionality.

Heidegger, too, takes this stance though his emphases 'existentialize' Husserl's conclusion by arguing that *dasein* is always in a 'with-world' (Heidegger, 1962). Even when there is no other around me, or in my presence, even when I have found some means to distance myself from or avoid others, I am still 'with-others' in that my stances, attitudes and actions arise out of the existential condition (or 'given') of *being-with*. My specific and particular stance to this given may be to embrace or reject others, love or hate a particular other, or a group of others, or all others, attend to or remain unaware of my impact upon one, or some or all others and theirs upon me. But whatever particular is evoked, it reveals the universal through which the particular has emerged.

Ontological and Ontic Expressions of Existence

In order to distinguish the particular from the universal, Heidegger writes of the *ontic* and the *ontological* aspects of existence. The *ontological* aspect refers to the universal 'givens' or structures of Being; the *ontic* aspect refers to the specific and particular means by which any universal given is expressed or embodied.

For instance, the *ontological* given of temporality may be expressed *ontically* through my fear of death, or my lack of concern for life-threatening danger, or my refusal to contemplate the future consequences of a current attitude or behaviour, or my leaving all necessary tasks to some unspecified future time.

We can now, perhaps, begin to discern that this Heideggerian distinction between the ontological and ontic may be of direct relevance to phenomenological psychology. The particular 'way of being' that we adopt, whether in general or in a specific instance, expresses not only my uniqueness it also reveals that this uniqueness emerges from, or is an expression of, universal existential 'givens'.

As phenomenological psychologists we are not promoting a stance that attempts to reduce the ontic to its ontological 'source' by seeking to explain ontic manifestations in ontological terms. What we can and should consider, however, is that our understanding of the ontic (especially in those instances when the ontic stance or behaviour is difficult to understand or appears to us to be bereft of understanding) becomes more adequate when we consider it in relation to its ontological aspect.

Explanation vs Understanding

Heidegger, like Husserl, was well aware of Wilhelm Dilthey's distinction between the natural sciences and what he termed 'the human sciences'. At the heart of this distinction lay 'the methodological difference between explanation and understanding' (Makkreel, 1995: 203, quoted in Cohn, 2002: 114). As Makkreel clarifies:

> The natural sciences seek causal explanations of nature – connecting the discrete representations of outer experience through hypothetical generalizations. The human sciences aim at an understanding... that articulates the typical structures of life given in lived experience. Finding living experience to be inherently connected and meaningful, Dilthey... developed a descriptive psychology... (Makkreel, 1995: 203, quoted in Cohn, 2002: 114)

This focus upon understanding rather than explanation (and with this the emphasis upon meaning) runs throughout phenomenology regardless of its diverse branches or emphases. For Heidegger, scientific enquiry lost much of its way when it placed its emphasis, if not exclusive attention, upon explanation alone. That loss was its very connectedness to Being. As Heidegger suggests, '[s]adness cannot be measured – but the tears which are formed as a result of psychosomatic connections can be examined quantitatively in various ways' (Heidegger, 1987: 105, quoted in Cohn, 2002: 53).

In part, following Heidegger, I have myself suggested that a very similar loss might be seen in the current state of contemporary Western Art which increasingly serves as a means for the artist to give expression to the unique ontic explanations of his or her particular way of being while paying little or no attention to, or even entirely dismissing, that ontological aspect through which a more substantive inter-relational understanding may be gleaned (Spinelli, 2001).

The divide between explanation and understanding, provoked by differing or competing tendencies, aims and goals, reveals that there exist differing 'ways to be' in our relation to Being. Heidegger paid substantial attention to this. One major distinction addressed by him sought to distinguish between *authentic* and *inauthentic* ways of being.

Authenticity and Inauthenticity

The terms *authenticity* and *inauthenticity*, as applied to Heidegger's writings, have caused great confusion and debate as to their meaning, not least because of the implied superiority or genuineness or truthfulness of one term (authenticity) over the other (inauthenticity). Hans Cohn, among others, has argued that the problem has been exacerbated by Heidegger's English translators (Cohn, 2002). In the German original, Heidegger is careful to select the term *'eigentlich'* (rather that *'authentisch'* which he could have used had he wished to emphasize a meaning paralleling that of the English 'authentic') to express his notion of what has been translated as authenticity. While difficult to translate directly into English, *'eigentlich'* expresses the opening up to, or ownership, of what is there. In this sense, Heidegger's use of 'authenticity' refers us to the capacity that each of us has to embrace Being as it presents itself to us as ours. *If I open myself to my experience of existing, I own that experience in that it expresses my particular way of engaging with Being*. This way of existing confronts me with the understanding of my part in what existence brings to me; it involves and implicates me.

In contrast, Heidegger proposed that an alternate way of being is also open to me. This *inauthentic* way emerges when I cut myself off from my engagement with Being because this way frightens or upsets or threatens or disturbs views and values and attitudes and assumptions that I hold, and wish to hold onto, regarding how I am to engage with Being and what that engagement may mean. This inauthentic view allows me to disown any sense of 'owned' involvement with or responsibility for what presents itself to my experience. I might deny that experience by suppressing it, for example, or by rejecting that it is mine in some way. This stance throws me into a way of being that is detached from what is there for me. As Mary Warnock expresses it, in leading an inauthentic existence:

> man ignores the reality of his own relation to the world. There is an ambiguity in his dealings with reality. He partly knows what things are, but partly does not, because he is so entirely caught up in the way other people see them, the labels attached to them by the world at large. He cannot straightforwardly form any opinion, and his statements are partly his own, partly those of people in general. (Warnock, 1970/1979: 57)

As inauthentic beings, we interpret ourselves as reactive victims to experience. This other-focused or *'they-self'*, as inauthenticity has been presented by various English-language commentators on Heidegger (Cooper, 2003; Macquarrie, 1972), has found the means to diminish, if not disengage completely, from the disturbing or anxiety-provoking implications of existence that present themselves. But in doing so, the inauthentic *they-self* has also imposed a way of being whereby 'it loses what it owns' (Cohn, 2002: 87).

For Heidegger, both authenticity and inauthenticity are human givens of existence. Our capacity for either is a universal attribute, as is our tendency to shift from one way of being to another – as with through the impact of dramatic or life-changing events such as the shock of a sudden catastrophe or the encounter with another who in some way 'shakes' our worldview. Equally, however, the shift from one way to another way of being may fall upon us unexpectedly and inexplicably with no discernible stimulus with which to explain the transformation that has been provoked.

What is important to understand is that the same or similar 'conditions' can generate a shift from authentic to inauthentic ways of being, or vice-versa, or, indeed, provoke no shift at all. The impact of a tragedy like the destruction of the World Trade Centre in New York City may have been experienced by some as a moment of illuminating authenticity, but it as surely induced an inauthentic stance in others. Equally, for some it may have had no impact whatever upon their currently adopted way of being.

Equally, such shifts remain *impermanent*. We do not *become* authentic or inauthentic in any fixed or final sense. While, as Heidegger suggests, we may 'fall prey' to inauthenticity most of the time, the possibility of authenticity is ever present.

Similarly, Heidegger makes it clear that authenticity is not necessarily a 'better' way to exist and, therefore, something for us to strive towards. Indeed, my very striving for authenticity can be seen as an expression of my inauthentic stance towards my being in that in my striving I remain closed to or detached from the way of being that is there for me.

Considered in these ways, the issue of authenticity and inauthenticity can be seen to have little or nothing to do with an aim for, or being 'blocked' from, personal empowerment, 'better living', self actualization and so forth. I shall return to this in Chapter 9 as part of my discussion on the similarities and divergences between phenomenological psychology and humanistic psychology since it is mainly through humanistic inter-pretations of authenticity or 'being authentic' that this misunderstanding has arisen. Hopefully, readers will now be clearer as to the existential-phenomenological meaning given to these terms and will have under-stood that they are attempts to *describe* rather than *prescribe* ways of being.

In this way, we can briefly return to the question of Heidegger's own 'fal-lenness' in relation to his public association with Nazism during the 1930s. Many readers have been shocked to learn of this and have subsequently questioned how it could be that someone who wrote so powerfully about authenticity and inauthenticity could fall prey to the particularly odious 'they-being' of Nazism. Perhaps readers can now understand that Heidegger's stance reveals all too clearly how any one of us can shift from one position to another in our way of being. Although we can, and should, remain critical of Heidegger's personal choice (not least because he never publicly regretted nor recanted his choice), this should not lead us to dismiss the power and worth of his ideas. It seems to be an all too common failing of human beings to be able to understand and communicate important 'truths' about human existence without always being able or willing to live with or act upon their implications.

Nonetheless, it has likely occurred to readers to ask why it should be that we would typically opt for a way of being that is inauthentic rather than authentic. What hidden values may there be in adopting inauthenticity as our principal mode of being? In order to provide an initial response to this question, we must turn to some of the other universal 'givens' of existence, or *existentials*, discussed by Heidegger.

Existentials

In *Being and Time* which is, for many scholars of his works, Heidegger's most important book (1962), he attempts to identify and describe various universally shared givens – *existentials* – that can be discerned about human existence (Steiner, 1978). As we have seen, authentic and inauthentic ways of being serve as one example of *existentials*. Among the various others that Heidegger highlights are: the inseparability of our inter-relational being-with others and the world in general, throwness and choice, anxiety (or *angst*), and temporality (or the awareness of our finitude).

These *existentials* are common to all *dasein* though how each of us responds to, and incorporates, them into our lives will be unique and specific.

Thrownness and Choice

As far as we know, we are the only animals capable of consciously choosing the meanings we give to our experience.

Whether or not we are partially or completely free from biological restraints upon our behaviour remains an ongoing debate. However, what is asserted by existential phenomenology is not a particular stance on this issue, but rather that it remains our choice to ascribe a particular *meaning* to any behaviour. Let me be clear about this: if I cross the road and get hit by a passing car, the existential-phenomenological view is *not* to argue that I chose this event in that I have the ability to control or determine the plethora of stimuli, such as a passing car, that impinge themselves upon me at any and every moment throughout my life. However, the significance and meaning I give to these stimuli, the interpretation I might make of any given event, the attitude I take towards it, the values with which I bequeath it, the impact upon my life that I make of it, ultimately, *the way I am in relation with the event*, is a matter of my choice.

Such a view, of course, is a direct extension and application of Husserlian intentionality. Existentialists, however, emphasize its *implications for being* since it is this basic acceptance of the freedom to choose our experience of being that is an integral aspect of all *dasein*.

Nevertheless, there exist conditions upon my being in its relation to the world over which I have no choice. Primary among these is my *thrownness*. I had no say, or choice, in my coming into existence. Rather, I was 'thrown into' the world. Similarly, I will have no say or choice in the fact that I will be, at some certain, if indeterminate point in time, 'thrown out' of existence in that I will cease to be as a human being.

During this indeterminate period of my existence, I am also 'thrown' into a particular body, a particular time, a particular culture, a particular set of prevailing socio-cultural attitudes and mores, stances and opinions. These, too, are beyond my choice. And, as well, throughout my existence I will be affected and impacted upon by any number of stimuli or events 'thrown' at me by the world that, also, are beyond my choosing.

As such, my existence is always *situated* in a structure, or set of 'thrown' conditions, whose presence I neither chose nor can truly control.

What remains always possible (if not inevitable) for me, however, is that within this thrownness, I choose its meaning and through it express my way of being-with thrownness.

This choice that I have to construe meaning is not always, nor even often, at a level where I can select differing options as to what an event might mean. The given conditions of my body, my time, my culture may well impose a non-optional meaning to which I ascribe my experience of being. In other words, while sometimes the meaning I arrive at can be selected from an option of choices A, B, C, or D (or more), in many instances, my choice rests upon: 'do I choose meaning A or do I choose meaning A?' As Heidegger puts it, my choice *'is* only the choice of *one* possibility – that is, in tolerating one's not having chosen the others and one's not being able to choose them' (Heidegger, 1962: 331, quoted in Cohn, 2002: 97). And, in similar fashion, we can now better understand Sartre's oft-quoted assertion that human beings are *condemned* to choose (Sartre, 1956/1991).

Both these conclusions seem to me to be a profound understanding of, and stance towards, the choice that is available, indeed inevitable, to all human beings, regardless of the various conditions of 'thrownness' in which we may find ourselves. From the standpoint of phenomenological psychology, this understanding of choice reveals how choice is not solely, or even primarily, a pleasant or desirable enterprise; we can begin to see that the attempt to abdicate from or deny choice may provide a desired reduction of tension from the often difficult and uncertain choices that present themselves to us. Further, this view of choice discloses how many of the disruptions and tribulations that provoke such pain and unease for us can be seen to arise when we insist upon claiming the ability to choose that which is not open to our choosing. Faced with the choice of 'A or A', many of us insist that it is our option to choose the non-existent option of B.

This is, of course, another way of viewing the issue of authenticity and inauthenticity. My authentic choice, and the possibilities that emerge through it, rests in my choosing or embracing that choice that is before me rather than adopting an inauthentic stance that assumes or insists that something other than that one choice can be mine.

Meaning and Meaninglessness

If we embrace choice in the existential-phenomenological sense outlined above, then we are faced with the awareness that we can no longer pre-suppose any definitive or ultimate interpretation or meaning other than that which presents itself to us as our choice. As we have already seen, phenomenologists argue that our interpretation of any event at any given point in time is dependent upon a number of experiential factors that imbue our interpretations with impermanence and fluidity rather than 'fix' them in time and meaning. If we accept this stance, we are immediately confronted with the meaninglessness (that is, *the interpretative openness*) of our experience of the world.

This very meaninglessness prevents us from asserting any indisputable finality, absolute truth or 'correctness' of one interpretation over any other. All sedimented beliefs, attitudes, rules, certainties must be forsaken in favour of disquieting uncertainty. This does not mean, of course, that we must give up our beliefs; rather we must acknowledge them as being just that – beliefs, or suppositions, by which we might choose to live our lives.

But, we might well ask, is there nothing that we can say with any certainty about our existence? Existential phenomenologists argue that there most certainly is, but that such certainties belong to the various aspects and conditions of 'thrownness' through which our choices emerge. Thrownness can be seen to be the source to all the beliefs, theories, meanings or rules that we might make about our experience of the world. For instance, our temporality – that each of us was thrown into and will at some indeterminate point be thrown out of the world as human beings – can be seen to be the source of our various convictions regarding the existence, or lack of it, of an after-life. We may hold a deep and abiding faith in an after-life or reincarnation or, alternatively, we may be entirely convinced of the inconceivability of either. Each stance, regardless of its opposition to the other, serves as a chosen meaning-derived expression of a way of being with temporality.

Once again, our stance towards meaning and meaninglessness can be considered in the light of authenticity and inauthenticity. From an authentic stance, we concede that all our choice-derived meanings are, and will remain, incomplete and uncertain and, in this sense of openness, meaningless. From an inauthentic stance, however, I can deny this conclusion and insist or convince myself of my ability to access meaning that is beyond my owned experience, that meaning exists without, or out of relation to, my existence.

Angst

How we are, or choose to be, in relation to the various existentials once again leads us to the adoption of either an authentic or inauthentic mode of being. It may now be clearer as to how it is that inauthenticity is the more dominant stance for us to take. From an authentic mode of being, our existence reveals itself as inevitably uncertain, unfixed in meaning, finite. This awareness is likely to be all too unbearable, disturbing, frightening. We can begin to see that in order to adopt an authentic way of being we are led to embrace an unavoidably anxiety-provoking existence. Our relation to and with this basic, raw, existential anxiety, or *angst*, as it is typically called in the literature of existential phenomenology, is once again made clear through the ways of authenticity and inauthenticity.

Regardless of whether our way of being is authentic or inauthentic, it is never devoid of angst. Through an authentic way of being we may face up to angst, but that will not remove or eradicate it from our experience of existence. Through inauthentic stances we may divert our focus from angst, but angst will continue to be present in our lives and through our relations in the form of any number of fear-provoking insecurities and debilitating symptoms.

From an authentic perspective, it is our embrace of uncertainty and openness to what is before us that permits us those 'leaps of faith' into the unknown. Our ability to open ourselves to beauty, to love, to truthful engagement with our selves and others, *and to value such as gifts of Being*, rests on the uncertainty, and hence angst, of their outcomes and consequences. Many practitioners of contemplative or meditative techniques, for example, claim to experience 'altered states' during which authentic uncertainty becomes acceptable and is the means to 'spiritual enlightenment'. Similarly, altered states brought about by drugs, sex, religious ecstasy and so forth may also induce temporary experiences of authentic acceptance of 'what is'.

Most often, however, uncertainty seems frightening, unacceptable, ultimately 'wrong'. In our insistence upon being certain of the outcome to our actions, and thereby evading the angst of being, we adopt an inauthentic way to our existence. In opting for inauthenticity we succeed in defending against, even temporarily denying, our experience of angst – but at a heavy cost. Rather than be rid of angst, we become caught up in various expressions of angst that structure the inauthentic mode. If, for instance, life *must* be meaningful and purposeful, then any doubts that may arise must be distinguished and disowned, as must the very *fear* that doubt might arise at some future point. If life *must* be secure, then anything that threatens my experience of security must be avoided, protected against, expunged from my relations. The great irony is that my very insistence upon the avoidance of angst turns me into an angst-ridden puppet in the hands of any number of fear-provoking, incomprehensible, puppeteers.

In our attempt to evade *angst*, we mimic the hysterical patients discussed in Freud and Breuer's *Studies on Hysteria* (1955/1971), in that, like them, as inauthentic beings we suffer from an understanding that we have hidden from ourselves. And further, again like those patients, through our symptomatic behaviours and 'neurotic' thought processes our yearning to reveal such knowledge to ourselves remains ever-present. To pursue the analogy a littler further, for existential phenomenologists the core hidden understanding is that we are free to face up to existence as we live it. That we do not, that we convince ourselves of other freedoms that are not ours to have or be, should not necessarily lead us to conclude that the human species is inherently self-destructive or perverse as some have suggested (Koestler, 1980). Rather, what should be clear now is that our denial of what we know, whatever its price, serves to protect us from the full angst-filled brunt of that knowledge. In so doing, the price we pay – inauthenticity – for the momentary illusion of security and certainty may seem worth its cost.

To paraphrase a line from Woody Allen's film *Manhattan*, as a means of summing up Heidegger's disturbing analysis of human existence: 'we're just too easy on ourselves.'

Jean-Paul Sartre: Beings in Conflict

If Husserl's philosophy centred on the phenomenology of essence, and Heidegger's lay in the phenomenology of existence, Jean-Paul Sartre's primary phenomenological inquiry fell upon the examination of human *freedom*.

Jean-Paul Sartre (1905–80), as philosopher, does not make easy reading. On the other hand, Sartre, as playwright and novelist, is a pleasurable, if disturbing, revelation. The three novels that make up his *Roads to Freedom* trilogy (Sartre, 1947a; 1947b; 1950) and plays such as *No Exit* (Sartre, 1989) are acknowledged masterpieces of twentieth-century literature. The publication in 1984 of his (rejected) scenario for John Huston's biographical film on Freud reveals penetrating critical insight on the development of psychoanalysis and, if flawed as a screenplay, my belief is that it would still have led to a far more interesting and exciting film than the one that was eventually screened (Sartre, 1984). His award of a Nobel Prize for Literature in 1964 (which he refused for both moral and political reasons) confirms his literary genius. As an introduction to his 'brand' of existentialism, Sartre's fictional works are a perfect starting point and I would urge interested readers to begin with them.

Like Heidegger, Sartre did not maintain the same philosophical position throughout the substantial output of his writings. Many of his works refer explicitly to 'phenomenology' (*Being and Nothingness* (1956/1991) for example, is subtitled *An Essay on Phenomenological Ontology*) but deal with issues that lie outside the focus of this text.

Additionally, Sartre is considered by many to be primarily a moral philosopher who, as both existentialist and Marxist, sought to unify both systems into a political ideology of freedom which gained him much notoriety during the 1960s but seems to have had little, if any, influence upon current political theory (Hayman, 1986). These issues, too, must remain largely outside our realm of discourse. For a much more complete account of Sartre's impact upon psychology and psychotherapy in particular, I refer readers to Betty Cannon's excellent *Sartre and Psychoanalysis* (1991).

As such, I've been highly selective in my discussion of Sartre; what follows, then, is not by any means a detailed analysis of Sartrean thought, but, rather, 'selected highlights' dealing with topics that I think bear most relevance on what has been argued previously and what is to follow.

Sartre's Existential Phenomenology

Although Sartre emphasizes his great debt to Husserl's writings, he is unwilling to assume, as Husserl originally did, that in following the steps of the phenomenological method our attempts to 'bracket' the various assumptions we have about the world will get us to 'the thing itself' as it actually is. In pursuing Husserl's arguments, Sartre is led to conclude that no amount of bracketing will ever be complete. In this, Sartre echoes contemporary phenomenological thought: ultimate reality is both unknowable and 'uncapturable' in any essentialist sense.

And, echoing Heidegger (though each author largely dismissed and possibly misunderstood the other's focus), Sartre argues that human beings do not *possess* freedom, they *are* freedom; like it or not, we are condemned to choose our mode of existence. Any attempted escape from this knowledge only leads to further anxiety and despair. One of Sartre's most famous epigrams accurately encapsulates his position: 'Man is a useless passion' (Misiak and Sexton, 1973: 76).

Richard Kearney's lucid exposition of Sartre's philosophy makes clear further points of correspondence between Heidegger and Sartre. Encapsulating Sartre's views on authenticity, Kearney writes:

> The authentic person... begins by acknowledging that there is no given self to be true to; that our existence precedes our essence; and that we invent ourselves as we go along. This means we make our own identity in and through our own decisions and actions. Accordingly our 'essence' is nothing other than that which we choose to be. We are what we are – good, bad, indifferent – not because we were born like that, or created so by God, or determined so by our environmental conditioning, genetic heritage, family upbringing or social and religious training, but because we *made ourselves* like that. (Kearney, 1986: 53–4, italics in original)

We can see from the above that Sartre here returns to and extends Heidegger's conclusions regarding existence. Where Sartre comes into his own, I believe, can be seen in his particular emphasis on the *conflict* between beings and its relation to our experience and acknowledgement of *freedom*.

Conflict, for Sartre, is expressed through the inevitable tension between the *a priori* of being – which cannot ever be fully contained or 'captured' in or as essence – and the opposing human tendency to define, essentialize, and 'capture' being so that being – my being, your being – becomes 'some thing', and hence is definable, finite, closed. Sartre employs the terms 'being-for-itself' (*pour-soi*) and 'being-in-itself' (*en-soi*) to distinguish these polarities of human existence (Kearney, 1986; Sartre, 1956/1991).

Being-for-Itself

Being-for-itself seeks to express all that is possible for us to be as human beings. It presents us with the freedom to be as we *can* be within the wide-ranging limits of our possibilities. Being-for-itself yearns to *transcend* the definitions, labels and habitual stances and attitudes within which we cloaked our uncapturable possibilities. It offers us the means to remain open to the potential essence-defying transcendence of our existence.

However, there is a price for this self-actualizing freedom: it is nothing less than the experience of *anguish*. Anguish of what? Most basically, it is the anguish that being-for-itself requires the loss of all substantive *meaning*. What Sartre is arguing here is that being-for-itself provokes the awareness that there is no fixed, reliable, certain objective criterion or value upon which we can base our chosen meaning as to what, how and who to be. Nothing – no rule, no law, no god, no scientific fact – nothing outside of our being is responsible for any and all emergent meaning given to our existence.

For Sartre, again like Heidegger, the freedom of being-for-itself does not lie at the *event level* – we cannot control nor truly initiate events. Rather, our freedom and choice become most apparent when our stance to 'what is there', what has emerged at an event-level, is to embrace it, accept it, 'say yes' to it, rather than adopt a stance that pretends and deludes itself into believing that 'something *else* is there for me'. Sartre's argument insists that *the price of a completely open stance to existence is meaning itself*. In this Sartrean understanding of being, no meaning remains, or is possible. All is flux, chaos, absurdity.

Being-in-Itself

Where then does meaning exist in the Sartrean view of things? Meaning exists as a property or expression of *being-in-itself*. It is through the inter-preted facticity of *being-in-itself* that we approach being from the stand-points of objectification, necessity and external or permanent truths, dogmas, facts, meanings. *Being-in-itself* continually moves us towards encasing and capturing our essence-transcending freedom – *essentializing* it through what Sartre describes as the *facticity* of existence – our bodies, our culture, our place within an historical framework. If *being-in-itself* provides us with meaning, or at least the possibility of construing some lasting, externally-founded meaning, so that thereby we can escape the anguish of freedom, it also has its price: we are brought to the experience of *shame* – the shame that is provoked by our willingness to adopt 'a servile unfreedom' (Kearney, 1986: 65).

All meaning directs us toward *facticity*: a constructed reality, an interpreted world made up of 'self', 'others', 'scientific laws', 'religious truths' and so forth. But for Sartre, our very search for and reliance upon meaning belittles us, makes us less than the being we are in our existence. It is this awareness, available to us all, that provokes our shame. In embracing *facticity*, and all the secure, if limiting, meanings that it permits, we deny the undefinable, filigree freedom that we both know and are.

For Sartre, we are nothing pretending to be something. And therein lies the source to all our experienced conflicts.

Inter-relational Conflict

What is crucial for Sartre is that our very awareness of, and response to, this personal or subjective conflict does not arise as a result of some internalized, isolated, *intrapsychic* mechanism of tension as might be suggested by Freud and all his subsequent followers. Rather, it is an *inter-relational* consequence (Cannon, 1991). For Sartre, self and other are inextricably bound together in an inescapable relationship. If my life-projects direct me towards the possibilities of being-for-itself, it is the presence and demands of others that serve to remind me of the choices I make to adopt a stance of being-in-itself.

When two people meet, a struggle begins between each person's desire to be perceived as a transcendent, actualizing subject and to avoid being captured as a defined and limited factual object. Each person wants the same and fears the same. As Kearney writes: '*in short, for one human subject to remain a* no-thing *the other must become a* thing. *Two nothingnesses cannot exist simultaneously*' (Kearney, 1986: 64, italics in original).

If Sartre is correct, then it must also be the case that inter-relational conflict is inevitable. The other remains inescapably my antagonist. Is there truly no way out?

Sartre certainly pondered a great deal on this and in his later writings he became more willing to consider a potential alternative relationship that, fraught with peril as it was, nonetheless permitted the *possibility* of an alternative possibility.

Being-for-Others

Sartre's beginning of a possible solution comes from Heidegger's insight that 'by "others" we do not mean everyone else *apart* from me – those against whom the 'I' stands out. They are rather... those among whom one is too' (Heidegger, 1962: 154).

Heidegger's insight was that one's very sense of 'I' – or more generally speaking, one's sense of self – is also an expression of 'other-ness'. Who I say I am is also a statement about who I am not; no real separation between the two exists.

The novel stance of *being-for-others* emerges as the result of a conscious being's ability to consider the world as it is perceived by another such being. *Being-for-others* rests upon the acceptance of a *mutuality* of being between beings. Through it we each come to recognize our inescapable reliance upon others for our very sense of self, our very ability to experience the choices we make with regard to our ways of being.

But make no mistake: for Sartre: 'conflict is the original meaning of being-for-others' (Sartre, 1956/1991: 364).

The move towards a *being-for-others* is not through the abdication or denial of conflict, but rather it is through the very acceptance of its inevitability and via the mutual embracing of its possibilities.

The possibility of *being-for-others* also permits each of us to consider our own conflicting aims and motivations in the light of the other's way of being towards conflicting stances. Not surprisingly, what often occurs is that both of us may well discover that our difficulties and differences be they subjective or between us may rest upon all-too-similar foundational values, beliefs, and projects that are *shared by us both*. Considered broadly, for instance, what is being suggested here is that while the worldviews of fundamentalist Christians and fundamentalist Muslims might initially seem to be in direct opposition to one another, more careful analysis might well actually reveal the source of mutual conflict to be as much (if not more) an expression of *shared* assumptions in their worldviews as they might be about the divergences between them.

This attempt provokes a novel experience: co-operation with one another not because we have *eradicated* the conflict between us, but rather because our attempt at 'being for' one another arises through the mutual recognition of the *inevitable* conflict between us. It is a 'fallen' sort of co-operation and resolution, to be sure: incomplete, always uncertain, and constantly straining to undo itself. In short, it could be seen as a sort of fun-house mirror image of the primary Christian message: 'don't do to others what you do not want done to yourself... for to do so *is* to do it to yourself.'

Bad Faith

As appealing as the *idea* of *being-for-others* might be, and as desirable might be the aim of directing our relations towards its possibilities, nonetheless Sartre found no actual evidence of *being-for-others* in the world he inhabited. It remained a possibility because it could be imagined and considered, but it was by no means an actuality.

Instead, Sartre saw that our most typical resolution to the inevitable existential conflict is that of self-deception or *bad faith*. In the stance of bad faith, an individual becomes nothing other than a 'thing', an object that has no control over its actions. These actions, when analysed, are seen as highly ritualistic and limited by the individual's beliefs about what can and cannot be done.

Such beliefs dominate our being, encase it in a 'must/should' moral order that achieves both a fragmentation in being and automation-like behaviour. Individuals in the state of bad faith deny a vast range of potentials, claiming them to be impossible as a result of the strictures imposed by society and biology. Class, culture, gender, parental upbringing, religious ideology – anything external to the individuals themselves – become worthy originating factors and excuses for their actions.

Without labouring the point, Sartre's notion of bad faith has many similarities to that of Heideggerian inauthenticity. But the power of Sartre's term rests with the brilliance of the examples he employs to demonstrate the state. Here, Sartre the playwright and novelist comes to the fore and presents us with illuminating, brutal, finely observed vignettes of individuals (often in the setting of Parisian café society) who are living exponents of beings in the state of bad faith. For instance, consider the following example:

> A girl who is taken to a restaurant by a man and who, in order to preserve the excitement of the occasion, and to put off the moment when she must face making a definite decision, saying either 'yes' or 'no' to him, pretends to herself that she does not notice his intentions towards her. There finally comes a moment when he takes her hand; and the moment of decision would be upon her, only at this very moment she becomes totally absorbed in intellectual conversation, and leaves her hand to be taken by him, without noticing it, as if he has just picked up some 'thing' any thing, off the table. She has dissociated herself from her hand, for the time being, and is pretending that it is nothing whatever to do with her. Her hand just rests in his hand, inert and thing-like. If she had removed it, or deliberately left it where it was, she would in either case have manifestly come to some decision. But by simply not taking responsibility for her hand and what happened to it, she avoided the need to decide; and this is Bad Faith. (Warnock, 1970: 102–3)

Or, alternatively, consider the following portrait of an all-too familiar waiter:

> All the movements and gestures of the waiter are slightly over-done. His behaviour is essentially ritualistic. He bends forward in a manner which is too deeply expressive of concern and deference for the diners; he balances his tray in a manner which is just a little too precarious. His movements are all of them like the movements in a mime or game. The game which he is playing is the game of being a waiter. (Warnock, 1970: 103)

As Warnock is right to point out, the power of such examples lies not only in the fact that each of us can recognize others who act in these ways, but that, if we are honest enough with ourselves, we are forced to confess: 'there am I' (Warnock, 1970: 103).

Put simply, the notion of bad faith reminds us that we lie to ourselves continuously. But, as ever, Sartre takes a different position on this dilemma. He argues that *the lie is the behaviour of transcendence*. That is to say, the fact that we *can* lie and that we can *know* that we lie, brings us to the awareness of the alternate possibilities of being open to us. This view, as with Heidegger's descriptive contrast of authenticity and inauthenticity, seeks to remove any prescriptive status to the notion of bad faith. To *know* that we are in bad faith reveals to us that we know already the alternative open to us. That alternative cannot be spoken of so directly as bad faith since to name it will serve to provide it with shape and substance, essentialize it so that it will only return us to bad faith. Like any movement whose aim is freedom, Sartre warns us, its tendency will be to 'capture itself' through definition, through various means of objectification and, by so doing, will become a movement not of freedom, but of oppression.

Nausea

There are also some parallels between Heidegger's notion of angst and Sartre's term *nausea*.

Should we somehow stop living in the state of bad faith, all the defences that we have built up around ourselves in order to be provided with the illusion of an essence-centred, meaningful, ordered and limited existence would be recognized as illusions. What would we be faced with then?

Firstly, argues Sartre, we would be confronted with a realization of our weakness, how difficult we find it to avoid being in bad faith, how easily we can each slip back into it. Secondly, we are confronted with the knowledge of the deception we have carried out both upon ourselves and upon others, we are forced to hold ourselves responsible for the lies told, the abuses we chose to enact, the myriad of ways in which we both trivialized and limited both our own being and that of others. At this point, Sartre argues, we are overwhelmed by an almost literal gut-wrenching nausea; if this is existence, it is sickening, revolting. The very knowledge of it induces a state of nausea in us.

Where Heidegger posits angst arising out of authenticity, Sartre conjures up the more vivid image of nausea; in either case, it is our avoidance of each that keeps us in particular states of unease that serve to reflect each of us a 'captured freedom'.

Sartre as a Moral Philosopher

The moral implications of Sartre's analyses of being are, I think, fairly obvious: whatever stance we adopt towards being confronts us with its inevitable inter-relational basis, even if that inter-relation is derived from conflict. Any inter-relation derived from a stance of bad faith inevitably limits or diminishes the existential possibilities of either self or other or, indeed, ultimately both self and other. As such it is open to moral analysis.

The political and social implications of this position are, of course, dramatic. If the actions of one group/nation/ideology/religion imperil the potentialities of being either of its own citizens/followers/believers or of the citizens/followers/believers of an alternative group/nation/ideology/religion, those actions are in bad faith and will ultimately imperil the potentialities of being of the nation/ideology/religion that enacts them.

I think it is unnecessary for me to provide examples to demonstrate the accuracy of this conclusion; unfortunately, we are faced with an over-abundance of such on a daily basis.

Although Sartre was a committed atheist, and particularly antagonistic to the Christian religion, it is interesting to note the initial similarity that might be drawn between his position and one of the two fundamental laws of Christianity, that is, 'to love others as one loves oneself'. At the same time, Sartre might well respond that it is again an aspect of bad faith to love others as if they were *nothing but* oneself. Instead, the real, and perhaps impossible, challenge is to love others *as others*.

Martin Buber: the Otherness of the Other

Sartre's analyses of relational conflict in many way lead us to the question of the status of the 'other' in our relations. We have seen that Sartre could only arrive at a point where he could imagine, as an act of imagination, a way of being-for-others. It was, initially, Martin Buber (1878–1965), writing contemporaneously to Sartre, who provides us with a critical alternative to, or extension of, Sartre's conclusion.

Throughout Buber's writings, there is continual attempt to distinguish 'persons' from 'individuals'. Buber's view of the person serves as an expression of what it is to be a human being – a being who inhabits an inseparable relation with the world, and is an expression of that relation. For Buber, being a person is far more than simply individuating. Being a person means being 'in real reciprocity with the world in all the points in which the world can meet man' (Kirschenbaum and Henderson, 1990: 63). Becoming an individual did not equate with making oneself more human and humane. Buber stated his position forthrightly: 'I'm against individuals and for persons' (Kirschenbaum and Henderson, 1990: 63).

Instead, Buber insists on reminding us that *we become ourselves through relation*. For Buber: 'in the beginning is relation' (Buber, 1970: 32).

Buber's now famous distinction between *I-It* and *I-You* inter-relations can be most directly understood in the following way: I can experience and relate to another as an object of my experience and self-consciousness and whose meanings can be reshaped and reformulated via the imposition of my preferred meaning stance. Alternatively, I can approach the other as a subject who is in a dialogical encounter with me and through which encounter inter-relational meaning possibilities unfold themselves to both of us.

The former stance is an *I-It* attitude that is grounded in separateness, manipulation and control. The latter is an *I-You* attitude that is grounded in inseparability and whose focus lies upon the meanings emergent *between* the persons. If the former demands that 'I' must fix myself in an attitude of authority, the latter equally demands that 'I' remain open to the reconstituting and redefining of my own meaning base via the attitude taken towards the other. To treat the other as merely another expression of 'I' succeeds only is my seeing the other as a projected image of my self. In such an instance, the relation that is fostered between us, however much warmth, care, and concern it may contain, still remains an *I-It* relation that equally objectifies both the 'I' and the 'It'.

In contrast, the *I-You* relation reveals that both 'I' and 'You' co-exist as an inseparable inter-relation whose truthful meanings are not 'handed down', directed or predetermined by one party to another. Buber argued that in order for us to approach an *I-You* encounter it is necessary for each of us to enter into a full dialogical relation with the other and, to 'live this situation not merely from his own end but also from that of his partner: he must practise the kind of realisation which I call inclusion... [Each]... must stand not only at his [or her] own pole of the bipolar relationship but also at the other... ' (Buber 1970: 178–9).

The *I-You* relationship is not necessarily about equality, or full reciprocity or empathy. It is much more about respect for the other in his or her *otherness* and involves practising what Buber termed *inclusion*, which rules out full mutuality. For many of us, the so-called attempt to enter into the other's *otherness* turns out, more accurately, to be an attempt to explain the other to ourselves as if his or her *otherness* no longer existed. This is more an act of possession, or denial, than it is of inclusion. The political and religious leaders of the various communities that exist in most multi-cultural cities, for example, might claim a stance of 'inclusion' between communities but it is evident that each community's *otherness* is either avoided or, more commonly, elevated in such a way that it prevents the possibility of inter-relational inclusion.

Buber's radical exposition of the different qualities of inter-relation seems to me to incorporate notions and ideas that can be found in both Heidegger and Sartre. What Buber is at pains to make evident, however, is the inter-relational foundation to all ways of being. While that view runs through Heidegger's and Sartre's writings as well, there is, at times a tendency in both – more pronounced perhaps in Sartre – to suggest an equal status to subjectivity, as if one were, at times, able to break out of relation or 'arrive at' relation through some individualistic or individual-izing process. Because of such misreadings of existential phenomenology, critics have argued against its implicit, if not explicit, solipsism and elevation of individual freedom and choice at the cost of others. Were their arguments not misplaced, I would agree with such critics as well.

One of the many valuable contributions to the literature of existential phenomenology made by Buber is that of expressing the foundational inter-relational condition of being in such a way that it cannot be misunderstood or confused with any or all of subjective analyses to which it contrasts itself. Indeed, Buber's emphasis on the *otherness* of the other may bring to light for many readers that which may have remained somewhat opaque in the discussion on Heidegger and Sartre. For this reason alone, Buber's contributions to existential phenomenology seem to me to be not only highly original but pivotal to its understanding.

Existential Phenomenology: a Summary

I am very much aware of the many major authors and contributors to existential phenomenology that I have failed to mention, much less discuss. That I have done so, should in no way suggest to the reader that such authors are in any way less important, or less original, than those whom I have discussed. Nonetheless, as brief and selective as this overview of existential phenomenology has been, it seems both useful and necessary to present a concise summary of the points considered.

Existential phenomenology stands in direct opposition to rationalist, idealist and materialist philosophies. It takes as its central focus of attention issues that revolve around the notion of existence, that is, issues concerning what and how it is to be in relation to the world and to others. Shaffer (1978) has deftly outlined the four main themes of existential phenomenology that have been the basis for my discussion. These are:

> (1) a person's unavoidable uncertainty when confronted on the one hand by a universe devoid of any clear-cut or easily fixed meaning, and on the other hand by the inevitability of his own eventual nothingness, or death; (2) his or her inherent freedom to choose the attitudes and actions that he or she takes in the face of this potentially meaningless situation; (3) the omnipresent constraints, or limits, that the person's situation places upon his or her freedom; and (4) the impossibility of successfully evading responsibility for whatever choices he or she makes. (Shaffer, 1978: 19)

To these, I would emphasize once again the inter-relational grounding through which existence emerges as *the* foundational phenomenological assumption that underpins all of the above four points.

Existential phenomenology argues that, if we are to face up to our potential for being, we must accept both our freedom and the 'thrown' or situated conditions that permit freedom's expression. This freedom lies in our ability, if not 'condemnation', to give meaning to our experience. As such, we are responsible for whatever we make meaningful about our unique and specific existence, that of the world, and that of others.

Faced with the unavoidable anxiety (angst) we experience when faced with this knowledge and its subsequent implications, we attempt to avoid it by placing a number of limitations (varying in extremity) which, while relieving our anxiety to a more or less bearable degree, lead us to impose limits on our potentials for being such that we become beings who are characterized by their degree of inauthenticity or bad faith. The only way out of this position is for each of us to cease denying our freedom and to face up to that freedom that is ours as it presents itself to us through and in our world relations.

Interestingly, although many of his theoretical ideas (centrally, the related notions of repression and the unconscious) have been rejected by many existentialists, including Sartre (Cannon, 1991), Freud, too, arrived at a highly similar general conclusion: for him, the aims of psychoanalysis were not necessarily, or even primarily, curative; rather they sought to make analysands more truthful and honest with themselves so that, if not necessarily emerging as 'happier' people at the end of analysis, they were certainly more capable of facing the vicissitudes of life (Gay, 1988).

Existentialist Influences on Psychology

Mention of Freud brings us to the consideration of the impact and influence that existential phenomenology has had on Western psychology.

Misiak and Sexton (1973) have referred to existentially oriented psychology as a movement whose principal aim is to provide existent schools of psychology with new approaches, insights, themes and methods with which to reassess, revise and make more adequate their views and conclusions regarding the understanding of human thought and behaviour.

A number of prominent and influential psychologists have written on general issues raised by an existential approach to psychology (principally, Binswanger, 1963; Bugenthal, 1981; Colaizzi, 1973; Farber, 2000; Frie, 1997; May, 1958; 1983; Valle and King, 1978; Van Kaam, 1966). Others, such as Allport (1955), Maslow (1968), Rogers (1961) and Rogers and Stevens (1967) have more or less aligned their own approaches to it. And still others (Fromm, 1956; Harré, 1998), while remaining allied to an established school in psychology, nevertheless readily admit the influence that existential thought has had upon their ideas and writings. Even so, these writers clearly pursue differing emphases and implications of existential thought and present interpretations which may not be readily agreed upon by other writers.

In spite of this lack of cohesion, the broad themes of existential phenomenology, that is, freedom, 'thrownness' or situatedness, choice, anxiety and meaning, form the nucleus of issues raised by existentially oriented psychologists.

Similarly, these writers stand united in their common interest in and pursuit of clearer theories of the various facets of human consciousness and take variants of the phenomenological method as their starting points to such investigation.

Lastly, existentially oriented psychologists take as a basic presupposition that human beings cannot be adequately understood or explained by a psychology that is modelled solely upon the natural or biological sciences. Rather it is through the remaking of psychology into a fully *human* science which, while not rejecting empirical data and investigation, nevertheless is required to develop new paradigms for investigation, that we gain an increasingly adequate understanding of ourselves.

Amadeo Giorgi's still highly influential book, *Psychology as a Human Science* (1970), for instance, presents a compelling case against the reductionist tendencies in contemporary psychology and offers initial steps towards the development of a more human-based approach which takes into account the unique features and problems that must be recognized when taking human beings as subject matter. Giorgi's ideas, and those of his contemporaries, spurred a novel and critical means to undertake structured psychological inquiry and research. I will pursue this point in the following chapter.

Because existential phenomenology raises issues broadly concerned with theories of personality, various levels of felt unease (or 'dis-ease' as some have termed such) and inter-relational conflict, it is not surprising that existential phenomenology's greatest psychological impact has been in the field of psychotherapy and counselling, as we shall see in Chapter 8.

As a final summing up of existential phenomenology, let me conclude with a précis of the final page of Philip K. Dick's novel, *Now Wait For Last Year* (1975). Set in the future, the hero, Eric Sweetscent, is having a discussion with a mechanical taxi driver. Eric's question to the Automatic Mechanism is whether he should leave or stay with his dying wife whose illness is inoperable even in the future from which Eric has just returned. The mechanical taxi driver's answer is unhesitant:

> 'I'd stay with her,' the cab decided.
> 'Why?'
> 'Because,' the cab said, 'life is composed of reality configurations so constituted. To abandon her would be to say, I can't endure reality as such. I have to have uniquely special easier conditions.' (Dick, 1975: 224)

Eric agrees and, as reward, receives a blessing from the Automatic Mechanism for having shown himself to be a human being. And with that the novel ends. As does this chapter.

7

Phenomenological Research

Few things have done more harm than the belief on the part of individuals or groups... that he or she or they are in sole *possession of the truth... It is a terrible and dangerous arrogance to believe that you alone are right... and that others cannot be right if they disagree.*

Isaiah Berlin

My aim in this chapter is twofold. Firstly, I will provide a brief overview of some of the central ideas of phenomenology and their relation to contemporary scientific enquiry. Secondly, I will focus upon the possibilities of phenomenologically related research in life sciences such as psychology.

Let me begin with a very brief overview of Human Science enquiry and some of its divergences from the more commonly studied 'Natural Scientific' approach adopted by the life sciences. Modern life science phenomenology is explicit in acknowledging its debt to ideas originating and derived from philosophical issues that, although directly traceable back to Plato, Kant, and Hegel, were specifically formulated at the start of the twentieth century by Edmund Husserl, the founder of phenomenology. His ideas regarding formal research studies were further extended by later phenomenologically informed researchers such as Paul Colaizzi (1973), Michael Crotty (1996), Amadeo Giorgi (1985), Gunnar Karlsson (1993), Steinar Kvale (1996) and Clark Moustakas (1994).

Human vs Natural Sciences

As noted in the previous chapter, it was Wilhelm Dilthey who first proposed a distinction between the Natural Sciences and the Human Sciences (Hodges, 1952). He argued that these different endeavours require different methodologies since the former are based upon explaining while the latter are based upon intuitive understanding. For much of the century just passed, the Human Sciences were all but forgotten or dismissed. But, more recently, this situation has begun to shift. The impact of this has been felt no more strongly than in the arena of psychotherapy research wherein persistent and recurring criticism continues to be made regarding the questionable value of psychotherapeutic analyses which are predicated upon natural scientific, modernist assumptions and which, in turn, are fashioned according to the dictates of a logico-empiricist methodology (Denzin and Lincoln, 1994; Kvale, 1994; Mahrer, 2000).

The dominant attitude towards psychology research claims to have as its aim the production of 'a body of facts… that can be objectively discovered using a methodology modelled on the natural sciences' (Kaye, 1995: 36). This natural scientific stance examines psychological variables by a) reducing them to observable, quantifiable elements; b) utilizing controlled experimental design; and c) seeking verification via replication. 'As a result… [psychology] has come to be treated for research purposes as an in principle lawful process, the components of which can be isolated, in which cause and effect can be empirically discovered and in which the critical variables lawfully related to change might be systematically established' (Kaye, 1995: 36).

Such a perspective, while initially appealing to some, is stripped of its allure when one considers its implications.

What is being revealed here is that this Natural Science approach to research both disconnects psychology from its appropriate context and is itself seriously disconnected from any valid form of investigation be it at either the outcome or process level. Indeed, what this kind of research does is address central questions of psychology by transforming them into something else which conforms to the dictates of a Natural Science paradigm. John Kaye, writing about the impact of this paradigm upon psychotherapy research in particular, nonetheless summarizes the broader impact upon psychology as a whole:

> Research within this frame necessitates either the reduction of the phenomenon being studied to quantifiable terms, or the selection for study of only those aspects of the phenomenon which can be converted into measurable terms… [T]his can only result in a partial picture… one which also misrepresents its holistic, contextual nature. (1995: 46)

What alternative do we have? To return to Dilthey, there is a Human Science approach available.

The Human Science view argues that an interpretatively-focused investigative activity 'cannot be accomplished by observing the individual as a complex mechanism geared to respond to certain conditions in regular ways; rather we have to get inside the forms of life and the socially normative regularities in which the person's activity has taken shape. This requires… [a]n empathic and imaginative identification with the subject…' (Gillett, 1995: 112).

When considered within the framework of psychology, Human Science research highlights our awareness that psychology inevitably involves the investigation and interpretation of *meaning*. This inevitability serves as the key distinguishing factor between the Human and Natural sciences in that the former perspective runs counter to the dominant positivist assumption of an objectively knowable, empirically derived reality subscribed to by the latter. Further, this distinctive hallmark of the Human

Sciences emphasizes the role of language as a primary constituent of 'reality'. This focus upon language is not solely restricted to notions of language within the spoken sense of the term. The attempt to make sense of another's worldview, according to Eugene Gendlin (1997) is not just a personal cognitive process but requires the participation of 'the lived body' as an authenticating and validating procedure that is 'responsive' to the bodily evocative dimensions that make words personally relevant. Further, this attitude opens investigations towards a recognition of aesthetic issues as possible lines of enquiry.

In general, as Denzin and Lincoln (1994) have argued, legitimate Human Science enquiry involves alternative notions to those of Natural Science enquiry. These include terms like trustworthiness, credibility, dependability, and confirmability and are intended to re-contextualize the Natural Science notion of validity within a Human Science arena. Similarly, while the notions of reliability and validity which remain central elements of a Natural Science research methodology are not directly employed by Human Science research, such approaches do rely upon the *verifiability* of the researcher's conclusions in so far as verifiability refers to 'whether another researcher can assume the perspective of the present investigator, review the original protocol data, and see that the proposed insights meaningfully illuminate the situations under study' (Churchill and Wertz, 2001: 259).

In addition, as Rom Harré has expressed it, the dominant Natural Science paradigm adopted by much of psychological inquiry rests upon the 'illusion of individual subjectivity' that cannot be maintained. 'Many psychological phenomena which have traditionally been ascribed to individual people are actually joint products of essentially conversational interactions' (Harré, 1991: 16).

Nonetheless, it must be acknowledged that these interpretative methodologies, even when they are employed appropriately, continue to be regarded with suspicion not only by those who elevate Natural Science research methodologies, but, more pertinently, by those who have substantial impact upon the kinds of research to be funded, emphasized and valued in both undergraduate and graduate psychology programmes.

Much of this resistance to Human Science research rests, I believe, upon the critical misunderstanding that interpretative and constructivist approaches lead research to the logical 'dead end' of an ongoing relative reality where all positions are to be treated and respected as being of equal value and merit. Were this the case, I would be as wary as anyone else about such enterprises. But this conclusion, happily, is patently misrepresentative of such forms of enquiry. Put simply, rather than lead us to extreme forms of relativism, such enquiry, as phenomenology has long argued (and as I have sought to demonstrate throughout this text) opens us to the implications of an inter-relational reality that exists within the context of discernible structures and boundaries and guidelines from which it is possible to arrive at positions of judgement regarding the relative adequacy of one stance in contrast to another. True, it may well lead to more intricate forms of understanding, but not to the sort of relativistic chaos suggested by critics.

Phenomenological Research: General Principles

Phenomenology, as applied to psychological inquiry, deals with the attempt to understand more adequately the human condition as it manifests itself in lived, concrete, experience. This includes not only the observable behavioural outcomes of experience but also the entire range of inter-relationally interpreted states of being including such instances as moments of joy, absurdity, anxiety, confusion, indifference, and so forth. In other words, phenomenological investigation includes all possible experiences available to human reflection. Phenomenology attempts to establish a more adequate set of criteria for the investigation of phenomena as we actually live them out and experience them. As Valle and King (1978) put it:

> [Phenomenology] seeks to understand the events of human experience in a way which is free of the presuppositions of our cultural heritage, especially philosophical dualism and technologism, as much as is possible. When applied more specifically to human psychological phenomena, [phenomenology] has become that psychological discipline which seeks to explicate the essence, structure, or form of human experience and human behavior as revealed through essentially descriptive techniques including disciplined reflection. (Valle and King, 1978: 7)

Recall that phenomenology initially was seen by Edmund Husserl as a practical or scientific philosophy that would allow a method of enquiry into all aspects of lived experience and mental activity. The task of phenomenological investigation became that of illuminating and disclosing the meaning structures of lived experience. Phenomenology takes the view that experience is not an internal, intrapsychic process. Rather than being 'inside our heads', experience is always concerned with and an expression of inter-relation. Experience is always already out in the world. As such, the study of experience is a legitimate and necessary psychological enterprise.

Phenomenology's exposition and clarification of every act of experiencing centres upon the twin standpoints of the experience's directional, or noematic, focus (its 'what-ness') and its noetic referential or contextual focus (its 'how-ness'). These foci serve to *structure* experience. Phenomenologically speaking, 'structuredness' refers to the meaningfulness of experience. The structure of a phenomenon is the commonality running through its many diverse appearances.

The primary task of phenomenological research is to illuminate and disclose the make-up, or way of being, of any given structure in its form of meaning. As such, if it is the task of the phenomenological researcher to disclose the experience of joy, or depression, or boredom or whatever other human experience that may be open to us, that task might well initiate investigation by eliciting particular instances of such experiences but only so that these may be utilized in order to approach a more adequate understanding of the experiential variables that constitute or structure the experience in general. As such, its focus on the subjective is only a stepping off point for its exploration of the more universal 'structuredness' of the experience.

As a clarification of what is being argued here, consider the following example provided by Valle and King (1978). Imagine that you are transcribing the musical notes that make up the melody from the first movement of Tchaikovsky's Fifth Symphony. If you then rewrite this melody as transposed by one octave, you will transcribe a quite different set of musical notes. Though the two notations reveal surface distinctions from one another, their underlying melody remains the same. While Natural Science derived psychological research typically focuses on 'the notes', phenomenological research seeks to disclose 'the melody', that is, more broadly speaking, the foundational structure of conscious experience.

As Colaizzi (1973) argues: 'without thereby first disclosing the foundations of a phenomenon, no progress whatsoever can be made concerning it, not even a first faltering step can be taken towards it, by science or by any other kind of cognition' (Colaizzi, 1973: 28).

Put succinctly, phenomenological research inquiry urges a stance that has been expressed by Knorr-Certina as that of turning 'the obvious into the problematic' (Knorr-Certina, 1981; quoted in Kaye, 1995: 30).

Phenomenological and Traditional Psychological Research: a Comparison

As we have seen, Husserl's aim was nothing less than to resolve one of the central problems that plagued Western philosophy, namely the split between subjectivity and objectivity and its implications for our statements about the nature and structure of reality. Husserl sought to create a truly scientific philosophy – not a philosophy of science, but, rather, a philosophy that would form the foundations of *any* scientific enquiry.

Most importantly for our purposes, Husserl developed a method of approaching the questions raised by scientific enquiry which, as we have seen, is usually referred to as 'the phenomenological method of reduction'. This method raises important, even crucial, objections to the many assumptions that underlie the 'Natural Scientific' approach to scientific enquiry that has so dominated Western thought.

Perhaps the most fundamental of these objections focuses on the naïve assumption of the Natural Scientific approach that we can speak with any certainty about the true, or objective, nature of reality. Instead, phenomenology argues, to put it simply, that we can never know the real world, only the interpreted world – the world that emerges through our reflections upon it. As such, all our statements about the world, or any aspect of the world – including, of course, ourselves – are, at best, approximations. We can never truly speak of 'facts' or with any final certainty because all our statements reveal limitations and assumptions that impede our ability to describe or understand things as they really are. Phenomenological research does not promise the sort of data that Natural Science methods generate. On the other hand, in eschewing the notion of a final statement on any focus of investigation, it provides an openness of possibilities, an open-mindedness in the exploration of any facet of human experience that may be highly desirable not just for its own sake but also possibly for its impact upon such issues as decision-making analyses, social change policies, and so forth.

As I have already argued, phenomenology stands in contrast to the Natural Scientific viewpoint and its underlying assumptions because the questions it poses and the methods it employs are grounded in a carefully articulated, but undeniably different, set of philosophical assumptions. It should be apparent that those looking for or expecting a form of research methodology that might be analogous to that which is employed by Natural Scientific assumptions will be disappointed in the possibilities of phenomenological research.

What then might be some of the most immediate implications of phenomenological research upon contemporary psychology?

Firstly, unlike traditional psychology, phenomenological psychology denies the possibility of truly objective observation and research. Rather, it assumes an indissoluble inter-relationship between the investigator and his or her focus of investigation. Both are said to *co-constitute* one another. The bases of co-constitutionality are *dialogue* and *disclosure*. Individuals and their world are always in dialogue with one another in that each is a necessary constituent to the construction of phenomenon-derived reality. Each is partly active and partly passive in relation to the other. Similarly, all inter-actions reveal, identify, define, in a word, disclose the co-constituents of the interaction. This fundamental assumption is most commonly expressed through terms such as 'figure-ground', 'self-other' or 'I-not I'.

A second major divergence rests on the notion of consciousness. In the more typical psychological research model the nature of consciousness *per se*, rarely surfaces as an issue. For phenomenological psychology, consciousness is central to all investigation since the primary aim of phenomenological investigation is to approach as adequately as possible direct and immediate experience.

Phenomenological research relies upon the phenomenological method in order that the researchers may more adequately attempt to suspend or to set aside their assumptions and preconceptions. In order to initiate this process of attempted *bracketing* researchers must first make their assumptions as explicit as is feasible. When investigators attempt to do this, they are likely to discover further previously unsuspected assumptions underlying their initial assumptions. As these emerge, these too are bracketed as far as possible. As such, the process of bracketing is never final. But the process itself leads one away from the Natural Science attitude that posits a subjective-objective stance and towards a phenomenological attitude that acknowledges and places acts of investigation *within* co-constitutionality. As Zaner (1970) points out, just as it is by consciousness that objects are made present, equally, it is by objects that consciousness is revealed and elucidated.

Thirdly, phenomenological research rejects the common notion of causality in its linear form. The focus of investigation is not therefore studied or understood in a manner that focuses upon explanations derived from events or circumstances that are claimed to be related in some causal chain of events that are perceived to be unidirectional from some point in the past to the present circumstances. The meaning of both past and present events may certainly be considered and both may prove interesting, but there is no justification for the assumption that the first event caused the second. Implicit in the above view is the rejection of standard research notions of control groups, dependent and independent variables, preliminary hypotheses, and so forth, since these all suggest, to a greater or lesser degree, the notion of linear causality.

Phenomenology's critique of the traditional methods of psychological investigation – that is to say, experimentation coupled with operational definitions – argues that such methods largely exclude, transform, deny, limit or denigrate human experience. John Rowan, writing about qualitative research in general presented this view in typical succinct style: '[t]reating people like things is methodologically wrong' (Rowan, 1998: 578, italics in original).

While traditional methods rely upon the isolation and manipulation of specified variables in order to discern causal explanations for particular events, phenomenological methods concern themselves primarily with exploratory strategies designed to accumulate an ever increasingly adequate description of any given phenomenon *as it presents itself* to one's experience.

From a phenomenological research standpoint, there is no demand on the researcher to define in advance any possible productive causality, nor is it the case that researchers must reduce their focus of investigation to a set of operational definitions that impose an immediate transformative bias upon the event under investigation and, further, serve to limit its range of definitional possibilities to those which remain open to particular forms of statistical analysis. Rather, phenomenological research acknowledges a multiple, even inexhaustible, range of definitional possibilities. And, once again, unlike traditional approaches it avoids taking a stance that demands the rejection of some data in favour of others because of competing, unique or mutually exclusive variants. Instead, the stance adopted by phenomenological research is complementary-focused such that all data – even the most idiosyncratic – are duly considered without the need to reject their meaning possibilities.

Unlike traditional research, the enterprise of phenomenological research is foundationally collaborative. Researchers and their participants (typically labelled *co-researchers*) are partners in the given enterprise whose meanings and purposes are openly revealed and discussed without any intent to deceive, misrepresent or obscure all or part of the process. The phenomenological researcher does not assume that the data will be contaminated by the co-researcher's knowledge, views or unplanned input.

In general, the principal methods of traditional psychological research – objective experimentation coupled with the use of operational definitions – largely exclude enquiry that is *directly* focused on human experience. But this is a primary area of concern to both the practice of and research in psychology since each demands the exposition and clarification of humanly lived experience. To put it another way, the phenomenological researcher must seek out a method of listening or investigation which neither denies experience, nor denigrates it, nor transforms it into operationally defined behaviour. Indeed, the method being sought aims to remain with human experience as it is experienced, and which seeks to sustain contact with experience as it is given.

While most psychologists seek to yield 'truth' (or, to be more precise, *statistical approximations* of truth) from their studies and experiments, phenomenological researchers focus upon the quest for statements of 'increasing adequacy' regarding the structure of an experience. This is not merely a question of semantics since this shift in aim allows phenomenological psychologists to include in their investigations those descriptive and qualitative variants of lived experience that empirically based research either fails to consider or, more likely, simply cannot consider within its quantitative parameters. As such, phenomenological research typically places central importance upon the investigation, description and clarification of *qualitative* variables. I state the obvious when I say that this important emphasis is rarely touched upon by those psychologists who work under the limitations imposed upon them by the Natural-Scientific approach to psychological research.

In general, the overall aim of phenomenological research is to provide increasingly adequate meaning statements rather than final laws or uncontestable truths. In this way, to extrapolate from the conclusion concerning the aim of psychotherapy arrived at by the inter-relational psychotherapist Leslie Farber (2000), phenomenology is more concerned with 'speaking truthfully' about an experience rather than focus upon the achievement of a final, or 'arrived at' truth.

The Methodology of Phenomenological Research

How is phenomenological research carried out? While the structured method devised by Paul Colaizzi that I summarize below provides an approach that I believe contains the key methodological characteristics of phenomenological research in general, it is essential to note that there exists *no one* phenomenological means to enquiry. The assumption of *a* method is a fallacy. Instead, each phenomenological investigator employs unique descriptive approaches derived from the phenomenological method. Again, as Colaizzi argues, 'each particular psychological phenomenon, in conjunction with the particular aims and objectives of a particular researcher, evokes a particular descriptive method' (Colaizzi, 1978: 53). In the general approach advocated by Colaizzi, this methodology can best be explained as a series of 'steps':

> *Step 1*: The researcher designs a brief unbiased statement or research question whose purpose is to specify the focus of investigation and to select appropriate co-researchers who are qualified (via their experience) to engage in a descriptively-focused enquiry. This step requires the researcher to engage in a preliminary process of self-investigation designed to expose his or her presuppositions regarding the phenomenon to be explored so that these can be 'bracketed' insofar as they are not inadvertently embedded within the starting statement or research question.

> *Step 2*: The researcher engages in a structured, focused enquiry with each co-researcher. This is typically carried out in a one-to-one interview usually lasting approximately one hour.

> *Step 3*: The interviews are transcribed verbatim.

> *Step 4*: The researcher reads each of the transcribed interviews (conventionally referred to as 'protocols') several times in order to gain a 'feel' for their content.

> *Step 5*: The researcher returns to each individual protocol and extracts those phrases or sentences that directly pertain to the investigated phenomenon so that by the end of this step the researcher has collected a list of *significant statements* from each protocol.

> *Step 6*: The researcher seeks to extract or spell out the meanings contained in each significant statement. This formulation of meanings, or movement from what is said to what is meant, is the most precarious interpretative part of the phenomenological research process and requires the researcher's creative insight to both remain true to the co-researcher's statement while at the same time seeking to draw out of it its embedded, often implicit, meaning.

> *Step 7*: Having formulated meanings from all of the significant statements derived from all of the protocols, the researcher now organizes the aggregate formulated meanings into clusters of themes that may be shared by one, some or all of the co-researchers. The themes may well be contradictory or even unrelated to one another and require the researcher's tolerance for ambiguity. Further, there may be formulated meanings that do not fall into clusters of themes in that they stand alone. These too are added to the final list of thematic elements.

> *Step 8*: The list of thematic elements is integrated into an exhaustive description of the investigated phenomenon.

> *Step 9*: The researcher returns to each co-researcher with the exhaustive description so that the co-researcher can respond to it in terms of its verifiability as a statement that captures the experiential structure under investigation.

Step 10: On the basis of the co-researchers' comments, amendments, corrections, novel additions, if any, the researcher produces a further, usually final, exhaustive description of the phenomenon. While never fully completed, in that the validation attempt will seek on-going refinement of any avowedly 'final' statement, nonetheless this step most frequently paves the way for further, and hopefully more adequate research. At the very least, it allows the researcher to go back to the original statement and to examine how well or poorly it reflected the co-researchers' actual statements, what previously unforeseen assumptions may have either remained within it or was left out that may be significant for future research.

As can be adduced, the starting point to any phenomenological investigation must lie with the clarification of the investigator's own involvement, biases, and aims. He or she must first clarify how his or her personal inclinations and predispositions influence his or her research project. For example, the phenomenological researcher's relative success in accurately describing or reflecting the co-researcher's world-views so that they may be clarified, considered, and evaluated is entirely dependent upon the more or less adequate attempt to bracket the researcher's noted biases and aims so that they do not transform the co-researcher's intended meaning. This research focused application of the phenomenological method exposes, among other things, the relative willingness or unwillingness of the investigator to acknowledge and respect the co-researcher's autonomy, authority, and experiential responsibility. It reveals both the power and powerlessness of the investigator and both acknowledges and clarifies the investigator's role in and impact upon the investigation. More generally, the 'factual truth' of his or her data becomes both relative and relational.

Needless to say, the process of phenomenological enquiry is exhausting, time-consuming, fraught with interpretative dangers, and never complete. At the same time, it is often exhilarating, surprising in terms of what emerges, intellectually and emotionally invigorating, moving and capable of provoking a level of intimacy between researcher and co-researcher that parallels that of psychotherapy and which reaches a depth of value and meaning to all participants that traditional research never begins to approach.

An Example of Phenomenological Research

Even so, one might well ask whether the adoption of a phenomenological approach to research is worth the effort. This seems to me to be a sensible question to ask and it remains for me to strive to convince the reader that the effort is worth making and that the gains are of critical importance.

My attempt at this task centres upon a necessarily brief sketch of some preliminary research conducted by myself and a number of psychotherapy trainees who were interested in carrying out a phenomenological investigation exploring the possible benefits, if any, of the psychotherapeutic experience for the client.

In considering our starting point, it was immediately apparent that we could not begin with or rely upon what definitions or reductions of this experience have been provided by traditional psychological research since these operational definitions eliminated the phenomenon's experiential aspects. Instead, as phenomenological investigators, we had to begin by approaching the phenomenon as closely as possible to the manner with which our co-researchers experienced it.

As such, we were faced with the task of first collecting from our co-researchers their descriptions of this experience. But how to go about this? Obviously, we would need to provide an appropriate focus, such as a set of questions or statements, that would initiate a descriptive exploration intended to elicit truthful statements regarding this experience by our co-researchers.

To start the refining of this enquiry, we centred our initial focus on an examination of our own concerns, approaches, and areas of interest in order to uncover at least the most conspicuous of our presuppositions about the investigated topic. As we did so, we discerned various beliefs, biases, hypotheses, attitudes and hunches that we held. From these we constructed a formal statement:

> The psychotherapeutic experience allows me to feel truly listened to in an uncritical manner so that I can honestly and in a non-defensive manner examine a variety of assumptions that I hold about myself. It allows me to explore how these assumptions pattern my life experience, and to consider the relative freedom I have to hold on to or begin to reduce the strength of these assumptions. It allows me to experience myself as source of my experience rather than as a reactive 'victim' to it.

Having carried out this preliminary step, the focus to our enquiry could be clarified. We could now construct a set of questions or statements that would allow us to explore whether our assumptions bore any similarity to the actual statements of our co-researchers. We chose to produce a set of questions that would address these assumptions but also, most importantly, would not be so leading (or misleading) that they would influence our co-researchers' statements to the extent that they created a kind of 'self-fulfilling prophesy'. Already, I think, we were confronting a fundamental bias that imbues a great deal of psychological research.

The questions generated included the following:

1. Please try to recall and then describe what, if anything, there was about your psychotherapeutic experience that made an impression upon you or which in some way affected or influenced you.
2. If there was anything in your psychotherapeutic experience that made an impression or which in some way affected or influenced you, what is it that makes you feel certain that it *did* impress, affect or influence you?
3. What was your experience of yourself before you began seeing your psychotherapist? During? Afterwards?

4. What differences, if any, could you detect in yourself after the psychotherapeutic experience was completed?
5. What, if anything, made the psychotherapeutic experience easy or difficult for you? Enjoyable or disagreeable? Worthwhile or irrelevant?
6. Is there anything you wish to add?

The success of such questions would depend upon how well they tapped into the co-researchers' experience as opposed to whatever theoretical knowledge either they or the investigators might have of it.

As can be seen, the questions were sufficiently open and broadly-focused so that anyone could be a co-researcher so long as he or she had experienced psychotherapy as a client and was willing and able to communicate his or her experience of this. As such, the actual size of the pool of co-researchers could be flexible. In this instance, eleven co-researchers replied to our invitation to engage in a structured interview.

Having completed the structured discussions, and transcribed each interview in its entirety, the following procedural steps were taken:

1. Reading Protocols

This step involved the careful reading and re-reading of the co-researchers' transcribed descriptions (or protocols) in order for the researchers to acquaint themselves with them.

2. Extracting Significant Statements

This step involved the researchers returning to each protocol and extracting phrases or sentences that directly pertained to the phenomenon under investigation. Several protocols might contain meaningfully similar statements and such repetitions were eliminated. For instance, co-researcher A spoke of his feeling 'at peace' by the end of a therapeutic session while co-researcher C spoke of 'the calm' that enveloped her in the last period of a session.

On the other hand, some statements contained particular specifics which were transposed to more general statements. For example, co-researcher F detailed a particular exchange between herself and her therapist which led to her feeling uncertain as to whether she could trust him and how she yearned for his having responded in another way so that she could have trusted him. The significant statement extracted from this was: 'verbal exchanges between therapist and client can engender both the gaining and loss of trust on the part of the client toward the therapist'.

Equally, some statements contradicted others. Co-researcher D expressed his shock at what he had revealed while co-researcher H 'knew ahead of time' that he would reveal closely guarded secrets and co-researcher B was surprised by how much she'd said but did not feel 'one way or the other' about this.

Finally, some statements were so unique that they appeared nowhere else in other co-researchers' protocols. Rather than exclude these (as is often the case in traditional research), we ensured that they were included in our list and were represented in our final statement.

3. Formulating Meanings

This step is difficult to delineate precisely since it involves the researcher's creative ability to intuit what has been stated specifically so that he or she might extract its implicit or foundational meaning. This is a precarious step because it involves moving beyond the explicit statement yet at the same time staying with the meaning contained within the statement so that the connections between both remain clear and concrete. Appropriate meanings are characterized by their avoidance of the imposition of theoretical/analytical interpretations and by their emphasis on descriptive interpretation. For example:

> *Protocol statement*:   Before I began, I felt that everyone except me was running my life, now I feel in charge.
> *Appropriate meaning*:   The psychotherapeutic experience allows the client to see him/herself as the source of his/her life-experience.
> *Inappropriate meaning*: The psychotherapeutic experience restrains the impact of the super-ego.
> *Or*:   The psychotherapeutic experience provides the means to a rational belief system.
> *Or*:   The psychotherapeutic experience allows for positive growth.

4. Extracting Clusters of Themes

This step involved the repetition of steps 1 to 3 for all protocols and the organization of formulated meanings into shared themes. Here we encountered similar difficulties regarding interpretation as were noted in the previous step. These were minimized by referring each extracted theme back to the original protocols in order to ascertain whether there was something added to or left out from protocols that in some way invalidated their intended meaning. In addition, this step acknowledged that contradictory, discrepant, and/or unique themes were acceptable and that a tolerance for ambiguity is necessary: 'what is logically inexplicable may be existentially real and valid' (Colaizzi, 1978: 61).

5. Exhaustive Description and Formulation of a Statement

In this step, all of the formulated meanings and thematic clusters were integrated so that an exhaustive description of the investigated phenomenon in as unequivocal a statement of identification of its formal structure as possible could be generated. The Statement derived from the research being described was formulated in the following way:

> The psychotherapeutic experience involves not so much the creation of new information but, rather, the discovery of a new way of living in one's own world. Regardless of their initial attitude to psychotherapy, all clients, at some

point in the sessions, feel confusion or are shaken by the experience or feel they must challenge its impact, even if the impact is a felt sense of 'wasting time' or 'going nowhere'.

The clients' most meaningful self-disclosures (as defined by the clients themselves) create a tension that is of substantial worth, whether or not it remains focused or unfocused, heard or misheard by the psychotherapist. Regardless of the style of psychotherapy, clients invest a central importance upon the psychotherapist and upon the relationship he or she engenders. Indeed, how the psychotherapist 'is' and responds to the challenges of the relationship (be they verbal exchange, silence, physical contact or its avoidance) is, for clients, the pivotal variable upon which psychotherapy is or is not deemed to be beneficial.

For most clients, the already known becomes seen in a new light allowing previously hidden meanings to the familiar to emerge. For some clients, the key term is 'change' (either positive or negative); for others, it is 'acceptance'. In all cases, while acknowledging its disruptive potential, the experience provoked a felt sense of an at least partial release of psycho-physical tension lasting anything between several hours to a still continuing occurrence.

While some clients' initial aims might be fulfilled, this is not always the case. For some co-researchers, the lack of fulfilment of aims is regretted; for others those aims lose significance or are seen as unrealizable fantasies, or are replaced by previously unstated or unseen aims. Some initial aims are exposed as false or as obscurants to more pertinent concerns.

All the clients who participated in the research claimed to have benefited from psychotherapy though benefit for one participant meant 'realizing what a "load of nonsense" psychotherapy is and being glad to get it out of my system'.

7. Co-researcher Verification

This step took the investigation back to the co-researchers in that our investigator findings in the form of the Final Statement were shown to the co-researchers in a face-to-face interview that was recorded in order to ascertain how adequately the Final Statement contained or 'captured' their experience. This step sought to verify from our co-researchers that our Statement captured adequately their statements. Alternatively, was there anything of importance left out by error or as result of incorrect interpretations? In addition, we wanted our co-researchers to tell us if there was there anything of significance that they had not considered or stated before which emerged via their reading of the Statement?

This last step may require the researcher to produce an amended Final Statement that incorporates new experiential information or that removes errors or that clarifies further the descriptions that have been provided. In our case, no amendments were required and the research was (temporarily) concluded.

Final Comments

Whatever the views arrived at by readers regarding the aims, uniqueness or worth of phenomenological research, my hope is that they have been convinced that phenomenological research is not, *per se*, anti-empirical.

While it questions the fundamental assumptions and investigative methodologies adopted by more traditional psychological approaches to research, it also seeks to provide an alternative to these that is structured, open to articulation, consistent with the overall understanding-focused stance taken by phenomenological psychology and whose conclusions remain open to an appropriate standard of verifiability.

Phenomenological research, as with phenomenology in general, rejects the Natural Science assumption that the meanings that can be given to or derived from any event reside in the event itself, independent of any human presence. Rather, phenomenological researchers argue, the meanings are imbedded in, and emerge from, the various inter-relations between the researcher, the co-researchers and the meaningful event. The underlying structure that shapes these meanings is shared, though the perspective from which the structure is experienced reveals the particular way of being adopted by each participant in the research toward the meaningful event. Hence, the researcher and the co-researchers engage in a collaborative enterprise, the ultimate purpose of which is to articulate with increased adequacy the shared structural character of the phenomenon under investigation.

In this way, contrary to what is often misrepresented as the aim of phenomenological research, it can be seen to be fundamentally focused upon the elucidation of inherent foundational structures that can be discerned in any specific example or instance of a particular lived experience rather than simply attempt a process of subjectively focused descriptive analysis emphasizing particularity or difference.

It is important for me to stress once again, however, that phenomenological research does not seek to impose *a* methodology upon structured enquiry. The means outlined in this chapter are intended to serve solely as possible examples and signposts with which to assist those who might wish to undertake this 'way' of investigation. In all cases, phenomenological research adopts Heidegger's dictum that the structure of any dasein is such that it 'never arrives' but is always only 'on the way' (Heidegger, 1962).

8
Existential Psychotherapy

I suppose I'm one of the symptoms of the times.

R.D. Laing

What influence phenomenology – and existential phenomenology in particular – has had and, increasingly, still has on general psychology is most apparent in the related professions of psychotherapy, counselling and counselling psychology.

This chapter will first of all consider phenomenological approaches to therapy in general and then go on to focus on two highly influential theoreticians, R.D. Laing and Carl Rogers, in order to demonstrate how each of these authors has incorporated and extended phenomenological ideas into his style of therapy.

In the years since the first edition of this book, it has become something of a convention among British proponents of phenomenology to refer to *existential phenomenology* when focusing upon current views or issues concerned with theory and to *existential psychotherapy* (or *counselling* or *counselling psychology*) when referring to practice-focused concerns. While I continue to retain a personal preference for *phenomenological psychotherapy*, my insistence upon this admittedly idiosynchratic view would be unnecessarily confusing to the reader. As such, I will follow the conventional view and focus attention upon existential psychotherapy. Nonetheless, given the specifically phenomenological focus of this text, I will concentrate upon those arguments and points of discussion that are more obviously derived from phenomenological insights originating from both the transcendental and existential branches of phenomenology. I must begin by emphasizing, however, that, rather than being a particular technique or method of therapy, existential psychotherapy more than anything else provides therapists with a set of foundational principles that serve as guidelines and 'meaning structures' which underpin their practice (Ruitenbeek, 1962). An important recent text by Mick Cooper, *Existential Therapies* (2003) provides a concise and clear account of both the diversity of existential therapies and those foundational structures which unite them. Similarly, texts such as Hans W. Cohn's *Existential Thought and Therapeutic Practice* (1997), Gion Condrau's *Martin Heidegger's Impact on Psychotherapy* (1998), Simon du Plock's *Existential Case Studies* (1997), van Deurzen-Smith's

Everyday Mysteries (1997) Strasser and Strasser's *Existential Time-Limited Psychotherapy* (1997), and my own *Tales of Un-knowing* (Spinelli, 1997) and *The Mirror and the Hammer* (Spinelli, 2001) provide readers with various attempts to configure existential-phenomenological theory into psychotherapeutic practice. Finally, Martin Heidegger's *Zollikon Seminars* (2001) remains essential reading.

If we accept that there exists a number of foundational principles and assumptions underlying existential phenomenology which are shared and to which existential psychotherapists subscribe, then it might be advantageous to first state these principles and assumptions. Here is my phenomenologically focused suggestion regarding what would be this list of chosen pivotal principles:

1. That a primary invariant aspect of human existence is the attempted construction of meaning – no matter how limited or inadequate – upon all reflections on our lived experience.
2. That all human meanings are intentionally derived in that meaning emerges from inter-relational acts upon, and reactions to, the 'stimuli' of the world.
3. That because they are intentionally derived, no meanings concerning any aspect of self/world inter-relations can ever be complete or fully 'captured'.
4. That both the attempt to accept or to avoid the multiple implications of the above point (3), as well as the persistent tendency to 'fix' or 'capture' meaning in spite of its intentional basis, provoke unease and insecurity in a being's self/world inter-relations.
5. That the existential underpinnings to the above point (4) lie in the awareness of the general time-limited or temporal constraints upon our intentional 'meaning making', as well as the inability to know the specific temporal constraints and parameters that situate each of us as an individual being 'in the world'.

Considered from a therapeutic focus, these five principles, taken separately and together, provide us with numerous practice-based implications and applications which, in turn, can be highlighted as critical features of existential therapeutic practice.

What is initially pivotal for the reader interested in existential psychotherapy to understand is that rather than stress yet another standard technique or set of practices, representatives of this approach hold that any over-emphasis on technique, or on practice in general, is one of the main obstacles to understanding the client and, thus, to any truly long-lasting outcome of therapy. It is the basic view of existential psychotherapists that 'it is not the understanding that follows technique, but the technique that follows understanding' (Misiak and Sexton, 1973: 87).

General Emphases in Existential Psychotherapy

The Aims of Existential Psychotherapy

As, I hope, will become apparent, if there is an ultimate aim to existential psychotherapy, it is to offer the means for persons to examine, confront, clarify and reassess their understanding of life, the problems encountered throughout their life, and the limits imposed upon the possibilities inherent in being-in-the-world.

Existential psychotherapists de-emphasize any directively generated 'curative' aims and place little value on any specific manipulative or re-educational techniques that seek to modify current behaviour. For existential psychotherapists, what other models have labelled as neurotic or psychotic defence mechanisms are more accurately understood as inter-relationally imposed blocks against authentic living brought on by the person's desire to deny and avoid the necessary angst that the possibilities of authentic living present to his or her general way of being, or *worldview*.

In order to emphasize that the role of the existential psychotherapist is not principally a medical/curative one, but, rather, that of stimulus to honest and revealing investigation of one's inter-relationally derived worldview, existential psychotherapists prefer the term client over that of patient. All this is not to say that clients might not emerge from therapy 'cured' of any number of symptoms or having learned how to modify their behaviour for their own 'betterment' – obviously this occurs in existential psychotherapy just as it does in most other therapeutic approaches – but this is not its primary aim or concern. Rather, as Emmy van Deurzen-Smith has put it:

> The existential approach to counselling centres on an exploration of some-one's particular way of seeing life, the world and herself. The goal is to help her to establish what it is that matters to her, so that she can begin to feel more in tune with herself and therefore more real and alive. Before the person can rearrange her lifestyle in accordance with her priorities she has to examine her own preconceptions and assumptions which stand in the way of her personal development. Much of what has always been taken for granted is therefore re-examined in the light of a search for truth about life. (1988: 27)

The Exploration of Lived Experience

Common to the various 'attitudes' within existential psychotherapy is the acknowledged emphasis placed upon the exploration of clients' consciousness and experience of being-in-the-world. In this way, clients' various embodied attitudes, values, beliefs, choices or assumptions regarding what it means and how it is for them to exist in and engage with themselves, others and the world in general can be exposed, examined, challenged and reconsidered in relation to the problems encountered throughout their lives, and the limits imposed upon the possibilities inherent in being-in-the-world.

This clarification of the client's worldview highlights the various world-view constituents' inter-relationship with, and impact upon, one another. From this perspective, the client's problematic presenting symptoms or disturbances cannot be isolated, or considered on their own, in isolation from the rest of the client's various 'ways of being'. Rather, it is argued, they reflect the wider possibilities and limitations of the client's chosen inter-relational stance toward both self and others (or 'the world' in general).

Attitudinal Qualities in Existential Psychotherapy

The existential psychotherapist's task centres upon a number of funda-mental attitudes that are derived from phenomenological inquiry. In brief, these require the therapist to make *the attempt* to

1. Set aside, or *bracket*, his or her own beliefs, theories, biases and assumptions;
2. Emphasize and explore the client's immediate conscious experience of 'being-with-another' (the therapist);
3. Focus the investigation upon its descriptive components rather than rely upon theory-driven interpretations.

This focus upon a descriptive attunement towards the lived world of the client forces existential psychotherapists to recognize that they are no longer able to be the detached objective observer/explorer/clarifier of some facets of their clients' lived reality. Rather, the existential psy-chotherapist is *implicated* via the inquiry in a way that the encounter between therapist and client, while undeniably focused upon the client, is, nonetheless, mutually revelatory. For both client and therapist, the encounter permits a conscious reflection of 'this is what and how it is to be who I am being in this relation'.

For the existential psychotherapist, the act of listening to the client is focused upon the client's self/world relations. In this way, the client's statements, concerns and disclosures are not considered in isolation but, rather, as explicit or implicit inter-relational statements that reveal the possibilities and limitations of being that emerge for the client through his or her values, beliefs, judgemental attitudes and affects.

The existential psychotherapist's task is not one of seeking to impose a directive change or to ameliorate the lived inter-relational world of the client, but, rather, to attempt to clarify it so that its explicit, implicit, and fixed or *sedimented* assumptions, values, and beliefs can be re-examined and reconsidered. In turn, this attempt reveals those disowned or *dissoci-ated* experiences, thoughts, behaviours and affects that serve to maintain the client's current worldview, even if these are experienced as being problematic, undesirable or even seriously debilitating symptoms.

The Dimensions of Worldviews

How can existential psychotherapists assist clients in clarifying their worldviews? One highly influential therapist, Ludwig Binswanger (1963), argued that an individual's worldview can be seen to consist of three dimensions: the Umwelt, the Mitwelt, and the Eigenwelt.

The *Umwelt* can best be described as the 'natural world with its physical, biological dimension' (van Deurzen-Smith, 1988: 69). Although each of us is limited by innate, biological invariants, we still provide unique meanings and interpretations of the physical world we inhabit. We might experience this physical dimension as being essentially harmonious, secure and pleasurable, or it may fill us with anxiety due to perceived dangers, doubts, injustices and so forth. Our attitudes to a wide range of variables within the physical dimension – our bodies, the weather, ecological variables and so on – rather than being seen as insignificant when mentioned in therapy, are duly examined and considered as valuable means to clarifying clients' meanings and concerns.

The *Mitwelt* dimension focuses on the everyday, public relations each of us has with others. The inferences each of us draws about our race, social class, gender, language, culture, the rules and codes of our society (and those who enforce those rules), our general work environments – all may lead us to develop a wide range of differing attitudes and values. We might feel empowered or invalidated by our public-world interactions, they may engender feelings of acceptance or rejection, dominance or submission, conformity or rebellion. The public world might be perceived as loving and respectful, or petty, spiteful and dangerous to the point where it must be avoided whenever possible. Once again, clients' stated perceptions of their dealings with the public world demand attention and investigation.

The *Eigenwelt* deals with the private and intimate relations each of us has with both ourselves and the significant others in our lives. How we view ourselves, the degree of self-confidence, self-acceptance and individuality we define for ourselves is an obvious area of concern as is the way we interpret our interactions with our family, friends, sexual partners – those 'intimate' beings in our lives upon whom we place so much significance and importance, and who seem to have the power to make our lives seem meaningful or meaningless, rich or arid, full or empty, secure or wracked with anxiety.

In addition to these three dimensions, a fourth – the *Überwelt* – has been suggested by van Deurzen-Smith (1988). This dimension 'refers to a person's connection to the abstract and absolute aspect of living' (van Deurzen-Smith, 1988: 97) and incorporates our ideological outlook on life, the beliefs we hold about life, death, existence – those beliefs which underpin or are a basis for all subsequent beliefs and interpretations. In voicing such attitudes and beliefs, clients are invited to examine and assess them more carefully, more honestly, in order that they might either 'own' them (perhaps for the first time in their lives) or come to realize that they can do so no longer and are in a position to consider and confront what beliefs they *do* hold.

All these dimensions are open to investigation and clarification; in doing so, clients confront the attitudes, assumptions and values they place upon each and, as a result, are more likely to make sense of the problematic 'symptoms' in their lives as extensions of, or defensive reactions to, any of these dimensions.

Four Inter-Relational Realms of Descriptive Inquiry

A related, though to my mind much more explicitly inter-relational, approach towards the investigation of the client's worldview has been suggested and developed by me in various papers and texts (Spinelli, 1994; 1997). This way of examination focuses initially upon four distinct *inter-relational realms*.

The first of these realms, '*I-focused*' inquiry, considers those views, statements, opinions, beliefs, demands, and affective feelings that express the client's experience of being him/herself in the current encounter with the therapist. *The I-focused realm of encounter* attempts to describe and clarify 'my experience of being "myself" in any given relationship'. It asks, in effect, 'what do I tell myself about my current experience of being me in this encounter?'

The second, '*You-focused*' realm, considers those views, statements, opinions, beliefs, demands, and affective feelings that the client places upon the other (the therapist) in the current encounter. The *you-focused realm of encounter* attempts to describe and clarify 'my experience of "the other" being in relation with me'. It asks, in effect, 'what do I tell myself about my experience of the other in any given encounter?'

The third realm, the '*We-focused*' realm, concerns itself with the explication of those facets of currently lived experience that emerge from the immediacy of current experience *between* client and therapist and that come into being via the encounter itself. *The we-focused realm of encounter* attempts to describe and clarify each participant's (i.e. the client's and the psychotherapist's) experience of 'us' being in relation with one another. In short, it asks each to consider 'what do I tell myself about the experience of being *us* being in relation with each other while being engaged in this encounter?' The *we-focused realm of encounter* is characterized by its **immediacy** – it is concerned with, and expresses, that which is being experienced 'in the moment' of engagement with the other from a person-to-person standpoint. As such, it expresses explicitly that inter-relational grounding that exists (and is more implicitly expressed) in *I-focused* and *you-focused* statements.

Finally, the *they-focused* realm of encounter centres upon the client's experience of how those who make up his or her wider world of 'others' (extending beyond the other who is the psychotherapist) experience their own inter-relational realms in response to the client's current way of being and, as well, to the novel ways of being that have presented themselves as possibilities to the client through psychotherapy. In brief, it asks the client to consider his or her way of being from the perspective of the 'others' in the client's world. Specifically, it challenges the client to consider the various facets of inter-relations between the client and these others as the client imagines *they* experience and interpret them. Further, it challenges the client to consider his or her worldview from the standpoint of the various facets of inter-relation between one other or group of others and a different other or group of others. The *they-focused* realm serves to extend the 'world-dimensions' of the therapeutic relationship beyond the confines of the consulting room. It is an explicit stance that can be adopted by existential psychotherapists to highlight the inter-relational dimensions of existence and to counter the more common psychotherapeutic tendency to consider the client in isolation, out of inter-relational context. The exploration of this fourth relational realm is particularly significant when, through therapy, the client has reached a point of considering and making choices about new found alternative 'ways to be'.

While existential psychotherapy attempts a descriptive exploration of all four realms of encounter in order that the therapist can attempt to 'stand beside', remain open to and in part 'enter', with increasing adequacy, the currently-lived world of the client, an explicit and overriding emphasis is placed upon the third (*we-focused*) realm (Spinelli, 1994; 1997; 2001; 2003). The existential psychotherapist's willingness to examine and consider what emerges experientially through this realm as being real and valid (rather than substitutive, symbolic, or 'transferential') serves to implicate his or her current manner of existence as expressed through the relationship with the client. Further, this focus serves to expose and clarify *in the immediacy of the current encounter* the self-same inter-relational issues that clients express as being deeply problematic within their wider world relations.

The Client's Way of Being in Psychotherapy

The examination and clarification of the four inter-relational realms serve to highlight the client's worldview both within the therapeutic relationship and with regard to the client's wider world-relations with self and others. At times, the client's experience of being with the therapist parallels his or her world-relational experiences of being. Just as significantly, however, the client's experienced way of being with the therapist may well contrast with his or her wider world relations and, in this way, serves to challenge both the sedimentations and dissociations concerning who and how 'I am expected or required to be (and not be) with others' or 'how others are expected or required to be (and not be) with me'.

In this way, existential psychotherapy can be most accurately construed as a structured form of *reconstitutive inquiry* in that it attempts to clarify that which is initially presented in a confused and fragmented fashion. By such acts of collaborative and clarifying dialogue, existential psychotherapy provides the potential for transformative experience.

Existential psychotherapy's insistence upon the inter-relational basis to all lived experience asks of the therapist and client to undertake a form of inquiry that *places the client's subjective experience within an inter-relational framework that requires the acknowledgement of others*. Within the therapeutic relationship, the therapist *is* the other in the client's current experience of being. As this other, the therapist acts as both the representative of all others in the client's wider world relations and, just as importantly, is also the other who challenges the client's worldview regarding others and their impact upon his or her way of being.

In focusing upon the various inter-relational realms, both the complementary and the symmetrical patterns of behaviour adopted by the client in order to maintain his or her worldview become clarified, just as the underlying embodied values, beliefs, meanings and felt experiences attached to such stances are more adequately discerned. But, it is apparent that, rather than specific behavioural skills or techniques, it is the existential psychotherapist him/herself who provokes this challenging form of enquiry.

The Existential Psychotherapist's Way of Being in Therapy

On reflection, it becomes evident that any hope of achieving this enterprise *must* begin from a standpoint of openness to and acceptance of the client's presenting way of being on the part of the therapist. To adopt any other stance which emphasizes a directive or manipulative change in the client's way of being, no matter how benevolent or concerned to ameliorate the client's distress, will only serve to maintain the client's underlying currently lived way of being towards self and others and, in turn, will allow the client to continue to avoid reflecting upon all clarificatory challenges initiated by the therapist.

It is via this first, and crucial, step of 'staying with' and 'attuning oneself to' the client's currently lived worldview – no matter how debilitating, restrictive, limiting, and irrational it may appear to be to the therapist (if not all others in the client's world) – that the existential psychotherapist, *simply via this client-attuned presence*, begins to challenge profoundly the client's expectations regarding how others are, how others expect the client to be, and how the client expects others to be with him or her.

Such attempts, which the great existential psychiatrist, Karl Jaspers, termed *not-knowing* (Jaspers, 1963) and which, more recently, I have myself referred to as *un-knowing* (Spinelli, 1997) make it the aim of the existential psychotherapist to seek to discern that which is *understandable within what is initially experienced as being un-understandable*.

Once the therapist's presence has begun to provoke a more open, honest clarifying process of worldview exploration by the client, then the therapist has earned sufficient trust to be able to focus upon the exploration of the client's experience of being with a particular 'other' (the therapist) so that the *experiential immediacy* of their current encounter can be considered in terms of the experiential resonances and contrasts it provokes with regard to the client's wider worldview. This dialogical process can then permit the inter-relational meaning of the client's perceived dysfunctions and disturbances to be more clearly explicated and reconsidered.

In adopting this stance, existential psychotherapy avoids bestowing upon the therapist the role of superior, objective instructor who distinguishes for the client those beliefs, attitudes and behaviours that are assumed to be 'irrational' and who attempts to replace them with 'rational' ones. Similarly, rather than present themselves as 'symptom-removers', 'treatment-providers', 'directive educators' or 'professional helpers', existential psychotherapists return psychotherapy to its original meaning: the attempt to 'stay with', 'stand beside' or attend to another. In attending to their clients, existential psychotherapists thereby make the attempt to provide them with the experience of being heard – and hearing themselves – in a manner that is non-judgemental and accepting of the stance they maintain. This attempt 'to accept the otherness of the being who is present' promotes the possibility of the clients' greater willingness and courage to confront the fixed, or sedimented, biases and assumptions they hold with regard to their relations with themselves, others and the world in general, and how these sedimented stances may themselves have provoked their current problems in living.

The Existential Psychotherapist's Attempts to 'Be-With' and 'Be-For' the Client

In order to assist clients in their investigation of their worldviews as optimally as possible, existential psychotherapists attempt a stance of openness and acceptance of the 'being there' of the client.

In their attempts at *being-with* the client, existential psychotherapists seek to give expression to their respect for and acceptance of their client's worldview as it presents itself in their current encounter.

In their attitude of *being-for* their clients, existential psychotherapists express their willingness to attempt a non-judgemental, descriptively focused entry into that worldview in order to disclose, together with their client, the underlying, often implicit and inadequately acknowledged, values, beliefs, assumptions, attitudinal stances and their accompanying felt, affective components that make up or provide a meaning-focused structure to the client's worldview.

While neither the attempt to be-with or be-for the client can ever be fully achieved, and remains an aim or attempt rather than a fulfilment, nonetheless the undertaking may well provoke one of the biggest challenges that the client is likely to experience: here is another who is not trying to distort, subvert, interpret, amend, impose upon the lived worldview but who rather is making the attempt to accept it as it presents itself in the immediacy of the inter-relational encounter.

Equally, through the attempt to be-with and be-for their clients, existential psychotherapists become better able to attempt the bracketing of their own meanings and interpretations of the world so as not to make it their task to value, judge or criticize their clients' experience, nor to instruct their clients as to how to live out their lives in ways which imitate and have the approval of their therapist.

Existential psychotherapists must maintain this awareness of the wide range of existential possibilities available to their clients and have the integrity (not to say humility) to allow their clients to arrive at their own decisions and make their own choices about how to live their lives. This, in turn, requires therapists to have a substantial degree of self-knowledge so that they are more aware of the biases and assumptions in their own lives in order to be better able to bracket them.

Similarly, existential psychotherapists attempt to bracket any personal feelings or attitudes that move them away from an open, non-possessive respect towards their clients' existential autonomy and integrity. They do not seek to impose or concede their own or their clients' inter-relational demands that are above and beyond the specific contractual conditions set down and agreed upon during their first session together.

A common example of such unacceptable demands is time. As has often been noted, a wealth of 'important' insights tend to occur to clients during the last few minutes of a session, making it 'reasonable' for clients to demand extra time in order to explore them. Various approaches have hypothesized the hidden or unconscious significance of this phenomenon. While not being categorical as to its true meaning, existential psychotherapists are in agreement with most other therapeutic approaches in their typical (though not totally inflexible) refusal to go along with such time-extensions either throughout the duration of the therapeutic contract or until such a point in the contract when both participants are better able to re-negotiate such amendments via the relationship itself. Readers particularly interested in these questions might it useful to read my forthcoming text dealing with the practice of existential psychotherapy (Spinelli, 2005).

The Emphasis on Descriptive Questioning

In the pursuance of the broad aims of existential psychotherapy, and in keeping with its underlying assumptions, questions posed to their clients will rarely begin with *why*, since attempts to answer such questions inevitably lead to theories and speculation on the clients' (and therapists') part, concerning hypothetical originating past 'causes'.

Rather, in focusing on questions having to do with the *what and how* of experience (that is, the noematic and noetic foci of intentionality) existential psychotherapists seek to assist their clients in striving to focus on their currently experienced conscious experience of being-in-the-world. In this way, it is argued, clients can more easily reflect upon their experience *as it is occurring in the encounter* rather than be generating unprovable hypotheses as to how they might have dealt with or understood their experience at various points in the past or would like to some time in the future.

This emphasis on the clarification of descriptive experience allows for more adequate and honest conclusions to emerge and increases the likelihood that clients will recognize the elastic nature of their experience and, thereby, re-acknowledge their role as active interpreters of, rather than passive reactors to, the 'givens' of life.

The Therapist as Attendant

As R.D. Laing has noted, the term 'therapist' is originally derived from a Greek word meaning 'attendant' (Evans, 1976/1981: xiix) and, as such a therapist should be a specialist in attentiveness and awareness. Existential psychotherapists explicitly remind their clients that, ultimately, the task remains up to them – the clients – to find their own meanings and truths, and, hence, to realize their role and responsibility in the choices they have made and will continue to make throughout their lives.

Unfortunately, one of the greatest obstacles encountered by the existential psychotherapist is that the vast majority of clients wish neither to hear nor to accept this argument. Most individuals who seek therapy have convinced themselves that someone else (the therapist) knows better than they do how to live out their lives. Feeling powerless, often expressing a deep self-hatred and loathing, such individuals want to be told what to do, who to be, how to change for the better, what technique they need to be taught in order to improve a particular aspect of their lives (for example, sexual dysfunctions, phobias, self-assertion and so on) or their lives in general so that they will somehow, magically, emerge 'cured'.

No therapist who adopts an existential-phenomenological orientation can claim to provide such results solely and directly; what *can* be achieved through existential psychotherapy, however, is the realization that such demands are impossible to satisfy and, more importantly, both limit and impair the client's experience of being-in-the-world.

The Emphasis on Existential Anxiety

Existential psychotherapists take the experience of anxiety to be a fundamental 'given' of being-in-the-world. The responses that individuals raise up in order to minimize, deny or repress intolerable levels of anxiety are, in themselves, central factors in subsequent experiences of sedimentation and dissociation, confusion, learned helplessness and denial of freedom. In other words, the great variety of unwanted and unpleasantly experienced 'symptoms' of which clients want to be cured are themselves defences against the acceptance of the various existential anxieties of being-in-the-world: temporality, meaninglessness, choice and so forth.

As such, it is not the 'treatment' of these symptoms that is central but, rather, it is the reconsideration of one's defensive, limiting beliefs that is the focus of existential psychotherapy. As Yalom has stated: 'existential psychotherapy is a dynamic approach to therapy which focuses on concerns that are rooted in the individual's existence' (1980: 5). The existential focus does not dispute that an individual's fears, denials and anxieties are likely to be operating at different levels of awareness. Nevertheless, its primary interest lies in the exploration and clarification of current conscious experience and the perceived conflicts inferred from this experience.

Unlike other therapeutic approaches, the existential stance argues that the sources of conflict in an individual's life are not due to instinctual demands that are not being sufficiently met or that are in conflict with opposing demands, nor are they directly due to conflicts with significant others, or to misunderstood, incomplete or improper learning experiences, but, rather, they lie with the ontological 'givens' of human inter-relational existence such as temporality, freedom, encounter, and meaning/meaninglessness, and the degree to which each individual responds to these either to minimize or to deny the anxiety they provoke via the construction and adoption of his or her worldview.

In his valuable text, *Existential Psychotherapy*, Irvin Yalom (1980) explores at length the various defences that might arise in response to the anxiety provoked by each of the existential 'givens'. Interested readers are strongly urged to refer to this text for its detailed analyses of these defences.

Let me just outline the types of symptoms that Yalom argues might arise from an individual's death anxiety. Yalom posits that there are essentially two modes of defending against this most basic of anxieties. One way is to convince oneself of one's 'specialness and personal inviolability' (Yalom, 1980: 115). That is to say, we might logically accept that, like everyone else, we will die at some point, but this rational understanding may be met with a more powerful, opposite belief that, whereas others may be doomed to die, we are somehow different, more important, 'special', and, as such, will be spared this fate. In order to convince themselves of their unique status, some individuals will enact all manner of 'death-defying' symptoms. For instance, the compulsive heroism characteristic of a writer such as Hemingway reveals the recurring need in such individuals to 'prove' this conclusion to themselves by testing themselves in more and more dangerous situations.

Equally, the workaholic, as well as being motivated by desires of 'getting on top of things', is convinced that no one else is capable of doing the work as successfully, or knowledgeably as he or she can. If no one else can match these set standards, the workaholic individual becomes more convinced of his or her indispensability – the world could not possibly survive their death.

Like the compulsive hero and the workaholic, the narcissist, the autocratic controller, the aggressor, all place their desires and abilities to control, determine, manipulate their world at centre stage. The power they convince themselves they have acts as a means to a deeper conviction: the more 'god-like' they appear to be to others and to themselves, then, like 'god', the more they can view themselves as immortal.

The other defensive road taken against death anxiety is characterized by Yalom as being that of 'the Ultimate Rescuer' (Yalom, 1980: 129–41). This ultimate rescuer may be perceived as a supernatural entity or force which guides, watches over and protects us at all times, which is omnipresent, and which often bestows 'ultimate' reward or punishment upon us. Most importantly, this version of the ultimate rescuer minimizes the power of death, reducing its finality to a mere turning point, or step, into another realm of experience. Alternatively, the ultimate rescuer need not be a supernatural entity, but another, albeit superior, human being. Religious and political leaders, charismatic personalities, the very personifiers of a cause or movement, may all be perceived as ultimate rescuers.

In either case, the ultimate rescuer fulfils the function of rule-maker, law-giver and meaning-constructor. If we believe in the words and deeds of the ultimate rescuer, if we follow the ultimate rescuer's ordinances, we gain an existential security: the world becomes an easy place to understand, all questions have their answers, our life is placed under the control of the ultimate rescuer whom we seek to emulate and serve and demonstrate unswerving allegiance to, even to the point of giving up our own life in his service.

If death has meaning and purpose, if it offers the promise of something better or finer, then it becomes more acceptable, less anxiety-provoking; it is the thought that death has no meaning, leads to nothing, that is unbearable and which the ultimate rescuer allows us to deny.

The price we pay for our beliefs in an ultimate rescuer is, of course, the loss of a great deal of what freedom we possess. Not allowed to think certain thoughts, to hold certain desires or to enact certain behaviours because they are contrary to the dictates of the ultimate rescuer, we lay ourselves open to a wide range of symptoms: masochism and depression, hysteria and fanaticism, obsession and ritual, may all follow from this defensive act.

Beliefs in our 'specialness' and beliefs in an ultimate rescuer often intermingle. While we can separate these beliefs for the purposes of discussion and analysis in a textbook, in real life it is not uncommon to note both influencing the behaviour of the same individual. We commonly tend, or gravitate, more or less to one defensive stance rather than towards the other, but both can and do coexist – after all, they share the same function and purpose.

The Anti-medical Stance in Existential Psychotherapy

In keeping with their view that the symptoms of mental disturbance are expressions of an individual's attempts to defend against central existential anxieties, existential psychotherapists argue that the problems of mental disturbances are principally rooted in *socio-ethical bases* rather than in medical ones; that medical forms of intervention and treatment at best provide only temporary alleviation from anxiety and, at worst, may induce an even greater psychic breakdown in the sufferer; and that, rather than being random, meaningless confusion, the behaviour of the disturbed individual is meaningful and revelatory of the anxieties that are being defended against.

This stance is perhaps the most far-reaching and controversial arrived at by existential psychotherapy since it contradicts the more generally advocated view that all symptoms are the direct outcome of physical illness and are to be treated as one would treat any other medical problem.

While some practitioners might be willing to concede that many neurotic symptoms may be tied to defences against the various 'problems of living' dealt with by existential psychotherapists and, as such, a neurotic might benefit from such therapy, they are likely to baulk at the notion that more severe forms of mental disturbance – the various psychoses, including schizophrenia – may also have their origins in these same anxieties and, like most neurotic symptoms, serve as meaningful if disturbing and excessively limited responses to these anxieties.

Existential psychotherapists have tended to react strongly against the 'physical disease' model of the mind and the reliance upon physical methods of treatments such as surgical, electrical and drug therapies that have become the norm in most Western hospitals. Similarly, existential psychotherapists downplay the overwhelming importance that their physicalist colleagues ascribe to bio-genetic factors in mental disturbance. Instead, many argue that while there may well be *correlates* between certain mental disturbances and the bio-genetic make-up of the individual, such factors are not in themselves directly *causative* of the wide-ranging variety and strength of individual responses to such stimuli. Existential psychotherapists argue that, rather than being problems open to medical treatment, mental disturbances reveal primarily 'being'-related issues. I will have more to say on this view in the following section.

On the basis of his theoretical insights and the impact of his ideas concerning the genesis and treatment of extreme mental disturbances, I would suggest that the most extensive attempt to introduce a phenomenological viewpoint into psychiatry was attempted by R.D. Laing. What follows is an attempt to summarize a number of his phenomenologically derived contributions to our understanding and treatment of the mentally fragmented individual.

R.D. Laing and Phenomenological Psychotherapy

During the 1960s and 1970s, R.D. Laing's highly original and forceful writings increasingly identified him as a particularly insightful and innovative spokesperson for a growing number of British psychiatrists who, in their adoption of an existential-phenomenological approach to their profession, became vociferous opponents of the prevailing ethos of physical methods of treatment of severe mental disturbances.

Like others such as Thomas Szasz (1970; 1974), (though admittedly for differing reasons) R.D. Laing (1927–89) rejected the disease model of mental illness and expressed open hostility to exclusively bio-chemical or genetic explanations of these disturbances. Laing criticized these forms of treatment on the principal grounds that, on the whole, they ignored the social context under which the various disturbing symptoms arose and so failed to give due consideration to their underlying meanings.

When reconsidered phenomenologically, these symptoms can be seen to be defensive reactions to basic existential anxieties. In this light, the often seemingly absurd and random statements and behaviours of severely mentally disturbed individuals take on new and clarificatory significance. Moreover, when considered in a wider social context, the symptoms reveal as much about the structure and demands of the society that the disturbed individuals grow up and live in as they do about the individuals themselves. Loose colloquialisms such as 'sick' or 'mad', or psychiatric terms such as 'paranoid schizophrenia' and 'manic-depression', make plain society's denial of shared responsibility in the production of the symptoms which these labels are assumed to define.

So long as a society holds on to medical models of mental illness, no examination and criticism of that society need be considered since the origins of the problem are considered to be primarily biological or genetic in nature, thereby minimizing – and exculpating – any socio-environmental factors.

An analogous, if extreme, example of the potential dangers in denying or minimizing environmental factors when considering social or mental disturbance can be seen in the Soviet Union's treatment of critics and dissidents during the late 1970s and early 1980s when it became an acceptable practice to place political prisoners of conscience inside mental institutions. It was argued that, if it is the case that Soviet society is the most politically advanced in the world, anyone claiming otherwise and who advances the cause of more regressive societies *must* be insane and, as such – progressive as the leaders of the Soviet Union claimed their society to be – their psychiatrists were urged to 'cure', rather than punish, internal dissidents.

Laing's interactions with individuals who had been labelled 'schizophrenic' led him to conclude that their inner experience and symptomatic behaviour could be understood as a defensive strategy that had been adopted in order to cope with 'close-to-impossible, existentially precarious situations' (Shaffer, 1978: 49).

'Normality' in Western society, for Laing, rather than proving a measuring stick to determine the relative mental health of an individual, as is often assumed, instead reveals an adaptability to bad faith or inauthenticity. Schizophrenics might be abnormal, but not necessarily existentially unhealthier than 'normal' individuals.

> 'Who is more dangerous,' Laing asked in a now famous example, 'the seventeen-year-old girl who claims that an atom bomb sits within her, or the nuclear strategist who helps the Pentagon find efficient means of destroying, within minutes, one hundred million people. The girl is diagnosed as schizophrenic and is institutionalized, whereas the Pentagon consultant is wined, dined, fawned over, and paid extremely handsome fees.' (Shaffer, 1978: 55)

The Schizoid Split

In *The Divided Self*, Laing (1960/1970) concluded that the basic anxiety that his patients defended against could best be understood in terms of *ontological insecurity*, that is, an insecurity about one's very relation to being. Ontologically insecure individuals experience a major *split* in their relations with the world. This split extends into two main relational dimensions.

At one level, the split being experienced reflects a felt sense of an internal fragmentation, that is, a split within one's sense of 'self' such that an irreconcilable rent is experienced between aspects of self that have been accepted and other aspects that appear to be alien and open to attempts at denial. At a second level, the person experiences an inordinate and precarious degree of dividedness between self and others who are perceived as being dangerous and destructive agents to self-autonomy.

The case of multiple personalities can be seen as an extreme example of ontological insecurity which the person attempts to cope with by literally creating multiple personalities to deal with this experience of internal fragmentation.

Similarly, the person who experiences a strong sense of alienation from the rest of society, who feels little or no contact with others, or who experiences what contact there is as being frightening, unpleasant and full of danger, will seek to maintain a distance from the world in order to avoid becoming in some way contaminated by it. The case of Howard Hughes (Drosnin, 1985) can be seen as a famous example of this split. Hughes constructed an ornate hierarchical system that allowed him to run his empire while at the same time avoiding any form of physical contact with virtually all of his employees. No one was allowed to be near him, no one could breathe the same air that he breathed, or touch the same objects that he touched. Any form of physical contact with others exposed Hughes to their 'killer germs'. 'Others', for Hughes, literally became dangerous to his life and health.

The existential split that Laing's ontologically insecure person experiences has been referred to as the *schizoid condition*. In the same way that Freud employed the term 'neurotic' to include everyday psycho-pathological symptoms rather than restricting it to specifically clinical cases, so too did Laing, in his later writings, make it plain that the term 'schizoid' was not to be restricted only (as his earlier analyses had suggested) to extreme forms of psychotic or schizophrenic 'splitness' since most (if not all) individuals experience some degree of schizoid splitness in their lives. The symptomatic, defensive behaviour of ordinary individuals differs only in degree – not in kind – from that of the 'abnormal' individual.

Like existential phenomenologists who focus on authenticity and inauthenticity, or on good faith and bad faith, as aspects of being-in-the-world, Laing presents an analysis of mental disturbances focusing on the degree of ontological security/insecurity in an individual's experience of life.

Laing did not, of course, argue that those individuals who come to be labelled 'schizophrenic' or 'psychotic' did not exhibit uniquely different, not to say bizarre, forms of behaviour; it was the assumed chaotic meaninglessness behind these behaviours that he disputed. Rather than being manifestations of medical disease, these symptoms could be better understood as expressions of, and defensive reactions to, ontological 'dis-ease' or insecurity.

When explored phenomenologically, these seemingly meaningless acts revealed attempts to deal with – even communicate – the frighteningly precarious existential condition in which such persons found themselves. For the individual who feels this level of insecurity, the experiences of life become 'a matter not so much of gratifying oneself as of preserving oneself' (Shaffer, 1978: 52).

Ontological Insecurity and Being-in-the-World

Rather than accept, and to some extent take for granted, one's very status of being-in-the-world, the ontologically insecure person *questions* it on three distinct levels: the level of existence (*that* one is), the level of essence (*what* one is), and the level of identity (*who* one is).

Faced with such insecurities, any interpersonal relations focused on self or others may easily be interpreted as highly threatening and, hence, to be avoided as much as possible for the sake of preserving what there is left of one's felt sense of one's own being. Under these circumstances, symptoms of withdrawal such as anti-social behaviour, excessive timidity and aloofness become more comprehensible. Even the extreme claims made by many schizophrenics that they are 'robots', 'unreal', 'someone else' or even 'dead' take on a sudden clarity.

The Fears of the Ontologically Insecure Individual

But what *are* the central fears of the ontologically insecure? Laing presents three specific conditions of fear as experienced by the ontologically insecure person, which, although ultimately linked in that they reflect anxieties about living, contain differing emphases in their expression.

The first fear, that of *engulfment*, focuses on anxieties related to feelings of being swallowed up, stifled, or being taken over by some alien external force. The fear of being controlled by some superior being whose powers force you to enact its wishes can be seen as an example of engulfment.

The second fear, *implosion*, shares certain similarities with engulfment in that it, too, is a fear of being taken over. In this case, however, the possessing agent resides *within* the individual and, little by little, takes control of its victim's thoughts and deeds. Here, the experience is one of being filled with something alien and dangerous. The individual who claims that there is some poison in his bloodstream or who is convinced that he has begun to emit disgusting odours, or who must wash away imaginary 'dirt' from his body expresses fears of implosion.

The third fear, *petrification*, focuses on fears of being turned into something lifeless, being somehow dead yet retaining the knowledge of once having been alive. Petrification refers to a fear of somehow being turned into inert matter that is no longer either truly alive or dead. The individual who claims 'I'm dead' reveals that this 'death' is psychological, even if the expression of this fear may well be via somatic symptomatology, such as the onset of partial or complete catalepsy.

It is in the schizoid's attempts at self-defence, Laing argues, that we see the origins of much of the strange behaviour that characterizes the psychotic or schizophrenic individual. Motivated by desires to defend against these fears, they act in remarkable, yet meaningful ways. Among their problems, unfortunately, is that very few of those who claim to seek to 'help' them find anything at all 'meaningful' in their behaviours. Interpreting ontologically based fears as signs of illness or madness, they succeed in further alienating the ontologically insecure individual from the world.

As I was preparing my notes for the above discussion, it occurred to me that these three fears are highly reminiscent of the archetypal themes of fictional and cinematic tales of horror. Being possessed by the devil, a demon or a mad hypnotist reveals the terrors of engulfment. A recent representative example of implosion can be seen in many of the films of David Cronenberg such as *The Fly*, wherein the principal character's own genetic make-up begins to alter his thoughts and appearance. Equally, once the 'poison' in Dr Jekyll's formula has been imbibed by him several times, it begins to 'fight' him until he can no longer control his alterations into Mr Hyde. As for petrification, simply consider vampires (often referred to as 'the undead'), zombies ('the living dead'), even the mythological monster Medusa (whose looks do worse than kill – they turn you into stone!). Might it not be that our continuing fascination with themes of horror is fuelled by the fact that they provide vivid, if safe, means to give expression to those very fears that, to some degree, we might all share? Whatever, for the schizoid individual, life may well be experienced as a series of vignettes from a horror story.

The Phenomenological Method and Laingian Therapy

In contrast to his more clinically oriented colleagues, Laing, like Karl Jaspers and Ludwig Binswanger before him, saw his task as that of deciphering the hidden meanings behind the behaviour of the mentally disturbed individual. Rather than intervene, dispute the individual's claims or numb the fears with medication, Laing observed and provided his presence, empathy and reassurance so that he could eventually reconstruct the individual's situation and understand the fears against which the person's felt sense of being was being defended.

In contrast to what might at first seem to be the more natural, more curative, step of preventing an individual from enacting bizarre, regressive or potentially injurious behaviour as soon as that behaviour is noted, Laing argued that the first task of the therapist is not to intervene, but to attempt to discern its meaning and defensive significance.

For example, imagine that in the middle of your conversation with someone who has been diagnosed as schizophrenic you note that he has begun to tug at his hair and that, over the next minute or so, the tugging increases to the point where it seems to you that if it is allowed to continue he will do himself serious injury.

If you adopted a medical approach you would conclude that this was behaviour symptomatic of his illness and you would, in all likelihood, attempt to stop it through some form of intervention. You might, perhaps, take hold of his hand and prevent him from continuing his action. This might succeed; on the other hand, it might anger him to the point of threatened violence. At this point, you might well decide that he required a sedative and called an orderly to assist you in keeping him still long enough for you to give him an injection or force-feed a pill down his throat – actions which are highly likely to make him even more angry and violent.

Laing's position urges an alternative approach: rather than intervene at the symptomatic level, you should be initially attempting to discern the meaning behind the symptom and its significance as a defence against the fears brought on by ontological insecurity.

Just as a child might respond to a perceived shadow-like 'presence' of danger or evil, the ontologically insecure individual devises a magical, ritualistic action which wards off the presence. The child who is frightened that there might be a monster under her bed enacts a specific ritual to make the monster disappear or become harmless. She might open the doors to her cupboard three times while reciting a made-up incantation, or she might skip around her room with her eyes tight shut, or she might require the counter-active, soothing presence of a teddy bear or some other favourite object which has the power – invested by the child – to conquer the monster or bring it to a standstill. Whatever the case, a specific ritual *must* be enacted in order to rid her of her fear.

Anyone's attempts to prevent the child from carrying out such rituals lead her to become increasingly more agitated and angry, possibly even violent. Similarly, any attempts at rational argument which seeks to deny the child's experience will not assuage the child. Even acts of punishment, though possibly temporarily successful in controlling her unacceptable behaviour, will not eradicate the child's fears – rather, punishment will increase them since, now, the child has reason to fear not only the monster under her bed but also the adult 'monster' who, in denying her experience, might actually convince her that the two monsters are in league with each other, or that they are one and the same.

The adult who is concerned that a child's rituals may lead to possible injury needs first to convince her that her behaviour is accepted as being meaningful, purposive and successful in warding off the perceived dangers. Presented with acceptance rather than denial, the child is likely to be more willing to explore and reconsider the dangerous presence, treat the adult as an ally, perhaps even begin to give expression to underlying fears in a more concrete rather than symbolic manner.

At the very least, the creative adult might even present the child with alternative social rituals for her to consider and attempt so that, even if her fears are not resolved, the rituals are no longer potentially physically harmful, nor are they likely to single her out as being aberrant or 'odd' in the eyes of others. So long as the child enacts rituals which are tolerated or even valued by adult society, both the rituals and the child will be no cause for concern; indeed the child's behaviour is more likely to be viewed as 'cute', rather than as symptomatic of mental imbalance.

In acknowledging the sense behind the ritual, the adult has at least opened the way for the child to express fears more openly; more significantly, in the long run, the adult, as representative 'other', shows the child that 'others' need not be further sources of fear but, rather, can be 'stimuli' for experiences of love and ontological security.

The person who has been labelled 'schizophrenic' might fear 'poison in the bloodstream' rather than 'a monster under the bed', but his fear is of the same shadowy presences as those imagined by the child. And, like the child, he has learned to defend against those fears by enacting rituals, such as 'tugging at his hair'.

If you decide to take interventionist measures like those of the adult above, you may succeed in stopping the behaviour temporarily through manipulative treatment (which is experienced as 'punishment' by the person being treated), but, inadvertently, you will also increase his fear and, worse, convince him that you, too, are dangerous and a threat to his being.

In essence, Laing's approach asks the therapist to acknowledge each person's experience; to provide a neutral, yet empathic stance that invites description, exploration and assessment of the fears being experienced and their underlying issues of insecurity; and, rather than 'infantalize' individuals further by taking action over their lives, to assume their right to autonomous action.

In following this procedure, the therapist disconfirms many of the fears and insecurities concerning others that fragmented individuals are likely to be experiencing, and allows the breaking down of any number of the defensive symptomatic reactions to others that they have felt a need to employ for self-protection. As a result of breaching these defences, individuals are more likely to regain a growing sense of integration and ontological security.

With regard to my example of the hair-tugging schizophrenic, by asking what he's doing, or by pointing out his action to him, or even by imitating it yourself, you might be told, for example, that through this sensory experience he is able to reassure himself that he still exists and that, hence, the greater his doubt, the more forceful the activity of hair-tugging needs to be.

Knowing such, it becomes evident that any preventative measures you might take would increase his doubts (and his fear-wrought insecurities) rather than allay them. It is only in your acceptance of his act, in your willingness to attempt to discern its meaning rather than treat it – and, by implication, the individual carrying it out – as 'sick' or 'mad', that its significance might become clearer to you.

Ultimately, your stance requires your respect for the person before you – a respect that makes a basic assumption that his or her actions, no matter how meaningless and confused they might appear to you, are his or her means of coping with terrifying fears, frightening insecurities. Destructive and physically harmful as his actions may seem to be, their aim is to *preserve* what she or he experiences is left of his or her being; misguided as they may be, his or her acts are attempts at self-survival rather than self-destruction, and, as such, though possibly ineffectual, they are by no means meaningless or 'crazy'.

The Schizoid Individual as Critic of Society

Some critics of Laing have accused him of 'glorifying' severe disturbances such as schizophrenia and of elevating the often bleak and pain-filled behaviours of these individuals into acts of bravery or mystical insight (Evans, 1976/1981). This, I think, is a serious misreading of Laing possibly resulting from his public statements to the general media in order to 'stir things up' in medical circles.

While not glorifying mental disturbances, Laing does argue against dismissal of the statements and actions of the mentally disturbed on the grounds that they are meaningless. Instead, he suggests that those who experience the world from an extreme schizoid condition might actually be capable of more clearly pointing out and clarifying the absurd and life-endangering acts of inauthenticity that characterize 'normal' living in industrial society. The extremely schizoid are not here being viewed as in some way 'superior to' or 'more heroic' than normal individuals; rather, all that is being stated is that, because of their deep fragmentation, unlike normal people they are less able to deny or defend against the shared anxieties of being-in-the-world. It is in this sense, and this sense alone, that the schizoid individual might be considered to be a 'seer' of some clarity.

The Aetiology of the Schizoid Split

Laing's hypothesis as to the origins of the schizoid split (Laing, 1960; 1961/1971; 1967; 1982; Laing and Esterson, 1964/1971) influenced substantially by the inter-relational theories of Harry Stack Sullivan (Barton Evans III, 1996) and John Bowlby (1979) in particular, posits that the schizoid split originates in our earliest interactions with others; it is the very structure of the family that nurtures both the normal and extreme variants of ontological insecurity.

Through our earliest interactions with the family we learn that certain of our behaviours are deemed to be good and others are judged as being bad. Good acts are valued and positively reinforced, bad acts are either negatively reinforced or, more commonly, punished by the family. For Laing, the term 'good' primarily equates with compliance to the family's wishes or codes of behaviour, whereas the term 'bad' refers to acts which defy or rebel against the family's code of conduct.

Laing's criticism is not that it is wrong for the family, or any other social institution for that matter, to seek to impose rules of conduct (for whatever reasons). Obviously, any social institution requires codes of behaviour. The problem which is of central concern to Laing arises when a social structure such as the family fails to make a distinction between one's actions and one's being. This distinction, Laing suggests (I think correctly), is rarely considered or made explicit.

Although the distinction between the statements 'what you are doing is bad' and 'you are bad for doing that' may seem superficial at first, their existential implications vary considerably, since, once one's being is directly linked to one's actions, any attempts to prevent, punish or deny them are equated to threats to one's being. Under the terms of this equation, schizoid fragmentation becomes inevitable.

If the child is told, for instance, that because he's acted badly, 'daddy doesn't love him', what the child is likely to understand is that he (or at least a part of him) has no right to exist in the physical world, and that, in order to maintain his very physical existence, the child must adopt a variety of fragmentatory defences. Equally, the child learns that others – even significant others – will either value or threaten his existence on the basis of what he does.

The issue is further exacerbated when we recall that the young child makes little, if any, distinction between mental and physical acts (Ginsburg and Opper, 1969). Even 'bad thoughts' become threats to one's existence and must be defended against.

As a result of the family's injunctions and rewards, we learn to define who we are and whether we have a right to be. The family, then, becomes not only the source of our 'good' or positive definitions of self, it also serves the function of defining those 'bad' or negative aspects of self which must not be allowed to be expressed (mentally or behaviourally) because to express them threatens not only our relations with the family (and others in general) but also our internal relations, that is, our very being.

Our attempts to deny the 'bad' self lead to fragmentation. Further, faced with the 'bad' self's inevitable appearance, we can only explain its presence on the basis of external or alien internal agencies. At worst unable to explain or control them, we might see no recourse other than to completely 'shut off' our capacity to experience. Here, then, lies the origin of the three schizoid fears discussed earlier.

Laing further argues that, however threatening the appearance of the 'bad' self may seem, our attempts to deal with the conflicts its presence generates lead to the development of an adult, autonomous identity. In other words, the conflicts arising from attempts to develop an autonomous identity that, for most of us, are characteristically pivotal identifying features of our adolescence, can be seen as our attempts to come to terms with the 'bad' self. The degree of our success in this task is reflected in the development of a relatively independent – if also relatively schizoid – adult.

Laing became convinced that the basis for severely schizoid individuals' symptomatology lay in their lack of any lasting development of an autonomous adult identity. The extremely schizoid have an arrested development since, in their failure during adolescence to incorporate the 'bad' self into their identity to some degree, they cannot achieve a sufficient level of autonomy. In perceiving the appearance of the 'bad' self as being overwhelmingly threatening to their existence, they strive to be 'good' all the time and seek the approval and love of their family.

If the power to decide that one is 'good' lies entirely in the hands of the family and the family's love is removed when one is 'bad', then the solution is obvious: one must simply never be labelled as 'bad' by significant others. Yet such a position is impossible to maintain when, most commonly during adolescence, one is faced with the conflicting demands of significant others. The solution for the great majority of us is that of the construction of an 'adult' self who finds some means to evaluate, choose and live with competing demands so that we can experience ourselves as more or less 'good' beings. In contrast, some of us, for various inter-relational reasons, fail to construct a relatively stable, relatively enduring, relatively 'good' felt sense of self. In such instances, the person is caught in a constant tension between competing expressions of being 'good' or 'bad'. In each case, the 'bad' self asserts its existence in verbal and/or behavioural outbursts that the 'good' self can neither explain nor fully or permanently 'own'. This erratic and incomprehensible struggle to both reject and own the fleeting felt experience of impermanent 'good' and 'bad' constructs of self is interpreted not only by the family and significant others during a person's adolescence as a symptom of 'madness', it is a view that, in part or as a whole is shared by the person who has been so labelled.

Laing's studies of the family structure of 'mad' persons revealed a particular intolerance of 'bad' behaviour in their children, an intolerance expressed in any number of ways which threatened the schizoid's sense of being. In response, the family might act as if the individual simply did not exist when the 'bad' self emerged (as in the case of Peter in *The Divided Self* (Laing, 1960/1970)), or, in their (claimed) inability to make sense of the 'bad' behaviour, insist that its genesis must be due to constitutional 'madness'.

In Ken Loach's film *A Family Life*, which presented these aspects of Laing's theory in a dramatized form, the 'mad' heroine's parents claim that their daughter used to be 'good' (that is, 'obedient'), turned 'bad' as a result of the rebellious, anti-social individuals she'd met, and that now she has been driven 'mad'. Overwhelmed by existential anxiety, too frightened to assert any autonomy because of the threat to her sense of being it produces, incapable of explaining her 'bad' thoughts and behaviours as being self-generated, their daughter can only collude with their conclusions – she *must* be 'mad' to behave as she does.

Laing's analysis of the schizoid split points out the existential dimensions which, though so often neglected in modern psychiatric theories which focus on exclusively organic variables, seem so central to the onset of 'mental illness' and to medical science's attempts to understand and treat it.

Laing's critics have argued that he minimizes the organic variables to the point of dismissal, thereby sidestepping the dramatic advances being made in the medical treatment of such extreme forms of mental disease as schizophrenia, senile and alcoholic psychosis, depression and so forth. Laing's response is that, whereas he acknowledges the organic factor as one among several, he sees no reason to assume that this factor is, in itself, any more *significant* than any other. More importantly, the insistence on the part of medical science that this factor is the originating or causal factor is a sedimented bias which hinders a more adequate contextual analysis of the problem.

> If I am disturbed, I may be disturbed spiritually, intellectually, emotionally, and physically. Many neurologists, once they find something, as they say 'organic', they think that's it... Until chemists and geneticists see the focus within the *context*, and realize there is an interplay between chemistry and social interaction we can't develop the theoretical speculation at a pure science level we must have. (Laing, in Evans, 1976/1981: 18–22)

The following example should clarify Laing's argument. A group of people are given the same dosage of LSD. For the sake of argument, assume that their physical constitutions are roughly the same so that their bio-chemical responses to the drug will not vary significantly. Each individual's experience of, and response to, the drug's effects will, nevertheless, be different. One individual may experience overwhelming fear; another may experience profound ecstasy. Yet another may find it impossible to control sudden feelings of joy and express them through unrestrained laughter, while still another may be flooded with feelings of abject misery and begin to cry like a baby. There may also be an individual whose behaviour shows no demonstrable change whatsoever, and so forth.

Even when the observed behaviour of one of these individuals shares a variety of features with that of others, the perceptions and memories which act as stimuli to the evocation of such behaviours will remain *unique* to each individual. In other words, each individual will *interpret* the chemical changes being experienced in a unique manner.

To argue that the drug alone directly caused all these reactions is both simplistic and misleading. The drug may have caused chemical changes to take place in the nervous systems of the individuals, but these changes had to be interpreted by each individual so that they could be acted upon in the way that they were. Similarly, providing an individual with an antidote that may counteract the drug's effects does not guarantee that other stimuli (be they chemical or otherwise), at some future point in time, might provoke similar changes in an individual's behaviour.

In the same way, it is, at best, naïve to suggest that an imbalance in the bio-chemistry of an individual, or some unusual combination of genetic factors is the sole or primary cause of an observed mental disturbance. Rather than being a direct cause-effect relationship, it is the interpretation given to the stimulus that will determine an individual's subsequent response. For all we know, there may be any number of individuals with the same bio-chemical imbalances or genetic combinations who never exhibit any signs of 'mental illness'.

Laing's view does not dismiss or deny possible bio-chemical or genetic factors in any mental disturbance. But it does argue against any tendency to view these factors as the sole or direct causes of that disturbance. Instead, Laing insists that the primary concern of the therapist should be the interpretations given by the disturbed individual to these, and any other, factors. By exploring the created meaning of the experience, testing out alternative explanations, and exposing the existential anxieties which provide the context for the disturbance, the 'mad' behaviour may well be better understood, alleviated, and possibly even extinguished.

Carl Rogers and Existential Therapy

It may seem, at least initially, odd to the reader that I choose to discuss various aspects of the work of Carl Rogers (1902–88) as an instance of existential psychotherapy. Certainly, strong cases can be made that the psychotherapeutic insights of various practitioners such as Ludwig Binswanger (1963; Frie, 1997), Medard Boss (1963; 1979), Viktor Frankl (1963; 1967) or Rollo May (1981; 1983), all of whom have been explicitly identified or identified themselves as existential therapists should take precedence over the work of an author whose primary impact was on the development of humanistic psychology and psychotherapy. While I am respectful of such arguments and do not in any way wish to imply that all of the above, and many other, existential psychotherapists should not be studied extensively, I want to make a case for including Rogers in this discussion.

First, it is evident that Rogers' way of thinking about and doing psychotherapy was derived from a series of very significant insights gleaned from both existential phenomenology in general and from the phenomenological method in particular. Second, it is also evident that a number of Rogers' interpretations of such deviate significantly from central phenomenological hypotheses and raise important distinctions between existential and humanistic approaches to psychotherapy. Taken together, it seemed to me that the particular and possibly unique phenomenological 'tensions' in Rogers' work serve to clarify pivotal features deeply relevant to psychotherapeutic applications for the reader. I have given a more extensive account of the relationship of Rogers' work to existential phenomenology in my book, *Demystifying Therapy* (Spinelli, 1994) but the briefer discussion both in this chapter and the next should prove to be sufficient at this introductory level.

Carl Rogers, the founder of *person-centred therapy* has had an enormous influence in the fields of counselling, psychotherapy and education (Rogers, 1942; 1951; 1964; Rogers and Stevens, 1967). Although most textbook accounts of Rogers' person-centred therapy fail to reveal his obvious indebtedness to the phenomenological method, Rogers himself made explicit reference to phenomenology as the primary basis for his approach (Evans, 1975/1981; Wann, 1964). It is this central aspect of Rogers' contribution to psychotherapy that I wish to examine.

The Rogerian Self-Concept

The concept of the self and the individual's subjective conclusions about 'self' are central themes running through all of Rogers' writings. Adopting an unequivocally optimistic view of human nature, he argues that all human beings strive for *self-actualization*, that is, 'the urge... to expand, extend, become autonomous, develop, mature – the tendency to express and activate all the capacities of the organism' (Rogers, 1961: 35).

Rogers hypothesizes that this urge might become less apparent, or 'contaminated', by self-imposed defences arising out of inauthentic interactions with significant others – principally, one's family – that lead to the subjective experience of fragmentation and restrict growth and development. Like Laing, Rogers sees the therapeutic process as an opportunity for clients to explore their experience of being in the world, expose fragmentatory defences, and begin to liberate and reintegrate their various potentials for being, thereby regaining a sense of their autonomy and allowing a more direct expression to their actualizing tendency.

Person-Centred Therapy

Decrying the medical orientation to therapy for much the same reasons as do Laing, Szasz and others, Rogers takes his criticisms one step further by insisting that the therapist's dependence upon, and therapeutic preoccupations with, *theory* while engaged in therapy result in a defensive and distancing intellectualization on the part of the therapist which itself hinders the client's steps towards reintegration.

Therapists cannot attend to both client and theory at the same time. Any attempts to do so will succeed only in distancing them from the special relationship required of successful therapy. Instead, for Rogers, the therapist's attitude and aim should be to enter the client's subjective world in order to experience it and to reflect it back to the client as accurately and concretely as possible.

This person-centred approach emphasizes an extreme reluctance to ask questions of clients and, in particular, to avoid asking those questions which, rather than seeking clarification of the client's current experience, involve hypotheses and ruminations concerning the client's remembered past experience. Further, the person-centred approach urges therapists not to make interpretative comments, offer advice or argue with the client's conclusions since these, too, hinder the therapist's ability to 'mirror the client's phenomenology as faithfully as possible' (Shaffer, 1978: 82).

Although Rogers takes an extremist stance on the issue of asking questions, it is evident that it is both a derivation and an extension of the phenomenological attitude which avoids asking questions related to assumed direct causality (that is, questions beginning with 'why') and focusing on questions designed to describe an individual's noematic and noetic experience (that is, questions beginning with 'what' or 'how').

Rogers' Three Necessary and Sufficient Attitudes

The person-centred approach insists that the therapeutic relationship must include three necessary attitudes or qualities on the part of the therapist that will allow the development of a unique and unthreatening relationship, opening the way for clients to expose, reconsider, and evaluate their subjective experiences of themselves and the world (Rogers, 1951; 1964).

The first of these attitudes is usually referred to as *unconditional positive regard*. Rogers identified the features of this attitude in the following manner:

> I hypothesize that growth and change are more likely to occur the more that the counsellor is experiencing a warm, positive, acceptant attitude towards what *is* in the client. It means that he prizes his client, as a person, with somewhat the same quality of feeling that a parent feels for his child, prizing him as a person regardless of his particular behavior at the moment. It means that he cares for his client in a non-possessive way, as a person with potentialities… it means a kind of love for the client as he is, providing we understand the word love as equivalent to the theologian's term *agape* and not in its usual romantic and possessive meanings. What I am describing is a feeling which is not paternalistic, nor sentimental, nor superficially social and agreeable. It respects the other person as a separate individual and does not possess him. It is a kind of liking which has strength, and which is not demanding. We have termed it positive regard. (Rogers and Stevens, 1967: 94)

This attitude of positive regard is said to be 'unconditional' in the sense that person-centred therapists strive never implicitly or explicitly to threaten to take away their positive regard from their clients regardless of what they think or feel about the clients' behaviour.

Person-centred therapists must be clear on the point that while what the client *does* is open to judgement (be it positive or negative), *who the client is* (that is, the client's being or 'personhood') must be accepted under all and any conditions (that is, unconditionally). This distinction, so often misunderstood even by those claiming to be person-centred therapists, is, initially, as difficult to understand as it is to accept.

As I discussed in my previous section on Laing's ideas, from our earliest interactions with others – and especially with significant others like our parents – most of us learn that their positive regard for us is *conditional* upon our behaviour.

If no distinction is made between 'being' and 'doing', an obvious lesson is learned: in order to be loved, one must be/do certain things and avoid being/doing others. This lesson leads directly to self-imposed limitation and fragmentation – certain potentialities of being *must* be avoided, rejected, denied or repressed because if they're not, one's being is threatened.

But how can a therapist, even a person-centred therapist, avoid giving only *conditional* positive regard? Although Rogers does not provide a specific prescription for the provision of unconditional positive regard, a clue can be ascertained from phenomenological theory. Recall that phenomenology argues that every experience contains both a noematic and a noetic component. Put simply (if not simplistically), every experience is made up of a 'story' (that is, *what* happened) and the affective components linked to the 'story' (that is, *how* what happened is interpreted and 'felt' by the experiencing being). If the therapist focuses primary attention upon the affective components rather than upon the 'story' elements of an experience, the giving of unconditional positive regard becomes far more likely to occur.

For example, a number of years ago I had a female client who had great difficulty in resolving a major issue in her life. In spite of her academic abilities and her parents' wishes for her to take up a grant she'd been offered to attend a prestigious university, her great desire was to enter the armed forces. As a consequence of the conflict she experienced, her anxiety had risen to such levels that she'd attempted suicide.

As my personal attitude to the armed forces is more than tinged with negativity, had I focused my attention on the noematic or 'story' element of her situation, I would have found it difficult to avoid judging her conflict as being somewhat ludicrous and might have been tempted to minimize the significance of her problem, and perhaps even 'side' with her parents. My client's noematic focus of experience was alien to me; her problem would never have arisen in my own life. On the basis of her 'story', her experience was one which, for me, made it difficult to attempt a stance of being-with and being-for her.

However, once I focused my attention on the noetic focus of her experience, I was far more willing and able to enter her lived-world of confusion, anguish, guilt, anger and incompatible desire. Consequently, having explored and partially resolved the various anxieties which created her conflicts, she was able to arrive at an owned stance towards her worldview and elected to join the navy.

Our differing 'stories' demand judgements that can either unite or separate us. But the affects that are linked to each are shared by all members of our species. In focusing on these unifying affects, both story-teller and listener acknowledge their humanity, recognize each other's being and are at least more likely to accept it *unconditionally*.

So long as we relate to and define individuals solely in terms of our own views of their behaviours and fail to consider the shared affective elements linked to them, we perpetrate the type of society that places its emphasis on conditional positive regard. In doing so, we foster schizoid defences that, in themselves, may act as primary influences towards the engendering of those very acts which we wish to eradicate.

The second necessary condition in person-centred therapy is that of *accurate empathy*. Here, the therapist is interested in grasping and adhering to the client's frame of reference as closely as possible in order to reflect back or (to use Rogers' term) 'to mirror' the client's experience as accurately and effectively as possible. To do so, the person-centred therapist refrains as far as possible from imposing personal and theoretical values and biases, since to do so would only lead to unwanted interpretation, judgement and prescription, each of which places obstacles in the way of the development of the desired relationship. Rather than engage in these divisive activities, the person-centred therapist *attends* to the client's statements and their underlying affects at a neutral and descriptive level so that the client may clarify and explore subjective experiences. This practice, sometimes referred to as active listening, promotes accurate empathy.

The third necessary condition of person-centred therapy is *congruence*, and, in Rogers' view, is perhaps the most important of the three variables. Congruence refers to the therapist's ability to be present and without façade, that is, to be a living embodiment of integration. The congruent therapist acts as role model for authentic being. Once again, it is not so much what the therapist does as it is the therapist's willingness to be as real, as transparent, as free of defences, as possible that, Rogers argues, provides clients with the necessary strength and willingness to engage in honest and accurate self-exploration and revelation.

As well as being necessary, Rogers argues that the three attitudes, or as they are sometimes called, therapeutic conditions, discussed here are also *sufficient* in themselves for successful therapy to occur. No other special-ized skills or knowledge are required of the therapist; indeed, as I've pointed out, these might actually impede rather than support the devel-opment of the therapeutic relationship.

At first, this stance might seem naïve or even dangerous to some. But, as Rogers has pointed out, this reaction reveals a view of therapy that empha-sizes 'doing' skills as opposed to 'being' qualities, and, as I have tried to demonstrate, Rogers sees the symptomatology of mental disturbance as orig-inating from a fragmentation in one's self-concept which imposes unneces-sary limitations on one's being-in-the-world. It is the degree of unity, or integration, in an individual's experiences of the world that either impedes or promotes self-actualization. The more capable individuals are in examining, accepting and integrating their subjective experiences, the more often they are likely to experience themselves as real, or authentic, beings-in-the-world.

Person-Centred Therapy as a Restatement of the Phenomenological Method

In theory, person-centred therapy seems to be simplicity itself. As Rogers himself once said of his approach:

> I can state the overall hypothesis in one sentence, as follows. If I can provide a certain type of relationship, the other person will discover within himself the capacity to use that relationship for growth and change and personal development will occur. (1961: 33)

However, in practice, person-centred therapy is perhaps among the most difficult to which to adhere.

Firstly, both clients and therapists must overcome what biases they hold concerning their roles and attitudes. Clients typically want to maintain the role of defenceless victim that they have placed themselves in and assume that the therapist will take over their lives (like an idealized parent) and, in so doing, resolve their problems, make decisions for them, provide them with the truth.

Secondly, therapists, having learned a wide number of theoretical approaches to, and skills-based techniques for, therapy, find it difficult not to offer to supply what the client wants and, in so doing, enter an unequal and experientially limited relationship with them.

Thirdly, and perhaps the source of greatest resistance, what person-centred therapy asks, initially of the therapist, but ultimately of both therapist and client, is that they engage in a relationship which almost certainly runs counter to any that has been sanctioned by society. Having learned to build up any number of defences which now seem essential to survival, the client is urged to examine and reconsider these defences not via the therapist's argumentative or manipulative skills but through the therapist's own willingness to *be* defenceless.

In many ways, these difficulties are highly similar to those encountered when attempting to practise existential psychotherapy. Indeed, I would argue that person-centred therapy is, in substantial part, a restatement of the essentials of the phenomenological method. The person-centred therapist, like the practitioner of the phenomenological method, attempts to bracket prior assumptions, biases and sedimented assumptions (*the rule of epoché*); focuses upon and describes (rather than seeks to interpret or explain) immediate experience (*the rule of description*); and avoids making hierarchical distinctions or judgements with regard to the value of one experience over another (*the rule of horizontalization*).

Such similarities are not superficial; both methods point to an attitude towards the investigation of a problem that demands an adherence to openness, accuracy, honesty and recognition of inter-relational involvement and attunement. Further, just as the phenomenologist admits the investigation to be an ongoing process, so, too, does the person-centred therapist accept that there is no end-point (except death) to the process of self-actualization. Finally, and perhaps most importantly, both focus on qualities of 'being' rather than 'doing' skills.

More generally, both accept as given the infinite varieties of interpretations that a situation might provoke, both take for granted the initial validity of all interpretations, and both, in their openness to 'being', make possible the experience of startling and potentially valuable insights.

As can be seen, Rogers' stance toward the psychotherapist's way of being with the client parallel or restate the phenomenological method. Would it therefore be appropriate to conclude that person-centred therapy is the same as existential psychotherapy?

My personal view is that at the level of practice what both approaches share surpasses substantially their divergences. At the level of theory, however, glaring divergences emerge.

Primary among these is Rogers' insistence upon viewing human beings as 'inherently good' and imposing a divide between this 'natural' state of affairs and the 'unnatural' appearance of 'evil' in human relations. This broad divide serves as the means by which Rogers can then make claims to distinguish between the 'real' self or being and his or her 'false' manifestations.

In brief, Rogers' views return us to a dualistic system which is ultimately open to objective analyses and within which the lived experience of the individual can be accessed, considered and restructured *in isolation*. It is evident that such perspectives run counter to the foundational principles of inter-relation as advocated by phenomenological theory. Further, these divergences raise questions as to how they might infiltrate and express themselves in the way of being with clients, or persons in general, advocated by Rogers.

Elsewhere, I have suggested that Rogers' philosophical assumptions impose a subtle 'conditionality' upon theory's seeming 'unconditionality' in that they permit Rogers to minimize or dismiss entirely those ways of being of the person that cannot, from his stance, be viewed as natural or good or real (Spinelli, 1994). In this way, Rogers steps quite some way away from the phenomenological method. As such, Rogers presents us with an apt reminder of how the recognition of similar practices should not lead us to conclude that the philosophical ground from which those practices emerge must also be similar.

The pivotal divergences between existential and person-centred psychotherapies clarify many of the areas of both significant agreement and disagreement between existential and humanistic approaches that many authors – and especially North American authors and theorists – have not, I believe, sufficiently distinguished. I will attempt some initial comparisons in the following chapter.

Existential Psychotherapy: a Summary

Within the existential psychotherapeutic relationship, the therapist is the other who serves as representative of all others in the client's wider world relations. But, just as importantly, the therapist is also the other who challenges the client's beliefs and assumptions regarding others and their impact upon his or her way of being.

The significance of this 'dual-otherness' on the part of the therapist provokes strong resonances with the notion of *schismogenesis* first introduced by Gregory Bateson (Parks, 1999). As Tim Parks explains in a recent article, Bateson's hypothesis evolved while observing the radically different complementary and symmetrical patterns of behaviour adopted by males and females of the Iatmul Indians. Bateson noted the inflexibility inherent in 'the process of reciprocally stimulated personality differentiation' (Parks, 1999: 43). He labelled this process schismogenesis and argued that schismogenesis was both a powerful and damaging process 'not only because it tended to violent extremes, but also because it could deny an individual any experience outside that promoted by this social dynamic' (Parks, 1999: 43). In order to 'correct' the destabilizing impact of schismogenesis, and thereby return some degree of stability to the tribe, its members were required to enact a bizarre series of highly specialized rituals which were referred to as *Naven*.

I would like to suggest, as an overall conclusion to this chapter, that existential psychotherapy provides a series of 'Naven-like' encounters designed to expose the rigid, inter-relationally imposed schismogenetic processes adopted by clients. In focusing upon the various inter-relational realms, both the complementary and the symmetrical patterns of behaviour adopted by clients in order to maintain their sense of 'self' and distinguish it from that of 'others' become clarified, just as the underlying meanings attached to such stances are more adequately discerned. But, it should be apparent that, rather than specific behavioural skills or techniques, it is the existential psychotherapist him/herself who provokes the 'Naven experience' via being the other who both reveals and challenges the client's schismogenetic patterns of being – initially, within the confines of the therapeutic relationship and, consequently, within the client's wider world relations.

But this Naven enterprise *must* begin from a standpoint of acceptance of the client's current way of being. To adopt any other stance, no matter how benevolent or concerned to ameliorate the client's distress, will only serve to maintain the client's sedimented way of being towards self and others. It is via this first, and crucial, step of 'staying with' and 'attuning oneself to' the client's currently lived worldview that the existential psychotherapist begins to challenge profoundly the client's expectations regarding how others are, how others expect the client to be, and how the client expects others to be with him or her. Once the therapist's presence has begun to provoke a more open, honest clarifying process of worldview exploration by the client, the *experiential immediacy* of their current encounter can be considered in terms of the experiential resonances and contrasts it provokes with regard to the client's wider worldview. This dialogical process can then permit the inter-relational meaning of the client's perceived dysfunctions and disturbances to be more clearly explicated and reconsidered.

9
Phenomenological and Humanistic Psychologies: Similarities and Contrasts

If it feels good, do it.

Anonymous slogan of the 'Me' generation

Over 25 years ago, when I first began to teach psychology courses, the vast majority of introductory texts made reference to humanistic psychology as the *third force* or orientation in contemporary psychology (the first and second orientations being those of behaviourism and psychoanalysis). Very little mention, if any at all, was made of phenomenological approaches to psychology. A cursory glance at current introductory texts will reveal that the situation has altered substantially. Texts now tend to refer either to a 'hybrid' third force, existential-humanistic psychology (Cooper, 2003), or just as likely simply highlight phenomenological psychology. However, although the section headings in these textbooks may have undergone a change of name, a comparison of their text summaries most often reveals only slight, if any, revision. Clearly the authors of such texts are assuming that the distinctions between one approach and the other are minimal, or that both humanistic psychology and phenomenological psychology refer to the same approach.

But are these assumptions correct?

The Origins and Development of Contemporary Humanistic Psychology

The earliest indications of the humanistic approach to psychology can be seen to have emerged contemporaneously with both the behaviourist and psychoanalytic approaches. The writings of Wilhelm Dilthey (Hodges, 1944) and Eduard Spranger (1928) during the first decade of this century protested against the tendency to link psychology to the natural sciences. Rather than pursue this reductionist tendency, these authors argued for the development of an *understanding* psychology that 'emphasized the dynamic nature and unique growth of each individual' (Misiak and Sexton, 1973: 108).

Parallel to this position, Gestalt psychology, while maintaining an experimental approach, emphasized its *holistic* stance and implicit dependence upon the phenomenological method as an essential means to psychological investigation (Koffka, 1935; Kohler, 1929).

It is also clear that major figures in the early development of psychology, individuals such as William James (1890) and G. Stanley Hall (1904), were strongly influenced by these movements in that their concerns lay with the investigation of subjective experience as a means of developing a scientific model of psychology that avoided mechanistic reductionism and preserved the distinctly 'human' qualities of its subject area. This argument continued to be advocated during the 1930s and 1940s by Gordon Allport (1955), Carl Rogers (1942) and Abraham Maslow (1968), among others.

It was only in the 1950s, however, that these various views coalesced into a formal movement of North American and European psychologists strongly critical of the dominant trends in the psychology of their time. Primary among their dissatisfactions was the limited and one-sided view of humanity that dominated psychology and which tended to base its 'explanations' on bio-physical models that either dismissed or minimized conscious experience and thereby 'dehumanized' and reduced human beings to relatively simple reactive mechanisms.

Instead, humanistic psychologists argued, psychology should focus on the *primary, 'human' dimensions* of our species, dimensions that emphasized the human being's liberation from the bio-physical restraints that control and determine the behaviour of the 'lower' species. Human creativity, decision-making, interpretation of stimuli, moral development – all these issues and more had been sorely neglected by the dominant trends, or else insufficiently 'explained away' via reductive models. Humanistic psychologists were intent on redressing the balance. The British psychologist John Cohen effectively summarized this stance in his influential text *Humanistic Psychology* (1958):

> the subject matter of psychology is distinctly human; it is not the 'mere lining of physiology.' Our first step should therefore be to study what is characteristic of man, the blossom rather than the root. (Cohen, 1958; quoted in Misiak and Sexton, 1973: 111)

However, humanistic psychology, as it now tends to be understood, only truly came to the fore during the 1960s, principally as a result of three separate, though related, factors significant to both psychology and Western culture in general.

The first of these was the growing disenchantment with both the behaviourist and the psychoanalytic models adopted by psychologists. For different reasons, each approach was beginning to be recognized as having seemingly in-built limitations which prevented a more complete understanding of human behaviour. In particular, the deficiencies in each model with regard to conscious mental processing had become increasingly apparent. Subsequent attempts to deal with this problem led to the so-called *cognitive revolution* within experimental psychology, the growing influence of *object relations theory* and *ego psychology* within psychodynamic approaches, and, not least, the rise of humanistic psychology.

At about the same time, the *human encounter movement* with its focus on self-discovery and the development of more 'liberating' ways to interact and communicate with oneself and others gained sudden popularity and massive media interest (particularly in North America). Loosely based on Kurt Lewin's *T-groups* (Rowan, 1976), encounter groups attracted an ever-increasing clientèle who demonstrated an unflagging willingness to indulge in a seemingly never-ending variety of techniques aimed at the exploration of one's potentials for being. By the end of the decade, this loose conglomerate of growth techniques became known as the *human potential movement*.

The third, and perhaps most significant, factor in the emergence of humanistic psychology was the rise of the youth-dominated *counter-culture*. Emphasizing its allegiance to 'new left' politics, its rejection of 'role-appropriate', 'establishment' thinking and behaviour, and its insistence on both freeing and expanding one's self-awareness via drugs, political, social and sexual 'consciousness raising', alternative lifestyles and so forth, it found its unity and strength in its protest against the war in Vietnam and adulation of rock-and-roll music.

The key feature in all three of these factors was a disenchantment with the norm, and a desire to develop more satisfactory, more relevant alternatives. Under such conditions, traditional approaches to psychology (as with everything else) became open to challenge; it is hardly surprising that a 'humanistic' psychology offering 'freedom, authenticity, and openness to experience' (Shaffer, 1978: 8) seemed worthy of serious investigation.

The Central Tenets of Humanistic Psychology

In his important text, *Humanistic Psychology*, John Shaffer (1978) outlines five basic principles, or emphases, that distinguish humanistic psychology from the other contemporary approaches. In summary, they are as follows:

1. Conscious experience is seen as the source of primary data. The recognition of the uniqueness of subjective experience allows for a greater sense of freedom and openness to one's potentials;
2. Rather than separating being and experience into various dichotomies, components, typologies, traits or functions, humanistic psychology retains a holistic and integrated view of human beings;
3. In spite of the bio-physical limitations placed upon them, human beings are essentially autonomous and experientially free;
4. Humanistic psychology insists on the genuineness of conscious experience and avoids taking a reductionist stance;
5. No complete, final, all-encompassing theory of human behaviour and experience is possible.

Phenomenological Psychology versus Humanistic Psychology

It should be evident that, on consideration, these five characteristic humanistic psychology emphases appear to be broadly in line with a phenomenological standpoint. However, on closer analysis, divergences begin to emerge.

The primary orientation through which humanistic psychology is typically identified today arose mainly as a result of the massive cultural and political unrest of the 1960s. Although this upheaval was world-wide, the focus and concerns of humanistic psychology have a peculiarly North American slant. As such, humanistic psychology's greatest impact has been on North American psychology. Various attempts to introduce it to Europe have been met with some significant resistance such that what ground it does seem to have gained is principally oriented in the therapeutic community in general and in the counselling movement in particular. In other words, much of humanistic psychology appears to be largely culture-bound to a broadly North American psychological perspective and bias that emphasizes pragmatic principles of individualistic freedom, growth and happiness and which focuses upon technique rather than centring upon the underlying philosophical assumptions from which the approach and its diverse applications are claimed to arise.

Put somewhat crudely, much of humanistic psychology reflects a North American attitude which, in its emphasis on technique, can be summarized as: 'if it works, do it'. Phenomenological psychology, on the other hand, firmly rooted in Continental European philosophy, takes a much more guarded stance which de-emphasizes technique and explores the wider implications of its ideology.

Yalom, for example, aware of this divergence, has labelled humanistic psychology as existential psychology's 'flashy American cousin' (1980: 17–21). More significantly, he has noted that while humanistic psychology has focused almost exclusively on individual freedom, choice and liberation, European existentialism, while acknowledging those features as requiring proper consideration, has also stressed the inherent limitations and 'tragic dimensions of existence' (1980: 19).

Echoing this view, van Deurzen-Smith has decried humanistic psychology's assumption that human beings are 'basically positive creatures who develop constructively, given the right conditions' (1988: 56). Instead, she reminds us, the existential attitude is 'that people may evolve in any direction, good or bad, and that only reflection on what constitutes good and bad makes it possible to exercise one's choice in the matter' (1988: 56–7). Both writers suggest a 'skewedness' in the humanistic approach; where phenomenology stresses a balanced consideration of both the unexplored potentials and inherent limits to freedom, humanistic psychology speaks less of limits and contingency than of development of potential, less of acceptance than of awareness, less of anxiety than of peak experiences and oceanic oneness, less of life meaning than of self-realization, less of apartness and isolation than of I-Thou and encounter. (Yalom, 1980: 19)

It is this imbalance, for example, that marks out Carl Rogers' stance. Whereas, as I've tried to show, his approach to therapy has its basis in the phenomenological method, his unwavering optimism as to the basic 'goodness' of human beings runs counter to the more guarded phenomenological stance as expressed by Yalom and van Deurzen-Smith, and, as a result, places him as firmly in the broad humanist camp as it does within the phenomenological orientation.

More generally, although phenomenology provides the primary considerations and philosophical bases to the wide (even confusing) variety of contemporary humanistic techniques, many of the developers and practitioners of these techniques have failed, on the whole, to adequately examine these bases fully and, as a result, have 'tainted' humanistic psychology with unnecessary, misguided, even potentially dangerous, overly optimistic tendencies.

The solipsistic excesses of the 'Me Decade' of the 1970s can be seen as direct results of this unbalanced perspective. Emphasizing only self-growth, self-development and self-interest without paying due consideration to the effects of such on others, most of the North American engendered techniques employed by humanistic psychologists clearly fail to acknowledge and duly consider phenomenology's conclusions with regard to the indivisible inter-relational nature of the self/other (or 'I'/'not I') relationship.

As a result, rather than promote co-operation, humility and shared responsibility, the great majority of humanistic techniques (if unwillingly) have fostered competition, self-aggrandizement and disdain for others' inter-relationally derived experiences. In their failure to give equal weight to a number of central phenomenological conclusions in their writings, teachings and techniques, many humanistic psychologists broke away from the very method (that is, the phenomenological method) that they claimed to follow or by which to have been influenced.

Lest my contention might sound unduly harsh to humanistically oriented readers, I wish to make it clear that my points are not meant to dismiss nor diminish humanistic psychology's contributions to the field. Recent texts such as *The Handbook of Humanistic Psychology* (Schneider, Bugenthal and Fraser Pierson, 2001) bear great relevance to both phenomenological psychology and psychology in general and deserve careful analysis revealing as they do the richness of contemporary views, not least with regard to a Human Science research focus. It is quite evident, for instance, that the ideas and work of Kurt Goldstein (1995) in particular deserve a great deal more attention by existential-phenomenological theorists and practitioners than they have received so far.

That a number of humanistic and phenomenological authors share important points of investigative contact with regard to such issues as the analysis of the therapeutic process and relationship (e.g. Alvin Mahrer, 1996) or the 'meeting' (or 'presence') between human beings (e.g. James Bugenthal, 1987) is also without doubt. That a continuing, respectful dialogue between such humanistic authors and those who adopt existential-phenomenological perspectives might take place seems to me to be not only desirable, but necessary. But the existence of shared per-spectives does not preclude the existence of divergent views.

What differences between humanistic and phenomenological psycholo-gies do exist are not merely, as some have suggested (Rowan, 2001) at the level of practice ('doing'). Rather, they are most clearly revealed when examining the underlying assumptions and values (what might broadly be termed as 'being qualities') that infuse their practice.

So, for instance, while major humanistic theorists such as John Rowan argue that existential therapy cruelly limits 'itself by not using the range of interventions made possible by the endeavours of humanistic practi-tioners' (2001: 448), I would instead suggest that 'cruelty' has nothing to do with the issue in that such restraints follow directly from the philo-sophical underpinnings and implications of the phenomenological method. To minimize or dismiss the importance of these underpinnings might permit some superficial similarities between approaches to emerge, but only at the cost of 'glossing over' crucial divergences. For example, Rowan (2001) provides a number of examples of the humanistic thera-pist's interventions when dealing with a client who continually speaks of his mother – asking the client to repeat a sentence several times in an increasingly loud voice, or suggesting to the client that s/he exaggerate the movement of his/her right foot. Without suggesting that such inter-ventions are in any way inappropriate for the humanistic practitioner, nonetheless they appear to me to be quite alien to the kinds of interven-tions that an existential psychotherapist might make since, rather than seek to address the 'dialogical way of being' of the client *as it is being expressed in the encounter*, they succeed in shifting the client to another mode of being and, thereby, express an implicit critique of the client's dia-logical way of being by the therapist who, in his/her role as 'other' in the client's world relations might well confirm – however inadvertently – the client's beliefs that the world is unaccepting of him/her as s/he is, and that, as such, the world knows better than s/he what is the appropriate way for him/her to be, and so forth.

Key Differences between Phenomenological and Humanistic Psychologies

Let me specify what I believe to be four key divergences between human-istic and phenomenological psychologies: 1) the centrality of experience; 2) the issue of actualization in general or self-actualization in particular; 3) the hypothesis of 'wholeness' and 'integration'; and 4) the status of 'the self'. I believe that these four concerns run throughout the whole of humanistic thinking, including, of course, Carl Rogers's person-centred approach that was discussed in the previous chapter.

Experience

Humanistic psychologists tend to speak of **experience** as a central aspect of the whole humanistic enterprise. Phenomenological psychologists would certainly agree that the question of 'experience' is crucial. I would also accept, as a valid critique, that existential-phenomenological authors have, at times, seemed to lose themselves in a somewhat arid and rarefied linguistic debate whose abstractions bear tenuous relationship to lived experience. As well, it is evident that humanistic authors such as Alvin Mahrer (1996) and James Bugenthal (1987) have provided important contributions to the debates surrounding experience. Notwithstanding, it is also the case that similarly important contributions exist in contemporary phenomenological literature focusing upon the dilemmas of consciousness (e.g. David Chalmers, 1997; Francisco Varela, 1996). But, even here, important divergences arise.

Humanistic authors seem to suggest the view that experience can be accessed in some undiluted fashion so that 'theory' (i.e. interpretation) does not get in the way. This, I think, is a characteristic attitude of the great majority of humanistic authors that seems to hearken back to an earlier attempt to separate thought from feeling or ideation from emotion.

In contrast to such assumptions, a phenomenologically derived position would not support such schismatic stances (in the same way as it would not support a 'split' between so-called 'subject' and so-called 'object'), not merely out of some abstract rationale but, far more importantly, because structured, experientially focused investigations reveal major limitations in this position *at a lived level*.

Instead, existential phenomenology suggests that our experience of experience is intentionally derived, expressive of an 'interface' between consciousness and 'the world'. For me to note or discern or speak of 'my experience' reveals an interpretative selectivity and reflection that has already taken place. In this way, to suggest some sort of pre-conceptual 'purity' to one's reflective experience is deeply misleading.

I find it strange that such an obvious point appears to be missed continuously by so many humanistic authors far more intelligent than I and can only suppose that it is missed because to accept it leads such authors to radically different, experientially derived conclusions to those held by the humanistic model about each of the remaining three issues I have highlighted as being crucial to the understanding and exploration of the divergence between humanistic and phenomenological approaches.

Wholeness, (Self-)Actualization and Authenticity

With regard to the issue of (self-)actualization, it becomes of little importance to dispute whether humanistic authors take an optimistic or neutral view on the matter. What is at issue is whether it is of much (theoretical and experiential) value to speak of (self-)actualization at all and that, perhaps, phenomenologically derived notions of inter-relational openness, disclosure and dialogue provide far more adequate attempts to reflect and evoke various features of human experience that the humanistic model has attempted to combine, and thus transform, into the hypothesis of (self-)actualization.

In similar fashion, the humanistic emphasis upon 'wholeness' or 'integration' is reconsidered by phenomenology from a standpoint that suggests that, at best, such an emphasis reveals only *one* aspect of lived experience and which permits the opposite and contradictory aspect of the *inevitable incompleteness* in all life experience to also be acknowledged and valued.

The humanistic re-interpretation of Heidegger's philosophical notion of *authenticity* encapsulates the dilemmas between humanistic and phenomenological psychologies and clarifies their divergent views on actualization and wholeness.

It is evident from their use of the term that most humanistic authors have altered the meaning of 'authenticity' so that it now expresses a person's subjectively felt experience of self-congruence and integration. In this way, authenticity has become more akin to an aspect of personality and which suggests an enterprise that one might wish to undertake with the aim of *achieving authenticity* or *becoming authentic*.

While humanistic authors obviously have the right to employ the word 'authentic' to mean whatever they might want it to mean, it is quite another matter for them to claim that they employ the term in the same way as do phenomenological psychologists. It is evident that this is not the case at all. Heidegger's term did not seek to express some subjectively felt state of experiencing being, much less imply that authentic being was in some way inherently superior to, or 'healthier than', inauthentic being. Nor did Heidegger propose that the striving for authenticity is in any way related to states of psychological balance, wholeness or congruence. His was a much more cautious, even neutral, position reflecting a way of being that emerges when a being is 'there' (that is to say, 'stays with', 'attends to', 'embraces') with the 'there of being' as it discloses itself. This stance of 'what is, is' has nothing whatever to tell us about health or personal growth or individual improvement. Indeed, there is not even anything to suggest the idea of making authenticity one's aim in life or something towards which a person may strive.

This is not to say that the phenomenological meaning given to authenticity is in any way superior to or more appropriate than that to which humanistic psychology has given it (or vice-versa). Only that they are different and that, in being different, they open up distinct alternatives for our exploration.

The Self

The differences in meaning arising from the phenomenological and humanistic use of the term 'authenticity' alert us to the fact that a further concern surfaces, in myriad ways, when considering the humanistic emphasis upon a singular, intrapsychic and 'real' self.

Writing about the self in a way that I believe encapsulates a widely-accepted humanistic stance, John Rowan asserts that 'the real self – the self which is to be actualised in self-actualisation – is not a concept but an experience. It is not something to be argued at a philosophical level, it is thing to be encountered at an experiential level' (2001: 457).

But, to repeat my earlier point: reflective experience isn't value-free, or concept-free or philosophy-free as is being suggested. Such a stance adopts a position that denies such pivotal variables as culture and history.

As was discussed in Chapter 5, the notion of the 'real self' that is being put forward is both a relatively recent historical development in Western thought and culture and remains significantly alien to a great many past and current cultures and societies who have no place in their worldviews for a singular, permanent, 'real' self (see, for instance, Dorrine Kondo's (1990) examination of modern Japanese self-constructs).

Readers will recall that existential-phenomenological theorists would argue that we don't directly experience our 'real self'. Rather, we interpret our experience from an *a priori*-biased and value-laden perspective that, in current Western culture, assumes the 'truth' in the belief in a 'real self' and which, in turn, requires that same belief in order to validate the inter-pretation we give to our experience.

It remains my personal view that humanistic theory's greatest diver-gence with phenomenological theory lies precisely in its somewhat unquestioning adoption and advocacy of a Western notion of a singular, intrapsychic, 'real self' which can be distinguished from any number of 'false selves'. I would further suggest that it is this adherence to such a notion which remains humanistic psychology's greatest philosophical weakness through which were provoked the solipsistic excesses of the 1970s and 1980s and which continues to permeate Western culture in all manner of ways, not least via the maintenance of an isolationist divide between 'self and other'.

The phenomenological critique of humanistic psychology's ideas regard-ing 'the self' is not some mere intellectual game, it has a direct impact upon our very way of engaging with our experience of being. To attempt to avoid the dualism of 'real' *vs* 'false' selves serves to not merely promote a less dissociated dialogical stance toward one's self-to-self relations, it also provokes a critical shift in one's sense of engagement with, and responsi-bility for, one's relations with others and the world in general.

Is this way of considering 'the self' more or less valid than the way pro-posed by humanistic psychology? I don't think any of us can say. But instead of validity we can speak of implications. For us as human beings, the phenomenological perspective challenges, at the very least, the stance of an isolationist self-centred, self-focused way of being and relating that runs rampant through our culture. In contrast, it provides some initial means to assess and consider possibilities that strive to place self in a self/world inter-relational context.

Unfortunately, due to the current confusion as to the distinction between phenomenological and humanistic psychology, many criticisms that are specific to particular aspects of humanistic psychology have been misguidedly presented as critiques of phenomenological psychology. This has often led to a naïve dismissal of phenomenological psychology by adherents of the remaining systems of contemporary psychology.

This is a particularly unwelcome development, not only because it rests upon false assumptions concerning phenomenological psychology, but, more significantly, because phenomenology's stated aim is not to deny the accomplishments of other approaches but, rather, to increase the adequacy of their investigations and theoretical models.

That there may be – perhaps insurmountable – theoretical and methodological disagreements between phenomenological psychology and the remaining systems in contemporary psychology does not deny the value of a phenomenological input to psychological thought. This issue forms the central concern of the following chapter.

10

Phenomenology and the Major Systems in Psychology

Though adjoining states are within sight of one another, and the sound of dogs barking and cocks crowing in one state can be heard in the other, yet the people in one state will grow old and die without having had any dealings with those of the other.

Lao Tsu

Husserl originally proposed the view that all the sciences could and should be constructed along phenomenological lines (Ihde, 1986a). During the final quarter of the twentieth century, for instance, various attempts to examine the benefits of this suggestion provided a variety of intriguing results: the rise and development of modern-day ethnomethodology as presented by Harold Garfinkel (Ihde, 1986a), is clearly indebted to phenomenological theory, as is Berger and Luckmann's highly influential text, *The Social Construction of Reality* (1966/1979). The authors of the latter text, for example, make this indebtedness explicit when they explain that the method they consider to be the best suited to allow the clarification of a scientific understanding of the process of ascribing meaning to everyday life is that of phenomenological analysis.

Similarly, Filmer, Phillipson, Silverman and Walsh, in their important text *New Directions in Sociological Theory* (1972) assessed positively the potential impact of a phenomenological alternative to sociological theories and research.

What unifies these 'new directions' in the various specialist fields just mentioned is a criticism of their sciences as being exclusively *noematic* in their orientation, and, thereby, able to arrive at only limited and insufficient conclusions; since noetic considerations are also clearly required, phenomenology offers a useful and rewarding starting point for future research.

As this text has argued, phenomenological investigation permitted the development of a unique and systematic approach to psychology. In addition, as this chapter will attempt to demonstrate, phenomenological psychology seeks neither to dismiss nor to diminish the contributions of other contemporary psychological systems. Rather, wherever possible, it attempts to reconsider and reassess their assumptions, both to point out their relative strengths and weaknesses and to incorporate significant findings obtained from phenomenological enquiry.

A case can be made that much of phenomenological psychology's language is somewhat esoteric and unwieldy. This may be so; nevertheless, it is its *ideas* that demand major consideration. As Erdelyi (1985) has shown, for instance, once the highly specific terminologies of psychoanalysis and cognitive psychology have been deconstructed, numerous important similarities and areas of agreement emerge and make inter-system communication and (at least partial) rapprochement more likely and potentially highly rewarding. There is no reason to suppose that similar benefits would not arise as a result of increasingly regular dialogue between phenomenological psychology and the dominant approaches.

Often, the conclusions arrived at by phenomenological psychologists challenge those held by other psychological systems. This is not because phenomenological psychologists judge the findings of the other schools as being 'incorrect' (a term which, like the notion of 'correctness', is avoided by phenomenology due to its implication of the ultimate knowability of 'truth' or 'reality'), but, rather, because their findings are often both limited and limiting.

In general, phenomenological psychology's criticism is primarily concerned with other systems' minimization or exclusion of conscious experience from their studies. This lacuna, phenomenologists argue, has harmed psychology, and restricted its practical applications. As Rollo May once wrote: 'we need a form of psychology that does not dwell on behaviour to the exclusion of experience, or experience without regard for behaviour, but centres on the relation between experience and behaviour' (1969a: 27).

An early attempt to explore the possible phenomenological contributions to psychology took place in the form of a symposium held at Rice University in 1963 and later published as *Behaviorism and Phenomenology* (Wann, 1964). I urge interested readers to refer to this important selection of papers, in particular R.B. MacLeod's contribution (Wann, 1964: 47–74) for its clarification of the centrality of meaningful constructions of experience to phenomenological investigation.

In what I hope is in keeping with the spirit of this symposium, I now wish to consider some areas of potentially useful dialogue between phenomenological psychology and the remaining major systems in contemporary psychology.

Phenomenological Psychology and Psychoanalysis

With its emphasis on questions of meaning and interpretation, as well as its focus upon lived experience, phenomenological psychology at first appears to be closer in its interests and applications to the various current psychoanalytic theories than to any others within contemporary psychology. In general, both approaches can be seen to consider the limits and potentials of human inter-relation, and to take the view that people are active interpreters of their environment.

On the other hand, a traditional psychoanalyst steeped in the ideas of Sigmund Freud and his immediate followers would point to a number of important differences and divergences between the two approaches. Freudian psychoanalytic theories stress the role of the unconscious, of our earliest infantile experiences, of the instinctual forces of Eros and Thanatos, and of the psychic conflict between id-ego-superego as prime instigators and determinants of conscious thought and behaviour. Equally, Freudian psychoanalysts (as well as those from numerous other major analytic 'schools' such as the Kleinian) argue that unresolved sexual and aggressive wishes lie at the heart of human motivation. On the other hand, following on from developments within object-relations theory, more recent attachment-based, intersubjective strands within psychoanalysis place greater emphasis on inter-relational issues (Atwood and Stolorow, 1984) and, by so doing, both explicitly and implicitly acknowledge their indebtedness to major existential-phenomenological authors such as Maurice Merleau-Ponty (1962).

As one of the most complete (and complex) systems within contemporary psychology, psychoanalysis provides a coherent – if highly controversial – theory of mind. Aside from surface agreements on issues of psychic conflict, the impact and significance of inter-relations and the worldviews derived from such, is there much of a meeting between psychoanalysis and phenomenology? As I see it, three critical philosophically derived obstacles stand in the way of any substantive rapprochement between psychoanalysis and phenomenology: psychoanalysts' reliance upon notions of linear causality, the accessibility of past events and the assumption of an unconscious mental system whose functions can be distinguished from, and impact directly upon, conscious experience. These three dilemmas are most acute when considering the more classically focused schools of psychoanalysis, such as the Freudian and the Kleinian. Nonetheless, they remain problematic for all contemporary approaches, though perhaps less intractably.

I have not the space here to detail the divergent views taken on these topics by psychoanalysis and phenomenology and I direct interested readers to texts such as Medard Boss's *Psychoanalysis and Daseinsanalysis* (1963), Betty Cannon's *Sartre and Psychoanalysis* (1991) and Hans Cohn's *Existential Thought and Therapeutic Practice* (1997) as well as my own *Demystifying Therapy* (Spinelli, 1994) for elaboration on these themes. Let me just state phenomenology's concerns in brief.

Phenomenology's Critique of Psychoanalytic Theory

Phenomenologists question the very possibility, much less its value, of understanding and predicting human behaviour on the basis of a notion of causality that is both linear (from A to B to C to D, and so forth) and unidirectional (from the past onto the present). This view of causality has been shown to be valid for regular, and hence simple, systems of movement and change and remains a pivotal assumption of a Natural Science approach to enquiry (though not when such enquiry is focused at a sub-atomic level). In contrast, phenomenology, while not rejecting causality as such, adopts views of causality that acknowledge human behaviour as being complex from a systemic perspective and thus requiring notions of causality much more akin to those that might be argued within recent developments in physics such as 'chaos theory' (Gleick, 1988).

With regard to the issue of the role of the past, as has already been discussed in Chapter 5, phenomenology considers the remembered past to be a selective construct whose primary function is that of validating the person's currently experienced worldview. In this way, rather than viewing the past as the source or originator of present experience, phenomenology reverses this position. Further, phenomenology argues that any divide between past and present (and, indeed, future) is both artificial and misleading and that, instead, one must investigate the current 'being' of a person from the standpoint of an indivisible inter-relational matrix composed of past events, current experience and future expectations.

As such, while phenomenological psychologists would certainly agree that past experience plays a major, even central, role in the person's current psychic life, they would also take the view that the past is a far more flexible construct, undergoing continual reassessment and reinterpretation. The *significance* of past events is by no means fixed, though this may, at times, certainly seem to be the case when our views and beliefs regarding a particular past event are deeply sedimented.

Whereas the psychoanalyst might seek to lead the analysand to an *acceptance of the past*, the phenomenological psychologist focuses on the description and examination of current experience as a possible means of liberating oneself from sedimented attitudes, values, stances, beliefs and behaviours that prevent one's *acceptance of currently lived experience*. In both cases, one's past is exposed to examination, but whereas the psychoanalyst seeks to establish causal links between past and present experience, the phenomenological psychologist eschews both the necessity for, and more importantly, the very possibility of, such links. The phenomenological psychologist seeks to expose the interpreted significance of past events in the light of current experience. This shift in perspective as with the related one of linear causality, if adopted by psychoanalysis, would free it from its somewhat outmoded mechanistic orientation without doing serious damage to its central emphases.

Equally, though the aims of these two processes might at first seem entirely dissimilar, it can be argued that in a broad sense both seek to allow individuals to be more honest and accurate in their perceptions of their experience.

Let me now turn to the vexing question of the unconscious. Like psychoanalysis, phenomenology suggests that persons resort to a variety of truth-distorting stances towards their experience of being. For instance, we might seek out the security of fixed external truths, permanent meanings, statements from on high concerning the true point and purpose to our lives. Alternatively, we might attempt to reject our experience via various forms of denial and dissociation. The appeal and frequency of such strategies lie precisely in that they serve to allay the unease and uncertainty of being-in-the-world. For instance, as was discussed in Chapter 5, clients who hold a fixed view of themselves, or a sedimented self-structure, that when experientially challenged through contradictory evidence or via experiences that expand its structural meaning boundaries might defend against such challenges by disowning, or dissociating, the lived experience so that the sedimented structure can be maintained.

In investigating such stances, phenomenology focuses upon persons' *conscious* experience of themselves-in-relation. Again, while not denying that much of experience remains unreflected, in that it is not properly clarified and attended to, it need not be the case that such phenomena require the hypothesis of a separate and distinct mental system whose primary mechanism of repression requires it to remain unavailable directly to conscious experience and, hence, unconscious.

Various phenomenologists have re-stated the question of the unconscious from a diversity of perspectives that reject the necessity of hypothesizing or imposing a separate mental system to that of consciousness. While Medard Boss proposed a reformulation that relied upon Heideggerian theory in general and the issue of inauthenticity in particular (Condrau, 1998), Sartre challenged the whole mechanism of repression upon which the notion of a psychoanalytic unconscious rested and suggested instead an alternative that centred upon his idea of unreflected consciousness (Cannon, 1991). I have myself suggested an alternative that reformulates the notion of the unconscious from the standpoints of dissociation of conscious experience and sedimentation of self-constructs (Spinelli, 1994; 2001).

In each of these cases, while by no means denying the experiential features and variables associated with bringing to conscious reflection that which has been previously distorted, denied or left unreflected, phenomenology simplifies and demystifies the underlying ideas associated with psychoanalytic notions of the unconscious.

As Grossman has argued, 'an unconscious desire is a desire which a person *experiences*, but which the person does not *recognize* for what it is' (1984: 56, italics in original). In other words, the psychoanalytic unconscious refers to a misidentification of experience for the purpose of temporarily reducing or removing the guilt-laden anxiety that would be generated from the correct identification of experience. Put in this way, the divide between psychoanalysis and phenomenological psychology becomes far less intractable since the issue now can be seen to revolve around patterns of meaning construction.

Phenomenological Psychology's Critique of Psychoanalytic Practice

In terms of its psychotherapeutic applications, the central technique of psychoanalysis – *free association* – can be seen as similar in many ways to the phenomenological method. Indeed, convincing arguments have been made that Freud's development of free association can be traced back directly to the profound influence that Brentano's lectures had upon him (McGrath, 1986). In attempting free association, analysands are instructed to allow their mind to flow freely, to speak of whatever comes into their thoughts no matter how trivial or absurd it may initially seem. In similar fashion, the phenomenological method directs us to bracket our beliefs and assumptions, to describe experience as accurately as possible, to avoid placing any immediate hierarchies of significance on our descriptions. The similarities are, I think, obvious.

Equally, though the aims of these two processes might at first seem entirely dissimilar, it can be argued that in a broad sense both seek to allow individuals to be more honest and accurate in their perceptions of their experience. Equally, I would suggest, both processes are best viewed as *attempts* rather than as achievable enterprises.

Another central process of psychoanalytic therapy, the development of the *transference relationship* between analyst and analysand, requires some degree of reinterpretation. Considered from a phenomenological perspective, the analysand's directing of deeply felt positive and negative emotions on to the therapist is not only, or necessarily, a regressive act through which the therapist becomes a temporary substitute for the analysand's past significant others. It is also (and perhaps more importantly) a demonstration of the analysand's growing respect for and trust in the therapist and of the analysand's acceptance that no revelation will threaten the analytic relationship and, by implication, the analysand's sense of being. As such, from a phenomenological perspective, the client's felt experience towards the therapist is neither symbolic nor substitutive. Rather, it is as direct and 'real' as any other interpretative experience and should be considered as such. That the client's stance and attitude towards the therapist may *share or correspond to* stances and attitudes that the client maintains towards others, present or past, general or specific, is neither unlikely nor surprising and certainly worth investigation. But this should in no way refocus the therapist's attention away from that which is occurring in its immediacy within the current encounter. Nor should it permit the therapist, as some psychoanalysts themselves have argued, to minimize or avoid the impact of the client's presence by invoking self-protective terms such as 'transference' when such presence is felt to be in some way challenging or disturbing (Spinelli, 1994). Further, it might also be the case that in those instances that psychoanalysts term as transference, the analysands are 'testing' their analysts' claimed open-minded neutrality towards them in order to ensure the truth of such claims (negative transference), and also under other circumstances, are expressing their desire to continue to explore and maintain this unique, unusual and highly desirable relationship via whatever means the analysand has learned to employ when dealing with others who provide only conditional regard (positive transference).

Once again, phenomenological psychologists take issue not with the necessity and strength of those lived experiences that have been termed as instances of 'transference'. Rather, their disagreement lies with the limited, and potentially misleading interpretative value of the term itself.

With regard to the traditional psychoanalytic 'metapsychology' and its notions concerning instinctual forces and existing conflicts between the hypothesized 'structures' of the mind, not to speak of the many theoretical concepts that make up the psychoanalytic view of the person (for example, concepts such as the Oedipus complex, castration anxiety and penis envy), it is first of all important to note that psychoanalysts themselves are by no means united in their acceptance of these concepts or on the relative importance of the role of each in the development of the human psyche (Grunbaum, 1984).

Freud, much to his credit, continually revised his theories when both theoretical inconsistencies and analytical data seemed to demand both major and minor revisions in thought, and was willing to accept some degree of divided opinion among his followers (Gay, 1988).

Phenomenological psychologists might well view many psychoanalytic conclusions as open hypotheses which, though neither proven nor disproven, might act as useful metaphorical ways of considering the workings of the mind. Nevertheless, they would also avoid considering such theories as 'invariants' of human experience until such a time as there was sufficient basis for such an assumption.

If there is a major division between the method of investigation adopted by psychoanalysis and phenomenological psychology, it lies in the former system's pronounced tendency to rely on explanatory-focused analytic interpretations and theoretical formulations that attempt to extract latent or hidden meaning from its manifest construct and of the equal, though opposite, tendency on the part of phenomenological psychology to maintain a focus that rests exclusively upon that which is manifest via descriptively focused interpretations.

True, phenomenological psychology has its own assumptions and, to some extent, a number of these might hold similarities to those of psychoanalysis. The psychoanalytic notion of a 'thanatos drive', for example, bears some (if initially seemingly superficial) resemblances to the existential notion of 'death anxiety' and both concepts might find some gain in being considered and contrasted in relation to one another. However, though no easier to 'prove' or 'disprove' than are psychoanalytic assumptions, there is, to me at least, a simplicity and experiential clarity within such assumptions that convince me of their greater adequacy. It takes little effort, for example, to experience at least some of the angst that the realization of one's embodied temporality brings forth. Similar attempts to experience, let us say, the Oedipus complex, require a good deal of meta-analysis just to discern its meaning and are as likely to provoke disbelief as they are to induce illumination.

Without denying the power of psychoanalytic insights, the phenomenological psychologist would argue that their adequacy might be limited in that, through their failure to apply the phenomenological method, they arrive at possibly misleading and biased interpretational conclusions. For instance, Freud's letters to his friend Wilhelm Fliess (Masson, 1985) reveal his tendency to generalize his own experience into a theory of universal validity. It is a measure of Freud's genius that so many of his conclusions *are* open, at least in part, to generalization. But, equally, it is also the apparent personal biases in his insights that have opened psychoanalysis to continuing controversy.

There have been various important attempts over the years to converge or reconcile psychoanalytic theory with phenomenology. Psychoanalytically oriented therapists such as Otto Rank (Lieberman, 1985), and Karen Horney (1966) among others, stressed the importance of inter-relational factors in personality development. More recently, Paul Ricoeur (1970) has attempted an admirable synthesis of phenomenology and psychoanalysis, and Robert Steele (1982) has argued the case for considering psychoanalysis as a hermeneutic science, that is, a science of 'meaning' thereby opening the way for more phenomenologically derived analyses.

The rise of *object relations theory* (Greenberg and Mitchell, 1983) within psychoanalysis has been revolutionary in its re-evaluation of psychoanalytic theory. Object relations theorists either disavow or diminish the importance of instinctual urges, preferring instead to focus upon the series of significant interactions in which individuals engage in order that they may form various interpreted relations with others, themselves and the world. Here, quite obviously, there is much scope for an illuminating dialogue between psychoanalysis and phenomenological psychology.

In terms of psychoanalytic theory in general, the impact and influence of social constructionist and post-structural thinking has challenged many of the most rigid interpretative stances taken by more traditional forms of psychoanalysis. Linguistic and metaphor–driven reinterpretations of various psychic processes, not least the psychoanalytic unconscious, such as those propounded by Jean Laplanche (Van Haute, 1995) are providing novel and noteworthy points of contact with phenomenological perspectives.

Most significant of all, I believe, has been the re-evaluation and extension of various *interpersonal theories* within psychoanalytic thought over the past decade. The work of Daniel Stern and his associates, most pertinently with regard to their idea of 'now moments' of meeting in the inter-relation between analyst and client, have begun to explore what I have termed as the 'the we-focus' in the therapeutic encounter in pertinent and exciting ways (Stern, 2004). Finally, the recent re-appraisal of Harry Stack Sullivan's interpersonally focused theory of psychoanalysis has provided a valuable means for significant dialogue with phenomenological theory (Barton Evans III, 1996). The initial impact of such an enterprise can already be assessed through the highly original and at times quite startling writings of Leslie Farber (2000).

Phenomenological Psychology and Cognitive-Behavioural Approaches

While it is feasible to consider similarities and areas of possible rapprochement between phenomenological and psychoanalytic theory, it would seem, at first, to be far more difficult, though potentially rewarding, to see what practicable benefit there might be in any dialogue between phenomenological psychology and cognitive-behavioural theory as well as its applied extension, cognitive-behavioural therapy or CBT.

Phenomenology and Behaviourism

After all, behaviourism arose in direct reaction to psychological schools that stressed the centrality of conscious experience. Declaiming the possibility that consciousness could be examined scientifically (that is, via experimental procedures derived from physical science), behaviourism both minimized and, in its most radical stance, rejected the role of consciousness in human behaviour. Instead, it focused its attention – for many years highly successfully – on both the observation and the manipulation of *external* or *overt* behaviour, and based its conclusions on data obtained from controlled experimental studies. Perhaps most importantly, a key element of behaviourist theory is the notion that we are, by and large, passive reactors to natural and culturally derived environmental stimuli which mould and shape our behaviour through conditioning and reinforcement.

Presented with such stances, what could phenomenological psychologists and behaviourists find of value from each other's approach?

It is important to recall that both approaches share a similar reluctance to provide theoretically based interpretations that invoke hypothetical structures or mechanisms. Instead, both (initially, at least) focus upon observation and description. In theory, behaviourists should have no qualms about the phenomenological method since its emphases follow closely the broad aims of behavioural research.

Both phenomenological psychology and behaviourism stress the importance of environmental stimuli as catalysts to action. Where there is disagreement, of course, is in behaviourism's claims that we are primarily passive reactors to directly experienced stimuli. Phenomenological psychology's stance, on the other hand, is to argue that we are active interpreters of the stimuli in that our response to them is intentionally determined through both innate invariants and individual experience.

In this disagreement, there exists much experimental data to support the phenomenological position. Of particular interest is the argument presented by Albert Bandura suggesting the basis for a 'reciprocal determinism' between environment and behaviour, thereby strongly contradicting behaviourism's uni-directional assumption (Yalom, 1980). Yalom points out that there exists a substantial amount of empirical research to support Bandura's contention (Bandura in Yalom, 1980: 271).

Such a position, of course, bears substantial similarity to that advocated by phenomenological psychologists who dispute the view that stimuli are directly observable. Instead, they argue, the stimuli themselves remain unknown and unknowable; rather it is the constructed meaning we add to stimuli, in order to make sense of our behaviour, that remains of importance.

It can also be pointed out that behaviourists are naïve in their assumptions as to what constitutes 'objectivity'. Their views reveal an adherence to a now outmoded stance derived from nineteenth-century theoretical physics. Current theories place doubt upon the traditional distinction between observer and observed. Even in a controlled experiment, the experimenter's assumptions, biases and expectations will, to some degree, determine the kinds of measurements made and even, as Rosenthal and his colleagues demonstrated in several controlled studies (Rosenthal, 1966), significantly influence the experimental results. In one famous study (and its two subsequent confirmatory replications), for example, it was shown that 'those experimenters expecting success ratings obtained them to a significantly greater degree than did those experimenters who anticipated ratings of failure' (Shaffer, 1978: 173).

Though behaviourists implicitly appear to suggest that we are 'slaves' to our environment, their actual attitude to this position reveals a major inconsistency.

What would a behavioural therapist do, for example, with a patient who claimed that she 'had no control' and was the passive victim of outside forces? I sincerely doubt that the patient would be congratulated for having seen the truth! Obviously, behaviourists hold some sort of sedimented (if unstated) beliefs concerning the experience of autonomy and (relative) freedom of choice. On the other hand, the phenomenological outlook, while acknowledging the uncontrollable limits to freedom, points out, nevertheless, its largely untapped and unacknowledged potentials.

Upon consideration, the most extreme behaviourist position on this issue (that is, B.F. Skinner's, as expressed in *Beyond Freedom and Dignity* (1971)) is, in a nutshell, that freedom is an illusion. Yet this conclusion requires clarification in that Skinner's critique is in reference to a definition of freedom which does not recognize *any* limits to or constraints on one's behaviour. As I hope I've already made clear, the phenomenological perspective, in its admission of the situatedness of freedom, falls outside Skinner's line of attack since it, too, criticizes optimistically naïve notions of individualistic and autonomous freedom. Interestingly, as Kvale and Grenness (1967) have argued, close comparison of the Skinnerian and phenomenological positions reveals (previously unseen) significant correspondences.

The major source of dispute between the two approaches lies, of course, in behaviourism's dismissal of consciousness since, its followers claim, any attempted investigation of inferred non-directly observable agencies such as consciousness threatens its objective, experimental stance. However, as Shaffer (1978) has pointed out, the distinction that behaviourism makes between private/subjective and public/objective events reveals a 'conceptual sleight of hand'. Shaffer argues (quite correctly, I think) that behaviourists 'must assume, however implicitly, some degree of correspondence between the research participant's verbal report and his actual perception' (1978: 175).

In spite of their dismissal of subjective experience, behaviourists depend on some degree of accurate correspondence between private experience and public report in order to provide validity and significance for their experimental data. Furthermore, as Koestenbaum (1973) has pointed out, all public statements begin as first-hand subjective experience; as such,

> to claim 'public verification' of my private experience is legitimate only to the degree to which all of us, as philosophers of science and students of human behaviour, agree on a fundamental philosophical assumption – namely that if each of our private experiences indicates a particular event to have occurred, we can then conclude that the event has actually taken place. (Shaffer, 1978: 176)

In brief, rather than rely upon *direct* verification, behaviourists actually depend upon indirect constructs or assumptions.

Most telling of all, I believe, critics of behaviourism have pointed to the paucity of *qualitative* data obtained from behavioural research; though vast in quantity, the great majority of behavioural findings tell us little of worth about ourselves. In a sense, having denied the importance of subjective data, their findings appear limited, alien, even 'soul-less'. In earlier chapters of this text I have tried to show how often confusing empirical evidence can benefit from phenomenological investigation. At the very least, the phenomenological method helps to expose experimenters' implicit, even hidden, assumptions, thereby allowing them to arrive at more adequate and descriptively accurate analyses and conclusions.

If, in the end, the major differences between behaviourism and phenomenological psychology remain irreconcilable, there still exists much scope for constructive dialogue (Ryback, 1972). Phenomenological psychologists, at least, can make great use of the data obtained by behavioural research – even if they must also dispute behaviourism's assumptions and conclusions.

Phenomenological Psychology and Cognitive-Behavioural Psychology

If behaviourism were still the dominant approach within academic psychology, the possibility of any substantial rapprochement with phenomenology would remain highly unlikely. However, behaviourism itself has undergone a substantial revolution over the past four decades such that the principal trend within contemporary psychology has fallen to a somewhat loosely bound 'conglomerate' generally labelled either as 'the cognitive school' or 'cognitive-behavioural psychology'.

Although still arguably a branch of behaviourism in that it adheres to the latter's principal methods for its own accumulation of data, the cognitive school in general, is far more open to the consideration of conscious experience and, more significantly, stresses the importance of the interpretational elements that mediate between stimulus input and behavioural response.

A great deal of what phenomenological psychology has concluded about perception, for instance, would find little dispute among cognitive psychologists. Similarly, the long-standing phenomenological assertion that there is a major distinction to be made between the unknown real world and the humanly interpreted object world has become an increasingly important hypothesis among a number of AI (artificial intelligence) theoreticians (Sortie, 1988). Along the same lines, cognitive theoreticians concerned with issues relating to memory would probably find that the phenomenological arguments in this area add valuable contributions to their research findings and, perhaps more importantly, clarify some of the confusion regarding the status of short-term memory recall and recognition. It would seem in fact that, for once, the difficulties of conjecturing potential areas of shared interest and possible mutual benefit are relatively minimal.

However, one of the central problems of positing areas of contact between phenomenological and cognitive psychologists lies in the lack of any truly unified approach or agreement concerning the realms of discourse that form the subject matter of cognitive psychology. More accurately, there exist *several* 'cognitive schools'. Although these share a common concern in the examination of cognitive processes (for example, perception, memory, concept formation), their assumptions and methodologies reveal significant disagreements and divergences of thought (Eysenck, 1984; Neisser, 1967; 1976).

In the first edition of this book, I highlighted Medcof and Roth's (1979/1984) summary of the three major weaknesses or 'unsolved problems' with which cognitive-behavioural theory must contend. Fifteen years later, while substantial effort has gone towards their resolution, they remain as problematic as before. In brief, these are: (a) the current lack of any coherent, integrated theory that links the various sub-theories united by their emphases on mediational processes; (b) the over-reliance on information-processing metaphors which, though partially useful, remain incapable of providing models of human behaviour that accurately represent human (as opposed to machine) information-processing; and (c) the failure to give proper consideration to the *emotional* content underlying human decision making.

There also exists, throughout the various cognitive approaches, a differing emphasis between those psychologists who are primarily interested in the study of the various cognitive processes *themselves* and those whose principal focus lies in the analysis of cognitive *processing*. Current circumstances suggest that a colloquium between phenomenological and cognitive psychology would be more beneficial with those cognitive approaches whose primary focus of interest lies in the study of 'the processes that come between stimulus and response' (Medcof and Roth, 1979/1984: 182).

One fairly obvious example of just such an area of co-operative exploration might well be that of emotion. There have already been several interesting, if by no means conclusive, experimental studies on cognitive factors in emotion and the modification of arousal via the alteration of cognition (Hilgard, Atkinson and Atkinson, 1987) whose results might best be interpreted and clarified from a phenomenological perspective (Strasser, 1999).

Schachter's cognitive-physiological theory of emotions (1964; Schachter and Singer, 1962) for instance, emphasizes the centrality of interpersonal variables in determining how we come to label, or conclude the presence of, a particular emotion. Feedback to the brain from physiological activity, argues Schachter, is insufficient in itself to allow for any clear identification of an emotion. Instead, individuals also require information gained from *past experience* in order to be able to give a particular interpretation, or meaning, to their current emotion. This view demonstrates striking parallels with conclusions derived from phenomenological investigation.

Although the study of cognitive processes and processing has become the dominant trend within contemporary psychology, the various cognitive approaches reveal a one-sided reliance upon, and interest in, noematic data and are somewhat disinclined to give proper consideration to the noetic variables within mediative processes. This weakness may have originated as a result of cognitive psychology's historical development as an extension of behaviourism and has persisted because noetic variables do not easily fit into the behaviourist-based experimental approach which much of cognitive psychology continues to advocate.

It is here, I think, that a phenomenological 'input', which stresses the co-presence and indivisibility of noematic and noetic foci in all intentional acts, might prove to be of the greatest benefit to cognitive research in general. In particular, it would seem to be especially useful to those orientations within cognitive psychology which focus on issues dealing with the various processing systems rather than upon their physiological bases and analogous hypothesized electronic parallels.

Phenomenological Psychology and CBT

Arguably, the greatest impact of cognitive-behavioural psychology has been in the field of psychotherapy. Although CBT has demonstrated experimentally its effectiveness with a wide range of disorders, it shares many of the recurring concerns raised with regard to cognitive-behavioural theory. Firstly, it is evident that CBT is not a unitary or unified system but that rather some 20 or so competing and at times quite contradictory approaches label themselves as CBT. Secondly, CBT continues to be criticized for its inability – or unwillingness – to state explicitly what is its foundational philosophy, in particular with regard to its theory of change (Mair, 1992). For example, in a recent review of cognitive-behavioural interventions with regard to alcohol dependence, Morgenstern and Longabaugh (2001) acknowledge the effectiveness of the therapy but argue that it remains a mystery as to what it is about the treatment that makes it so.

At the same time, like phenomenological psychologists, CBT theorists increasingly view persons as active agents who derive meaning from the world via inference and evaluation. However, a critical difference between the two approaches can be seen in CBT's common assertion that client distress is the result of *misinterpretations* of situations. Phenomenological psychology takes a much more cautious perspective on this and tends to view such 'misinterpretations' as meaningful – if often restrictive – responses to the uncertainties and anxieties of inter-relation.

In spite of the many claims made on its behalf by the first generation of practitioners, CBT has failed substantially to live up to its claims of methodological and outcome-oriented superiority over alternate approaches and models (Fewtrell and O'Connor, 1995). As such, over the years, the (over) emphasis on the behavioural tasks and directive interventions given by CBT has tended to be replaced with 'softer' attitudes and approaches increasingly centred on the quality and impact on outcome of the therapeutic relationship itself. At the more extreme end, more radical stances and approaches have evolved within the model. Initially at the fringes of acceptability by CBT practitioners, these have tended to gain more and more ground in recent years and are having, and will surely continue to have, significant impact upon CBT as a whole.

The most extreme of these developments can be found in *constructivist* CBT approaches and here the interface with phenomenological psychology becomes far more apparent. Radical constructivist systems such as the post-rationalist model proposed by Vittorio Guidano (1991) and Robert Neimeyer and Michael Mahoney's (1995) social constructionist influenced approach each emphasize the inter-relational aspects of the therapeutic relationship and follow closely the attempt to 'stay with' and respect the meaning system of the client, no matter how irrational it may appear to be. Similarly, Attribution theory (Schaap et al., 1993), and Dialectical Behaviour Therapy place substantial focus on the currently lived experience of the client and promote views that place the possibility of beneficial behavioural change within the context of the acceptance and exploration of 'what is' as it is presently interpreted by the client (Linehan, 1993).

Perhaps most notably, Acceptance and Commitment Therapy (ACT) has emerged as one of the most significant of recent attempts to reconfigure CBT (Hayes et al., 1999). ACT's major deviation from more classical CBT approaches lies in its explicit acknowledgement that the endeavour to change or remove 'misinterpreted' thoughts that have arisen in the person's attempt to cope may well be counter productive and even dangerous. Rather, ACT concentrates on the clarifying and opening up of the meanings expressed within the 'misinterpretation'.

This undertaking on the part of the ACT practitioner to 'stay with' the client's currently experienced meaning brings to the foreground a much more focused *inter-relational* perspective. This stance suggests a valid 'meeting point' for phenomenological and ACT theorists and practitioners. At the same time, it does remain the case that ACT continues to employ explicitly directive interventions that, from a phenomenological perspective, run counter to its stated enterprise. Nonetheless, as with the other radical constructivist reworkings of CBT, there exists solid ground for worthwhile dialogue with phenomenological psychology.

The possibilities inherent in such discourse have been explored by David Fewtrell and Kieron O'Connor in their important text, *Clinical Phenomenology and Cognitive Psychology* (1995). The authors' stated aim to highlight 'potential clinical roles of cognitive psychology and the phenomenological perspective… [in order]… to illustrate how they can co-exist as complementary modes of enquiry' (Fewtrell and O'Connor, 1995: x) is highly encouraging and serves as a notable starting point for theorists and practitioners from both approaches whose interests lie in 'enrichening the role of both within the context of psychopathology' (Fewtrell and O'Connor, 1995: viii).

Towards a Unified Psychology

Throughout contemporary psychology, there are serious attempts being made to find areas of unity among the various disparate approaches. For example, there have been several important texts published which seek some convergence between two or more schools of thought (Erdelyi, 1985; Fewtrell and O'Connor, 1995; Kegan, 1982; Stern, 1985, 2004).

Though by no means an unbiased observer, it would seem to me that phenomenological psychology stands in the vanguard of this movement. Although it retains distinctive features that provide clear contrasts with other contemporary approaches in psychology, phenomenological psychology remains an 'open' system which is both capable and willing to incorporate relevant data obtained by other systems.

Piaget has argued that every interaction with the world involves the complementary processes of assimilation (that is, dealing with the stimuli of the world through one's currently available structures) and accommodation (that is, changing one's structures in response to the varying stimuli of the world). Through such processes, we increase the adequacy of our adaptive responses (Ginsburg and Opper, 1969). In much the same way, phenomenological psychology, in its ability both to assimilate and to accommodate to the 'stimuli' of the other psychological systems, increases not only the adequacy of its own assumptions and conclusions, but also (potentially) those of the other systems.

It is, I believe, this very 'adaptive' openness that allows phenomenological psychology to provide pivotal contributions to increased communication and substantial rapprochement between all the contemporary systems in psychology.

11

A Critical Overview of Phenomenological Psychology

As far as we can discern, the sole purpose of human existence is to kindle a light of meaning in the darkness of mere being.

C.G. Jung

A Summary of the Phenomenological Orientation

The founder of the philosophical movement known as phenomenology was Edmund Husserl. Strongly influenced by a number of ideas concerning conscious experience proposed by his teacher, Franz Brentano, Husserl set about developing a philosophical system that sought to clarify both the nature of consciousness and its relation to reality.

Husserl's central argument was that we do not experience the physical world as it actually is in its 'pure', or 'real', state, but that the world we experience is an *interpreted* world that has been shaped both by in-built biological invariants and by the experience-based values, beliefs, attitudes and biases and the embodied affects which accompany them. Our world-view both structures the world we experience and, at the same time, is structured by the influences of the world upon us. This interweaving process, *intentionality*, runs through all of our interactions with and relations to the world and from which the meanings we designate and instill upon our lived experience arise.

The 'real' world, though it exists independent of our consciousness of it, remains obscure and is, ultimately, unknowable.

Intentionality explicitly refers to the directional nature of consciousness insofar as consciousness is always *of some thing*. In this sense, intentionality serves as a descriptive psychology of conscious processes (Ihde, 1998). However, at a more significant level, intentionality can also be understood to be the *foundational correlational rule* of phenomenology (Ihde, 1998). In this latter sense, intentionality points towards the inter-relatedness and interdependence of what a Natural Science tradition refers to and separates as 'subject' and 'object'. From the standpoint of intentionality, however, neither term makes sense in and of itself, nor can one be dealt with, defined and understood in isolation from the other. Considered from the standpoint of existence, the experience, knowledge and understanding of either the subject or the object can only emerge via this correlational *a priori*.

As such, the notion of intentionality reveals that both 'self' and 'other' (or, more generally, 'the world') are made meaningful, or are opened to disclosing investigation through their interdependent, co-constitutional relations. Each of us is actively involved, or implicated, in attempting to make meaningful our experience of the world – including our experience of self, of others, and of all those features, processes and dialogical ways of being that make up our lived reality.

Every intentional act contains both a noematic and a noetic focus. While clearly allowing for the development of (partially) shared constituents in the interpretations of the world arrived at by individuals who have built up similar culturally and linguistically derived schemata, nevertheless, each individual's experiential focus also contains unshared variables (such as those derived from that individual's unique set of lived experiences). As such, while human beings share the self-same means or ontological givens ('existentials') through which our interpretations are structured, the actual interpretations each of us derives from these 'existentials' reveals a *unique* expression or means of disclosing what and how it is 'to be human'. In this way, as Heidegger would have it, each being is both the way to and expression of Being.

Husserl developed a method – since known as the phenomenological method – that attempts to bracket, or set aside, immediate biases and sedimented beliefs; to describe the immediate items, or existentials of conscious experience; and to avoid imposing an initial hierarchy on these described items in order that any subsequent interpretations may become increasingly adequate, or offer a closer (if still incomplete) approximation of either the essence or the being of the focus of any investigation. As such, the goal of the phenomenological method is not to expose and explore what is truly or ultimately real – since that remains an impossibility – but, rather to clarify both the specific variables and universal invariants, or existentials, of humanly experienced phenomenal reality.

In brief, then, phenomenology is an investigative science whose primary concerns lie with issues both of essence (transcendental phenomenology) and of existence (existential phenomenology).

Phenomenological Psychology

Since the study of inter-relational experience is a central defining characteristic of phenomenology, it is obvious that many of its concerns bear a direct relevance to psychology. Phenomenological psychology (which, like phenomenology, stresses both transcendental and existential orientations or areas of interest) applies the phenomenological method in order to pursue a more adequate understanding of the central concerns of psychology. As a separate and specific system within contemporary psychology, phenomenological psychology stresses an interactive, Human Science focused approach to enquiry and, equally, is characterized by a strong reluctance to impose hypothetico-reductive models on the study of human beings. Its one central assumption of intentionality presents human beings as active interpreters of their experience of the world rather than as passive reactors to both bio-physical and environmental forces while at the same time acknowledging the inevitable role and impact of the world in shaping the very means through which our investigations are structured.

Phenomenological psychology has had, and continues to have, significant impact on the related fields of psychotherapy, counselling and counselling psychology as well as psychiatry. Major practitioners such as Karl Jaspers (1963), Ludwig Binswanger (1963), Medard Boss (1963; 1979; Gion Condrau, 1998) and R.D. Laing (1960/1970) have applied both the phenomenological method and key existential notions to therapeutic intervention, thereby deriving non-medical models for therapy that focus on the elucidation of meaning rather than upon interventionist 'cures'.

In relation to other academic systems in psychology, phenomenological psychology neither dismisses nor denies their various contributions. Instead, in its critical analyses of these systems' separate biases and assumptions, whether it be upon the specific area or topic of focus, or, just as importantly upon the methods and means through which investigations are carried out, phenomenological psychology clarifies possible areas of divergence, convergence and of mutually beneficial exploration.

Most recently, and perhaps most significantly for the future development of phenomenology, there has been both significant and substantive phenomenological input to the area of *consciousness studies* in general and cognitive science in particular. Hugely significant extensions, amendments, reconsiderations and applications of phenomenological insights are being argued out and challenged in texts and journals by self-identified phenomenological authors as diverse as Francisco Varela (Varela et al., 1993), Ralph Ellis (1995), Galen Strawson (1997) and David Chalmers (1996). While it is true that many of the debates between one another and with those who adopt differing perspectives are specifically focused upon the philosophical consideration of the so-called 'hard' and 'easy' problems of consciousness, it remains the case that such debates have returned the subject of consciousness to a central position within psychological enquiry. There is no doubt in my mind that phenomenological psychology will continue to fuel and provide avenues of inquiry for future debates. But equally, I also have no doubt that phenomenological psychology will, in turn, be influenced and reconfigured by the findings that emerge from such inquiries.

Nevertheless, I would be misleading the reader if I failed to give due consideration to the many criticisms that have been levelled at phenomenology in general and, in particular, at its psychological extensions. It is to the most significant of these that we must now turn our attention.

Philosophical Criticisms dealing with Possible Logical Inconsistencies within Phenomenology

As my academic background has suffered from scant philosophical training, I am particularly indebted to Reinhardt Grossmann's text *Phenomenology and Existentialism* (1984) and Richard Kearney's *Modern Movements in European Philosophy* (1986), both of which clearly state and rebut the principal logico-philosophical critiques of phenomenology. I wholeheartedly encourage those readers interested in exploring the philosophical ramifications of phenomenology to read these important texts; in the meantime, I am afraid that they must remain satisfied with my summary of what have been seen to be the three principal philosophical challenges to phenomenology and their rebuttals.

Are All Mental Phenomena Intentional?

This first philosophical criticism is directed more towards Brentano's (1995) argument that all mental phenomena are directed towards 'some thing'. This argument became the basis for Husserl's notion of intentionality. However, various philosophers have criticized this view by demonstrating that such phenomena as feelings and sensations are not intentional in that they are not directed towards an object. They argue that awareness of feeling and sensing *is* intentional in that it is the *experience of some thing*, but the phenomena themselves need not be. As such, Brentano's thesis holds only if it is limited to the argument that all mental *acts* are intentional. As it turns out, this latter view is precisely the position adopted by all branches of phenomenology and, as such, this criticism can be relatively quickly dispensed with.

The Problem of Non-existent Objects

A second philosophical argument has to do with the problem of imaginary or non-existent objects and their relation to intentionality. Put simply, this argument suggests that if I am capable of imagining a non-existent object, let's say, 'moon cheese', how could I possibly have come up with its mental image via intentionality? If my consciousness is not directed towards an object (as intentionality insists it must be) and I am still capable of imagining 'moon cheese', then there must be something erroneous about the phenomenological notion of intentionality.

According to Grossmann, the best resolution to the issue was devised by one of Brentano's students, Kasimir Twardowski. Twardowski argued:

> We must sharply distinguish between two questions. There is, firstly, the question of what a given idea represents, what its object is. There is, secondly, the quite different question of whether or not this object exists. Every idea has an

object or, more generally, every mental act has an object. Thus the intentional nexus always holds. But not every object exists. Thus the intentional nexus does not always connect with an existent. (Grossmann, 1984: 49)

In other words, the rebuttal of this criticism demonstrates that the notion of intentionality accommodates all mental acts. In my example, although 'moon cheese' is an imaginary object, were I to attempt to describe its various properties and constituents I would find that those properties bore an important relationship to properties of intentionally experienced objects that would not be considered to be imaginary. That I may have found a creative way to combine various properties such that I invent a new and imaginary object out of them in no way places doubt on the phenomenological notion of intentionality.

A gryphon, to employ another example, is an imaginary creature composed of the head and wings of an eagle and the body of a lion, but I can only imagine or describe a gryphon if I have the necessary awareness of the properties or constituents from the non-imaginary objects (that is eagle and lion) that make up the creature.

The Problem of Infinite Regress

A third philosophical issue disputes the existence of mental acts by arguing that, in assuming that there *are* mental acts, we are led to assume further the implicit existence of prior mental acts (which made us aware that there were mental acts) and which, in turn, lead us further and further back until we are in a cycle of infinite regress. Therefore, this argument would tell us, to speak of mental acts assumes an infinity of mental acts, and since an infinity of mental acts doesn't occur in our experience, one single act cannot occur either. Hence, we can deny the existence of mental acts.

As Grossmann makes explicit, this argument assumes two implicit points: firstly that a mind is aware of all its mental acts *as they occur* and, secondly, 'that to be aware of a mental act is itself a mental act' (1984: 51). If one or both of these points can be rejected, then the critics have lost the argument.

Most phenomenologists have attempted to dispute the second point and, in doing so, have developed somewhat convoluted and circuitous strategies that are not entirely satisfactory resolutions of the issue. On the other hand, argues Grossmann, the first point can be shown to be open to rejection. The mind is *not* aware of its every occurring act. The act of experiencing makes us aware of whatever there may be in our minds at any given moment, but we do not 'experience this experience itself' (Grossmann, 1984: 53). A mind, at any given moment in time, both experiences and is aware of certain consequences, or objects, of this act of experience. We can be aware of certain objects of experience at any given moment in time, but not of the act itself.

To put it another way, at any given moment in time we can be consciously aware of certain experiences, but *the act of experiencing* itself remains outside our conscious awareness. As such, we are *not* aware of our every mental act and, thus, the criticism of infinite regress can be dispensed with.

Psychological Criticisms

The most vociferous opponents of phenomenological psychology have tended to represent it as 'an anachronistic reversion to outdated doctrines, incompatible with the scientific character of psychology, and harmful to its progress' (Misiak and Sexton, 1973: 54).

Equally, behaviouristically oriented critics have argued that both the methodology and the conceptual basis of phenomenology are of little use or interest to any modern-day psychologist whose aim is to manipulate and predict behaviour from a standpoint focusing on generalizable rules which emphasize similarities in behaviour or mental processing.

Such critics have also put into question both the possible significance and effectiveness of phenomenological theory and its application by raising the issue of the non-explanatory nature of phenomenological data and querying the validity and reliability of such data. Similarly, they have fuelled their arguments by pointing out the seeming paucity of 'appropriate methods and techniques of investigation, overdependence on verbal descriptions with their inherent limitations, ambiguity of phenomenological concepts and sometimes the esoteric language of phenomenologists' (Misiak and Sexton, 1973: 54–5).

In their defence, phenomenological psychologists have argued that the long neglect of the issue of human inter-relatedness in academic psychology has not only severely put into question the validity and reliability of psychology's own accepted views and positions, but has also restricted psychology to issues that hold little value and relevance to anyone outside the field.

In its neglect of the issue of inter-relational experience, psychology has not only lost its 'soul', in a metaphorical sense, it has lost its original purpose and has focused instead on the construction, analysis and interpretation of ever more ornate and esoteric experimental studies whose far from unusual lack of replicability fuels research and fills the pages of the various (little-read) learned journals of psychology.

Phenomenologists argue that, as a science whose purported aim is the understanding of the person, psychology's starting point *must* be the exploration of human experience. They do not wholly dismiss the findings and methodologies of the other approaches; more accurately, they argue that the progress of psychology requires a more fundamental investigation of the attitudes and assumptions that underlie psychological explorations.

I have already spoken in the previous chapter of the difficulties engendered by the *language* of phenomenology. I only wish to reiterate the point that these linguistic problems prove to be far less difficult to deal with in a climate where there exists a greater willingness to explore issues of common concern and interest.

Before I examine the major psychological criticisms in greater detail, I want to provide a more general rejoinder that should clarify the general thrust of a phenomenological response to these arguments.

I hope that, on the basis of the various topics discussed in this text, unbiased readers will recognize that, unlike the claims made by its critics, phenomenological psychology is neither an anachronistic reversion to outdated introspectionist doctrines, nor is its stance incompatible with a scientific approach to the understanding of human beings.

While it is true that phenomenological psychology takes conscious experience to be its primary concern, its interest lies not with subjectivity per se but with the central inter-relational mechanism of intentionality and its role in determining the 'reality' that we interpret and upon which we base our actions. In this, phenomenological investigations lead to the discovery of a number of inter-relationally derived 'invariants of experience' that are universally shared by our species and, just as importantly, expose the many sedimented beliefs that both cultural and individual biases impose and which serve to distort and diminish our understanding of ourselves and our world.

Now, let me address the arguments with greater specificity.

Phenomenological Psychology as a Return to Introspectionism

Many critics (Wann, 1964) have assumed that phenomenological psychology is the modern-day equivalent of earlier psychological *introspectionist* approaches whose limited value to psychology was exposed long ago. This incorrect association has emerged because phenomenological psychology and introspectionism share a basic focus upon consciousness (a term which both behaviourists and, until recently, neo-behaviourists have sought to expunge from psychological language).

That the principal subject matter of both approaches is conscious experience is not being denied. However, their purposes in engaging in such studies are markedly different. In introspectionist studies, well-trained observers focused upon their subjective reactions to external stimuli in order to note various characteristics in their impressions, and sought, ultimately, to reduce their subjective experiences to the simplest mental elements – that is, to sensations, feelings, images. They also attempted to examine certain attributes of their experiences, such as their quality, intensity and duration. In contrast, in a phenomenological study, no assumption concerning the composition or attributes of impressions is permitted.

Moreover, while in an introspective report, objects and meanings were excluded, in a phenomenological study they are essential. The phenomenological psychologist is interested in the meaning that stimuli or situations have for the observer; introspectionists, on the other hand, primarily analysed impressions of various stimuli and provided reports that focused upon their sensory experiences.

The distinctions between the two approaches might perhaps be made more obvious to the reader by example. For instance, consider the notion of self, or 'I', which was discussed in Chapter 5. Introspectionist theorists studying the self typically began from the (arguably erroneous) assumption that there is a constant self (which might be divided into various components), and, through which, we experience the world. As such, the starting point of the introspective approach is the 'I'. The phenomenological approach, on the other hand, would attempt to avoid any immediate assumption of a pre-existing 'I' that acts as the source-point or originator of experience. And indeed, as we have seen, this stance has led phenomenology to adopt a view of 'I' that construes its appearance as a consequence or product of reflective self-consciousness.

Such differing stances lead, as I have already argued, to quite different analyses and issues of concern. As such, though it is true to say that both introspectionism and phenomenological psychology are concerned with the issues of consciousness, it is, nevertheless, also important to understand that not only are the methods employed by each system vastly different, their scope and focus of investigation are clearly distinct from one another.

The debate regarding phenomenology's relation to introspectionism reveals a continuing misunderstanding that is important to make explicit. Whereas introspectionism concerned itself with issues of *subjectivity*, phenomenology is concerned with the *inter-relational grounding in all human experience*. In this, phenomenology does not view subjectivity as a basic 'given' of human experience. Instead, it is more accurate to view subjectivity, from a phenomenological perspective, as one particular consequence of inter-relational experience in that what is termed as 'subjectivity' only emerges from a *prior* inter-relational grounding. Rather than being equal possibilities or options, as some have suggested, or equally, as is implicit in a good deal of humanistic theory that the inter-relational can only emerge once a person has attended sufficiently to his or her subjectivity, phenomenology asserts the primacy of inter-relatedness as the basis to the emergence of uniquely-lived experience.

Phenomenological Psychology and Environmental Stimuli

Cognitive-Behavioural psychologists stress environmental factors, as exemplified by cultural and social variables, as primary, even causal, stimulus determinants of human behaviour. Phenomenological psychologists also stress environmental variables as stimuli to behaviour, but insist that such stimuli are first *intentionally interpreted*. It is these interpretations of stimuli that initiate specific behaviour, not the stimuli in themselves.

Each of us develops more or less sedimented biases and outlooks which result both from the development of culturally sedimented schemata and from our unique experientially based interpretations of environmental stimuli. Our cultural, social and moral considerations are not simply due to socio-cultural environmental influences; they are also the direct results of this interpretative process. This perspective leads to the consideration of human beings as active interpretative constructors of their experience and not, as behaviourists suggest, as passive reactors to environmental stimuli.

The implications of the phenomenological argument can be seen to have immediate practical and social relevance. For, as active interpreters of our experience, we are led to acknowledge our experiential responsibility as beings-in-the-world. The acceptance of responsibility reorients one's *being* experiences; in turn, this new perspective may well allow for the alteration of one's behaviour.

Phenomenological Psychology's Stance on Interpreted Realities

A common critique of phenomenology questions the phenomenological conclusion that reality, as experienced by each of us, is a construct brought about by intentionality. For many critics of phenomenology, this idea seems to be patently absurd (Dreyfus, 1982; Wann, 1964) in its implications. They might argue that, on the basis of phenomenological theory, if, for example, someone were to decide that a brick wall before her no longer existed, she should be able to walk through it with no injury since it was not part of her constructed experience. Obviously, such critics point out, were such a person to put this assumption to the test, she would quickly discover its fundamental error.

This criticism, rather than placing doubt upon the phenomenological argument concerning constructed realities, reveals the critics' misunderstanding of the argument. Phenomenologists do not dispute the existence of a physical reality separate from our conscious experience of it; their point is simply that our experience of reality must always be situated within intentional interpretations.

With regard to the specific example employed above, phenomenological psychologists would argue that the object that has been labelled as 'a wall' is an intentional construct. What that wall *actually* is in its real state is unknown. However, that it exists, that it *is*, regardless of what interpretation is made of it, is not in doubt. Nonetheless, it remains important to note that while the person who we might see as 'walking into the wall' cannot 'erase' the physical presence of whatever is there that we have termed 'the wall', the interpretation she makes of the experience, in short what it means to her, need not necessarily be 'I have walked into a wall'.

The clarification of this basic misunderstanding of phenomenological theory once again brings to light the major divergence between phenomenological psychologists and cognitive behaviourists. Where the great majority of cognitive behaviourists speak of 'responses' to stimuli (thereby implying passive reaction), phenomenological psychologists employ terms such as 'construction' or 'interpretation' in order to make explicit the mediative events that lie between stimulus and response.

Phenomenological psychologists hold that this interpretative model of human behaviour is far more adequate than that proposed by cognitive behaviourists. The cognitive behaviourial model is partially correct in stressing the importance of environmental stimuli, but it is also naïvely misguided in not realizing that our responses are not to the stimuli themselves but, rather, to our current interpretations of them.

Phenomenological Psychology's Stance on the Experience of Unique Worlds

Related to the criticism just discussed is the equally misunderstood argument concerning the phenomenological conclusion that each of us experiences a unique perspective of the world. Experimentally oriented critics (Gibson, 1950) have argued that this cannot be the case since their results demonstrate that, for example, we perceive the same things and can communicate quite clearly and (seemingly) accurately with others about what we have perceived. If so, where is the evidence of 'uniqueness' that phenomenological psychologists take as being so central to their approach?

Phenomenological psychologists *do* argue that our assumption of a shared reality is an illusion since what each of us perceives is the result of a combination of both species specific 'structural givens' or existentials and unique experientially derived intentional constructs.

Those of us who share a similar language or cultural perspective may develop mental frameworks which, in influencing the labels we impose, as well as our general attitudes towards those labels, may lead us to assume that our perceptions are shared with those of others. At the same time, the diversity of perspectives and attitudes between persons sharing similar socio-cultural influences that is apparent in any given situation makes clear that what is perceived as shared (be it noematically or noetically) is at best partial and that alongside every shared experience, unique perceptions will emerge if they are given due attention and structured enquiry. Similarly, while it may be the case that substantial attention is given by phenomenological psychology upon the unique variables that make up a person's worldview, this is not because such are considered to be inherently more significant or more worthy of inquiry, but because the other systems of psychology either minimize or deny these variables in their studies. In addition, existential phenomenology takes the view that it is precisely via the study of a particular way of being (ontic analysis) that the investigator is directed to the universal, or ontological, structures of Being.

Criticisms Concerning the Scientific Status of Phenomenological Psychology

Contrary to the common assertion that phenomenology is antagonistic to, or disinterested in, psychological research, phenomenology continues to play a major role in the development of qualitatively focused approaches to research (Churchill and Wertz, 2001; Giorgi, 1985; Karlsson, 1993). At the same time, phenomenology's view of suitable paradigms for psychology research stands in direct contrast to the Natural Scientific viewpoint and its underlying assumptions.

First, unlike traditional Natural Science psychological research models, phenomenology denies the possibility of truly objective observation and analysis. Rather, it assumes an indissoluble inter-relationship between observer and observed. Second, phenomenology places conscious experience, as central to all inquiry since its primary aim is to arrive at a description of the 'structure' of conscious experience. Third, phenomenological research rejects standard research notions of control groups, dependent and independent variables, preliminary hypotheses, and so forth, since these all suggest and rely upon, to a greater or lesser degree, the notion of linear causality.

Instead, phenomenological research is principally *qualitative-interpretative*, focusing upon descriptive methodologies that seek to remain as faithful as possible to the data of experience. In other words, it seeks to understand rather than to explain, and, by so doing, it searches for meaning rather than seeks to collect facts. As Gunmar Karlsson has clarified this distinction:

> In line with logical empiricism, traditional psychology neglects to study meaningful experience in a 'direct' way. Instead, one *operationalizes* variables so as to turn them into observable facts. [Phenomenology] rejects the idea that there exist objective facts... The 'objectively' given fact is always present in relation to... a constituting and meaning-imbuing subject... (Karlsson, 1993: 16, original emphasis)

While the notions of reliability and validity, which remain central elements of a Natural Science research methodology, are not directly employed by existential phenomenology, the approach relies upon the *verifiability of* the researcher's conclusions in so far as verifiability refers to 'whether another researcher can assume the perspective of the present investigator, review the original protocol data, and see that the proposed insights meaningfully illuminate the situations under study' (Churchill and Wertz, 2001: 259).

In general, the phenomenological method, which lies at the core of all phenomenological analyses, reveals an underlying scientific attitude to investigation and, either explicitly or implicitly, has been adopted (albeit under a variety of terminologies) by all other approaches that claim scientific status. Although this would at first suggest that the phenomenological method is no more than a basic 'truism' of science, I have shown that, at least in the area of psychology, this 'truism' has not been applied sufficiently even within 'hard' experimental psychology (for example, in the investigation of perception) with the result that numerous unnecessary sedimented assumptions have led investigators to form distorted and misleading conclusions.

The wider debate surrounding the status of 'objectivity' is not simply a psychological issue. Since the beginning of this century, primarily as a result of the Einsteinian and quantum revolutions in physics, our understanding of objectivity has undergone radical change (Capra, 1982; Zukav, 1980). For instance, one central feature of modern atomic physics is the notion that 'we cannot talk about the properties of an object as such. They are only meaningful in the context of the object's interaction with the observer' (Capra, 1976: 144). As such, the role of the scientist is no longer that of the passive observer whose measurements reflect an objective reality; rather, the scientist is, more accurately, an active participator, who, through specific measurements and subjective interests or goals, sets temporary (and arbitrary) limits upon an uncertain universe.

This view, of course, alters the notion of 'objectivity' quite drastically. Rather than state 'facts' or 'final truths', physicists can only speak in terms of probabilities which allow for increasingly adequate theories and conclusions that *approach* 'truth' or 'objective reality' – but can never achieve such.

Along similar lines, both Bohm's (1980) and Pribram's (1971; 1976) corresponding theories positing a 'holographic' universe, as well as the evolution of various approaches to causality from a complex-system standpoint (such as 'chaos theory' (Gleick, 1988; Wilber, 1982)) reveal an indebtedness to phenomenological theory of which the authors may or may not have been aware.

Some Phenomenological Critiques of Phenomenology

While it remains my view that phenomenology is more than capable of responding to the more common critiques presented of it, this should not suggest that no substantive critiques remain. This is far from the case and what follows seeks to summarize those critiques that seem to me to be most pertinent.

The Overextension of Phenomenology

Let me first address what is, for me, a much more critical concern. For want of a better term, I have chosen to label it as *the tendency to overextend* existential-phenomenological thought and practice.

This tendency might be most simply and directly expressed as 'they're all really just existential-phenomenological thinkers and practitioners'. What it refers to is the attempt to subsume into the category of existential-phenomenological thought and practice a substantial number of disparate, if highly influential, individuals, ideas and movements in order to declare some degree of intellectual ownership that overrides all other similar attempts by others.

So, for instance, while it is undoubtedly the case that there exists a great deal of stimulus to existential-phenomenological inquiry in a number of the key works by Friedrich Nietzsche, it is quite another matter for anyone to suggest that Nietzsche was some sort of crypto-existentialist or 'nothing other than' an existentialist. It is undoubtedly the case that Nietzsche explored a number of themes that have subsequently become pivotal areas of existential-phenomenological inquiry. In this sense, he might well be seen, as I have suggested in this text, at least in part as a forerunner, or herald (or, as he might prefer, a 'prophet') of existential phenomenology. Problematically, however, for those who wish to see Nietzsche as nothing other than this, it must be pointed out that, equally, and again in part, he can be seen to be *the* major herald of psychoanalysis (Ellenberger, 1970; Kaufman, 1980b, 1980c). That he may have been an author who significantly influenced both existential phenomenology and psychoanalytic thought, and, pivotally, was also an author who was concerned with much more than that which has influenced both seems to me to be something worth remembering and acknowledging.

As with Nietzsche, a similar argument could be made of Kierkegaard, and any number of other authors and philosophers. For instance, one eminent existential author has written that '[p]eople like Socrates or Jesus of Nazareth can be seen as existential thinkers who set themselves against the brutality and bigotry of their respective cultures...' (van Deurzen-Smith, 1997: 3). Well, again, that Socrates and Jesus may have, in part, considered issues and themes that are also the shared concerns of existential phenomenology is one thing, to call them 'existential thinkers' seems to me to be quite another matter.

Certain themes that existential authors have made central to their investigations have been examined and considered by a very wide variety of thinkers. Some of these have even arrived at certain conclusions that are in substantial agreement with conclusions derived from existential-phenomenological inquiry. Clearly, a mutual study and sharing of ideas and conclusions is both valid and of great potential value to all parties. Just as clearly, it is evident that even in those instances where agreements arise, shared insights and ideas should still not permit one system to define the other as 'nothing but' a mirror of, or the equivalent to, itself.

I raise this concern because such claims of 'ownership' seem to me to have increased in parallel with the growth and acceptance of existential phenomenology within psychology and I personally find them to be diminishing and disrespectful attempted take-overs by, and ill-considered over-extensions of, existential phenomenology. Further, I believe that they do damage not only to the views being taken over but also to existential phenomenology itself.

It remains necessary to point out that any dialogical enterprise, be it between cultures or individuals or ideas, does not ever take us back to where either we or the other may once have been but, rather, opens us both to novel inter-relational possibilities of being-in-the-world. That we might both arrive – or appear to arrive – at similar places should not permit us to minimize the significance of our having set out on our journeys from distinctively different 'locations' and carrying quite different sorts of concerns, aims, and 'baggage'. While all 'roads' may be the same 'ROAD', it would seem to me to be arrogant folly for us to declare that existential phenomenology is '*THE* ROAD'. But, it seems to me, that is precisely what some adherents and proponents of existential phenomenology *do* say whenever they promote the claim that theory/person/thinker 'X' is properly subsumed within existential phenomenology.

Postmodernity and Beyond

The concern just expressed leads directly to my second critique. If asked: 'what is the status of phenomenological psychology, or phenomenology in general, within the wider realm of contemporary thought?', my personal view is that phenomenology is immediately confronted with two highly significant counter-movements that require its attention.

On the one hand, phenomenological psychology is faced with an assortment of viewpoints and contentions that might be labelled post-structural, postmodernist, social constructionist and/or narrative/discursive approaches each of which, while either explicitly or implicitly acknowledging its indebtedness to phenomenology for having provided a foundational starting point or direction for its particular stance, nonetheless is also unhesitant in criticizing phenomenology for its unwillingness or inability to confront the full force and implications of dialogical relativism and inter-relation upon notions of 'truth', 'reality', 'ethics' and 'morality' (among many other themes).

On the other hand, an opposite 'post-post-structuralism' of sorts has also arisen whose proponents espouse the value of a new 'objectivism' as a response to the moral and explanatory impasse wrought by both 'liberal' and 'extremist' relativist stances (Hacking, 1999; Nagel, 1998).

What is obvious is that phenomenology must seek to provide an adequate response to both of these critical perspectives if its views are to continue to be treated with the respect and seriousness that I believe they deserve. But to do so, contemporary phenomenology must renew its commitment to an open-minded readiness to be receptive to and willing to reconsider potentially disturbing alternatives presented to it via its inquiries.

My own sense is that phenomenological psychology's strength lies in what has been perceived by critics on either side of the constructionist divide as its major weakness: its adoption of a stance that is neither solely objectivist nor solely relativist but rather stands between or 'holds the tension' between the two extremes. A recent review of Terry Eagleton's new book, *After Theory* (2004) clarifies my stance. As a leading proponent of the relativist perspective, Eagleton has raised powerful concerns and critiques regarding its limitations. He writes:

> Cultural theory as we have it promises to grapple with some fundamental problems, but on the whole fails to deliver. It has been shame-faced about morality and metaphysics, embarrassed about love, biology, religion and revolution, largely silent about evil, reticent about death and suffering, dogmatic about essences, universals and foundations, and superficial about truth, objectivity and disinterestedness. (Eagleton, 2004, quoted in Lodge, 2004: 41)

The 'new orthodoxy' of relativism has largely begun to seem something of a dead end to many because it 'denies the validity of universals and first principles' (Lodge, 2004: 40). As I have sought to argue throughout this book, this tendency is precisely what phenomenology has avoided. At the same time, as I have also sought to demonstrate, phenomenology has also provided a major critique of more classical forms of objectivity which have imposed an inevitable dualism in our investigations of human existence. Perhaps, as it has done so in the area of consciousness studies, phenomenological psychology can be seen to provide a viable and valid alternative to these limiting extremes.

Final Comments

Having presented the principal critiques of phenomenology in general, and of phenomenological psychology in particular, I hope that I have succeeded in raising doubts about their strength. If readers have been sufficiently convinced by my arguments that they are willing to consider the phenomenological alternative more seriously and to weigh up its possible implications and benefits to psychology with greater accuracy and open-mindedness, then I think I will have been granted all that an author can reasonably expect from his readers.

As well as all the obvious limitations that are set within the writing of an introductory text on *any* subject area, a written introduction (indeed, any expository work) dealing with phenomenology suffers from the added burden that, ultimately, it is the *doing* of phenomenology that both clarifies its central ideas and removes much that at first appears to be obscure and difficult in its language and methodology.

As Ihde (1986a) has pointed out, without *doing* phenomenology it may be practically impossible to gain a proper understanding of its most significant implications. This is not to say that one may not find it useful to learn about the history, concerns and methodology of phenomenology through the reading of its major hypotheses and conclusions. This is, of course, a standard element of any intellectual enquiry. Nevertheless, without initiating an 'experiential' attempt to understand the basic thrust of phenomenological enquiry, one runs the risk of both misunderstanding and failing to recognize its potential value to areas of scientific exploration such as psychology.

Like any other investigative science, phenomenological psychology relies upon observational and experimental data in order to arrive at its conclusions. Phenomenological psychology is not 'merely' experiential, but its ideas are best clarified through experientially based investigations.

I hope that the various points raised throughout this text are intriguing enough for readers to initiate their own experientially oriented 'experiments'. On the basis of my own experience, I can report that such attempts are eminently worth the effort. For instance, as a psychologist, I find myself, today, amazed (and amused) that I have become intrigued by topics in psychology that I once found impossible even to feign any interest in. Similarly, while I was once dominated by outlooks and biases that essentially dismissed the findings and hypotheses of one approach, or overvalued those of another, I can now consider the various approaches far less defensively and, more significantly, all the more critically with regard to their theoretical and methodological assumptions.

These experiences, I believe, have led to my becoming a better lecturer in, and practitioner of, psychology and psychotherapy and have convinced me of the significance of phenomenological theory.

Interestingly, since I began to teach an introductory course in this area almost 25 years ago, it has become somewhat commonplace for students to approach me with enquiries as to where they can pursue further studies in phenomenological psychology since, as many of them have put it, it is this approach more than any other that they have taken that 'feels like what psychology should be' and which provides them with renewed enthusiasm for their subject area.

Though sympathetic to their requests, I have had to inform them that, unfortunately, phenomenologically oriented graduate programmes in psychology still, today, remain relatively uncommon. Happily, there is every indication of significant change regarding this. In the UK, there exist already two academic and training institutes which provide advanced programmes in existential phenomenology and, as well, in existential psychotherapy and counselling psychology. Similar institutes either exist or are in various stages of development in the United States, Canada, Australia and throughout Continental Europe. Just as significantly, many established psychology programmes have begun to include phenomenological psychology as part of their course curricula.

The first edition of this book concluded on the following note:

> Ultimately, on a broader level, the 'doing' of phenomenology must have significant impact on one's life in general and one's relationship to the world. It does not take much to realize that, although our age is characterized by its multiplicity of advances in science and technology, both nations and their individual members remain so divided by their beliefs and attitudes that the very existence of all living things has come under serious threat of annihilation.
>
> If each of us were willing to apply the phenomenological method to the various private and social interactions in our lives, if we were all momentarily to bracket our sedimented outlooks and beliefs in an attempt to enter each other's frameworks of being with mutual openness and respect, we would be likely to find that highly similar elements of concern and fear underlie our separate and seemingly antagonistic actions. Under such circumstances, although the many and varied problems of the world would not be instantly resolved, we could at least begin to disassemble many of the barriers that stand in the way of such a goal.
>
> In shifting from an 'I *or* you' position to one which provides for the consideration of 'I *and* you' options, we would set into motion a major revolution in all forms of social behaviour, ranging from small group interactions such as contained within the family and pair-bonding, to the workings of industry, education, welfare, government and, ultimately, to the interactions between nations.
>
> Without doubt, such changes require us to shift our philosophical and psychological assumptions. My personal conviction is that, should it ever come about, this revolution would be, in its broadest sense, one dependent upon *phenomenological* insight (Spinelli, 1989: 192).

As I come to the end of this second edition, I am all too aware that the growing tide of religious and secular fundamentalism which had begun to become so apparent in 1989, but which seemed to be counter-balanced by a powerful resurgence of political and social liberation against oppression of every sort, has, in the intervening years, reached levels that far surpass anything that most of us would have imagined as a possibility, much less a lived reality.

In this brutal world we have created, where the pursuit of death has been elevated above life and justice has come to mean little more than military power, if phenomenological insight has any meaning at all it must surely be that of illuminating that which is there for us and, by so doing, reveal those human – and humane – possibilities that still remain.

References

Adams, M. (2002) 'Reflections on reflection', *Existential Analysis*, 13 (2): 204–13.

Allport, G.W. (1955) *Becoming*. New Haven, CT: Yale University Press.

Allport, G.W. and Cantrill, H. (1934) 'Judging personality from the voice', *Journal of Social Psychology*, 5: 37–55.

Asch, S. (1952) *Social Psychology*. New York: Prentice-Hall.

Asmall, I. (1997) 'Existentialism, existential psychotherapy and African philosophy', *Journal of the Society for Existential Analysis*, 8 (2): 138–52.

Atwood, G.E. and Stolorow, R.D. (1984) *Structures in Subjectivity: Explorations in Psychoanalytic Phenomenology*. Hillsdale, NJ: The Analytic Press.

Barrett, W. (1958) *Irrational Man: A Study in Existential Philosophy*. New York: Greenwood Press.

Bartlett, F.C. (1932/1967) *Remembering*. Cambridge: Cambridge University Press.

Barton Evans III, F. (1996) *Harry Stack Sullivan: Interpersonal Theory and Psychotherapy*. London: Routledge.

Benoit, H. (1955) *The Supreme Doctrine: Psychological Studies in Zen Thought*. New York: Viking Press.

Berger, P. and Luckmann, T. (1966/1979) *The Social Construction of Reality: a Treatise in the Sociology of Knowledge*. Harmondsworth: Penguin.

Bergson, H. (1907/1911) *Creative Evolution*. London: Macmillan.

Bergson, H. (1911) *Matter and Memory*. London: Allen and Unwin.

Binswanger, L. (1963) *Being-in-the-World: Selected Papers of Ludwig Binswanger*. New York: Harper Torchbooks.

Bohm, D. (1980) *Wholeness and the Implicate Order*. London: Routledge and Kegan Paul.

Bolton, N. (ed.) (1979) *Philosophical Problems in Psychology*. London: Methuen.

Boss, M. (1963) *Psychoanalysis and Daseinsanalysis*. New York: Basic Books.

Boss, M. (1979) *Existential Foundations of Medicine and Psychology*. Northvale, NJ: Jason Aronson.

Bowlby, J. (1979) *The Making and Breaking of Affectional Ties*. London: Tavistock Publications.

Braude, S.E. (1991) *First Person Plural: Multiple Personality and the Theory of Mind*. London: Routledge.

Brehm, J. (1966) *A Theory of Psychological Reactance*. New York: Academic Press.

Brentano, F. (1995) *Psychology from an Empirical Standpoint*. London: Routledge.

Buber, Martin (1970) *I and Thou*. Edinburgh: T. and T. Clark.

Bugenthal, J.F.T. (1981) *The Search for Authenticity: an Existential-Analytic Approach to Psychotherapy*. New York: Irvington.

Bugenthal, J.F.T. (1987) *The Art of the Psychotherapist*. New York: Norton.

Cannon, B. (1991) *Sartre and Psychoanalysis: an Existentialist Challenge to Clinicalmetatheory*. Lawrence, KS: University Press of Kansas.

Cantor, J. (1976) 'Individual needs and salient constructs in Inter-personal perception', *Journal of Personality and Social Psychology*, 34: 519–25.

Capra, F. (1976) *The Tao of Physics*. London: Fontana.

Capra, F. (1982) *The Turning Point: Science, Society, and the Rising Culture*. London: Wildwood House.

Chalmers, D. (1996) *The Conscious Mind: in Search of a Fundamental Theory*. New York: Oxford University Press.

Chalmers, D. (1997) 'Moving forward on the problem of consciousness', *Journal of Consciousness Studies*, 4 (1): 3–46.

Cherry, E.C. (1953) 'Some experiments on the recognition of speech with one and two ears', *Journal of the Acoustical Society of America*, 25: 975–9.

Churchill, S.D. and Wertz, F.J. (2001) 'An introduction to phenomenological research in psychology', in K. Schneider, J.F.T Bugenthal and J. Fraser Pierson (eds), *The Handbook of Humanistic Psychology: Leading Edges in Theory, Research, and Practice*. London: SAGE Publications.

Clifford, M. and Walster, E. (1973) 'The effect of physical attraction on teacher expectation', *Sociology of Education*, 46: 248.

Cohen, J. (1958) *Humanistic Psychology*. London: Allen and Unwin.

Cohn, H.W. (1997) *Existential Thought and Therapeutic Practice; an Introduction to Existential Psychotherapy*. London: SAGE Publications.

Cohn, H.W. (2002) *Heidegger and the Roots of Existential Therapy*. London: Continuum.

Cohn, H.W. and du Plock, S. (eds) (1995) *Existential Challenges to Psychotherapeutic Theory and Practice*. London: SEA Press.

Colaizzi, P.F. (1973) *Reflection and Research in Psychology: a Phenomenological Study of Learning*. Dubuque, IA: Kendall/Hunt.

Colaizzi, P.F. (1978) 'Psychological research as the phenomenologist views it', in R.S. Valle and M. King (eds), *Existential-Phenomenological Alternatives for Psychology*. New York: Oxford University Press.

Condrau, G. (1998) *Martin Heidegger's Impact on Psychotherapy*. Vienna: Mosaic.

Cooper, M. (2003) *Existential Therapies*. London: SAGE Publications.

Coopersmith, S. (1967) *The Antecedents of Self-Esteem*. San Francisco: Freeman.

Coren, S., Porac, C. and Ward, L.M. (1978) *Sensation and Perception*. New York: Academic Press.

Crabtree, A. (1985) *Multiple Man: Explorations in Possession and Multiple Personality*. Eastbourne: Holt, Rinehart and Winston.

Crider, A.B., Goethals, G.R., Kavanaugh, R.D. and Solomon, P.R. (1986) *Psychology*, 2nd edn. London: Scott Foresman.

Crotty, M. (1996) *Phenomenology and Nursing Research*. Melbourne: Churchill Livingstone.

Damasio, A. (2000) *The Feeling of What Happens: Body, Emotion and the Making of Consciousness*. London: Heinemann.

Davenport, W., Brooker, G. and Munro, N. (1971) 'Factors in social perception: seating position', *Perceptual and Motor Skills*, 33: 747–52.

Deaux, K. and Emswiller, T. (1974) 'Explanations of successful performance on sex-linked tasks: what's skill for the male is luck for the female', *Journal of Personality and Social Psychology*, 29: 80–5.

DeJong, W. (1977) 'The stigma of obesity: the consequences of naive assumptions concerning the causes of physical deviance'. Unpublished doctoral dissertation, Stanford University, CA.

Denzin, N.K. and Lincoln, Y.S. (eds) (1994) *Handbook of Qualitative Research*. London: Sage.

Deurzen-Smith, van, E. (1988) *Existential Counselling in Practice*. London: SAGE Publications.

Deurzen-Smith, van, E. (1997) *Everyday Mysteries*. London: Routledge.

Dick, P.K. (1975) *Now Wait For Last Year*. London: Panther.

Diener, E., Fraser, S., Beaman, A. and Kelem, R. (1976) 'Effects of de-individuation variables on stealing among Halloween trick-or-treaters', *Journal of Personality and Social Psychology*, 33: 178–83.

Dion, K. (1972) 'Physical attractiveness and evaluations of children's trangressions', *Journal of Personality and Social Psychology*, 24: 207–13.

Dion, K. (1977) 'The incentive value of physical attractiveness for young children', *Personality and Social Psychology Bulletin*, 3: 67–70.

Dreyfus, H.L. (1982) *Husserl Intentionality and Cognitive Science*. London: MIT Press.

Drosnin, M. (1985) *Citizen Hughes*. London: Arrow.

Duncan, S. (1974) 'Some signals and rules for taking speaking turns in conversation', *Journal of Personality and Social Psychology*, 23: 283–92.

Duncan, S. and Niederehe, G. (1974) 'On signalling that it's your turn to speak', *Journal of Experimental Social Psychology*, 10: 234–47.

du Plock, S. (ed.) (1997) *Case Studies in Existential Psychotherapy and Counselling*. Chichester: Wiley.

du Plock, S. (ed.) (2002) *Further Existential Challenges to Psychotherapeutic Theory and Practice*. London: SEA Press.

Duval, S. and Wicklund, R. (1972) *A Theory of Objective Self-Awareness*. New York: Academic Press.

Eagleton, T. (2004) *After Theory*. London: Penguin.

Ebbinghaus, H. (1964) *Memory*. New York: Dover.

Edelman, G. (1992) *Bright Air, Brilliant Fire: on the Matter of the Mind*. London: Penguin.

Ekman, P. (1975) 'Face muscles talk every language', *Psychology Today*, Sept: 35–9.

Ekman, P. and Friesen, W. (1971) 'Constants across cultures in the face and emotions', *Journal of Personality and Social Psychology*, 17: 124–9.

Ellenberger, H.F. (1970) *The Discovery of the Unconscious: the History and Evolution of Dynamic Psychiatry*. New York: Basic Books.

Ellis, A. and Whiteley, J. (eds) (1979) *Theoretical and Empirical Foundations of Rational–Emotive Therapy*. Monterey, CA: Brooks/Cole.

Ellis, R.D. (1995) *Questioning Consciousness: the Interplay of Imagery, Cognition and Emotion in the Human Brain*. Amsterdam: John Benjamins.

Erdelyi, M.H. (1985) *Psychoanalysis: Freud's Cognitive Psychology*. New York: Freeman.

Evans, R.I. (1975/1981) *Dialogue with Carl Rogers*. New York: Praeger.

Evans, R.I. (1976/1981) *Dialogue with R.D. Laing*. New York: Praeger.

Eysenck, M.W. (1984) *A Handbook of Cognitive Psychology*. London: Laurence Erlbaum Associates.

Fantz, R.L. (1961) 'The origin of form perception', *Scientific American*, 204: 66–72.

Farber, L. (2000) *The Ways Of The Will: Selected Essays*. New York: Basic Books.

Farber, M. (1962) *The Foundation of Phenomenology*, 2nd edn. New York: Paine-Whitman.

Ferrare, N. (1962) 'Institutionalization and attitude change in an aged population'. Unpublished doctoral thesis, Western Reserve University, OH.

Festinger, L. (1954) 'A theory of social comparison processes', *Human Relations*, 7: 117–40.

Fewtrell, D. and O'Connor, K. (1995) *Clinical Phenomenology and Cognitive Psychology*. London: Routledge.

Filmer, P., Phillipson, M., Silverman, D. and Walsh, D. (1972) *New Directions in Sociological Theory*. London: Collier-Macmillan.

Frankl, V.E. (1963) *Man's Search for Meaning: an Introduction to Logotherapy*. New York: Washington Square.

Frankl, V.E. (1967) *Psychotherapy and Existentialism*. New York: Washington Square.

Freedman, J. and Combs, G. (1996) *Narrative Therapy: the Social Construction of Preferred Realities*. London: W.W. Norton.

Freud, S. (1960/1980) *The Psychopathology of Everyday Life*. Harmondsworth: Penguin.

Freud, S. and Breuer, J. (1955/1971) *Studies on Hysteria*. Harmondsworth: Penguin.

Frie, R. (1997) *Subjectivity and Intersubjectivity in Modern Philosophy and Psycho-analysis: a Study of Sartre, Binswanger, Lacan and Habermas*. Lanham, MD: Rowman and Littlefield.

Friedman, M. (ed.) (1964) *The Worlds of Existentialism: a Critical Reader*. London: University of Chicago Press.

Fromkin, H. (1968) 'Affective and valuational consequences of self-perceived unique-ness deprivation'. Unpublished doctoral dissertation, Ohio State University.

Fromm, E. (1956) *The Art of Loving*. New York: Harper.

Gay, P. (1988) *Freud: A Life for Our Time*. London: Dent.

Gendlin, E.T. (1997). *Experiencing and the Creation of Meaning*. Evanston, IL: Northwestern University Press.

Gergen, K.J. (1971) *The Concept of Self*. New York: Holt, Rinehart and Winston.

Gergen, K.J. (1991) *The Saturated Self: Dilemmas in Identity in Contemporary Life*. New York: Basic Books.

Gergen K.J. (1999) *An Invitation to Social Construction*. London: SAGE Publications.

Gergen, K. and Wishnov, B. (1965) 'Others' self-evaluations and interaction antic-ipation as determinants of self-presentation', *Journal of Personality and Social Psychology*, 2: 348–58.

Gibbins, K. (1969) 'Communication aspects of women's clothes and their relation to fashionability', *British Journal of Social and Clinical Psychology*, 8: 301–12.

Gibson, E.I. and Walk, R.D. (1960) 'The "visual cliff"', *Scientific American*, 202: 64–71.

Gibson, J.I. (1950) *The Perception of the Visual World*. Boston, MA: Houghton Mifflin.

Gillett, G. (1995) 'The philosophical foundations of qualitative psychology', *The Psychologist*, 8 (3): 111–14.

Ginsburg, H. and Opper, S. (1969) *Piaget's Theory of Intellectual Development: an Introduction*. Englewood Cliffs, NJ: Prentice-Hall.

Giorgi, A. (1970) *Psychology as a Human Science: a Phenomenologically Based Approach*. New York: Harper and Row.

Giorgi, A. (1985) *Phenomenology and Psychological Research*. Pittsburgh: Duquesne University Press.

Gleick, J. (1988) *Chaos: Making a New Science*. London: Heinemann.

Goffman, E. (1959/1972) *The Presentation of Self in Everyday Life*. Harmondsworth: Penguin.

Goffman, E. (1967) *Interaction Ritual: Essays in Face-to-Face Behavior*. Chicago: Aldine.

Goldenberg, H. (1998) 'Fact or fiction? The relationship of "fact" and "narrative"', *Journal of the Society for Existential Analysis*, 9 (2): 71–83.

Goldstein, K. (1995) *The Organism*. New York: Zone Books.

Gordon, C. and Gergen, K. (eds) (1968) *The Self in Social Interaction*. New York: Wiley.

Grant, E. (1988) 'A pen by any name?', *Psychology Today*, May: 16.

Greenberg, J.R. and Mitchell, S.A. (1983) *Object Relations in Psychoanalytic Theory*. London: Harvard University Press.

Gregory, R. (1981) *Mind in Science: A History of Explanations in Psychology and Physics*. London: Weidenfeld and Nicolson.

Grossmann, R. (1984) *Phenomenology and Existentialism: an Introduction*. London: Routledge and Kegan Paul.

Grunbaum, A. (1984) *The Foundations of Psychoanalysis: a Philosophical Critique*. London: University of California Press.

Guidano, V.F. (1991) *The Self In Process*. London: Guilford Press.

Gurwitsch, A. (1966) *Studies in Phenomenology and Psychology*. Evanston, IL: Northwestern University Press.

Gurwitsch, A. (1982) 'Intentionality of consciousness', in H.L. Dreyfus (ed.), *Husserl, Intentionality and Cognitive Science*. London: MIT Press. pp. 59–71.

Haber, R.N. (1969) 'Eidetic images', *Scientific American*, 220 (4): 31.

Haber, R.N. (1970) 'How we remember what we see', *Scientific American*, 222 (5): 104.

Hacking, I. (1995) *Rewriting the Soul: Multiple Personality and the Sciences of Memory*. Princeton, NJ: Princeton University Press.

Hacking, I. (1999) *The Social Construction of What?* London: Harvard University Press.

Hall, G.S. (1904) *Adolescence*. New York: Appleton.

Hampden-Turner, C. (1981) *Maps of the Mind*. London: Mitchell Beasley.

Handley, N.K. (1996) 'Anxiety: an existential perspective', *Journal of the Society for Existential Analysis*, 7 (2): 27–49.

Harding, M. (1999) 'Using language', *Journal of the Society for Existential Analysis*, 10 (1): 82–101.

Harding, M. (2003) 'Delusions of references', *Existential Analysis*, 14 (2): 186–202.

Harré, R. (1991). 'What is scientific about psychotherapy?', *BPS Psychotherapy Section Newsletter*, 11: 14–17.

Harré, R. (1998) *The Singular Self: an Introduction to the Psychology of Personhood*. London: SAGE Publications.

Harré, R. and Secord, P. (1972) *The Explanation of Social Behaviour*. Oxford: Basil Blackwell.

Hawley, P. (1971) 'What women think men think: does it affect their career choice?', *Journal of Counseling Psychology*, 18: 193–9.

Hayes, S.C., Stroshal, K.D. and Wilson, K.G. (1999) *Acceptance and Commitment Therapy: an Experiential Approach to Behaviour Change*. New York: Guildford Press.

Hayman, R. (1986) *Writing Against: a Biography of Sartre*. London: Weidenfeld and Nicolson.

Hebb, D.O. (1966) *A Textbook of Psychology*. London: Saunders.

Heidegger, M. (1962) *Being and Time*. New York: Harper and Row.

Heidegger, M. (1993) 'What is metaphysics?', in D.F. Krell (ed.), *Basic Writings* (revised edition). London: Routledge.

Heidegger, M. (2001) *Zollikon Seminars: Protocols-Conversations-Letters*. Evanston, IL: Northwestern University Press.

Heron, W., Doane, B.K. and Scott, T.H. (1956) 'Visual disturbances after prolonged perceptual isolation', *Canadian Journal of Psychology*, 10: 112–22.

Hilgard, E.R., Atkinson, R.L. and Atkinson, R.C. (1987) *Introduction to Psychology*, 9th ed. New York: Harcourt Brace Jovanovich.

Hochberg, J. (1970) 'Attention, organization and consciousness', in D.I. Mostofsky (ed.), *Attention: Contemporary Theory and Analysis*. New York: Appleton Century-Crofts.

Hodges, H.A. (ed.) (1944) *Wilhelm Dilthey: an Introduction*. London: Routledge.

Hodges, H.A. (1952) *The philosophy of Wilhelm Dilthey*. London: Routledge and Kegan Paul.

Hoffman, D.D. (2000) *Visual Intelligence: How We Create What We See*. New York: Norton.

Holland, N. (1985) *The I*. London: Yale University Press.

Horney, K. (1966) *New Ways in Psychoanalysis*. New York: W.W. Norton.

Hubel, D.H. and Wiesel, T.N. (1962) 'Receptive fields, binocular interaction and functional architecture in the cat's visual cortex', *Journal of Physiology*, 195: 215–43.

Hughes, R. (1980) *The Shock of the New*. London: BBC Books.

Husserl, E. (1929/1969) *Formal and Transcendental Logic*. The Hague: Nijhoff.

Husserl, E. (1931a) *Ideas: General Introduction to Pure Phenomenology*, vol. 1. New York: Macmillan.

Husserl, E. (1931b) *Cartesian Meditations*. The Hague: Nijhoff.

Husserl, E. (1948/1973) *Experience and Judgement*. London: Routledge and Kegan Paul.

Husserl, E. (1965) *Phenomenology and the Crisis of Philosophy*. New York: Harper Torchbooks.

Hyman, H. (1942) 'The psychology of status', *Archives of Psychology*: 269.

Ihde, D. (1986a) *Experimental Phenomenology: an Introduction*, Albany: State University of New York.

Ihde, D. (1986b) *Consequences of Phenomenology*. Albany: State University of New York.

Ihde, D. (1998) *Expanding Hermeneutics: Visualism in Science*. Evanston, IL: Northwestern University Press.

Jacobsen, B. (2003) 'Is gift-giving the core of existential therapy?', *Existential Analysis*, 14 (2): 345–53.

James, W. (1890) *The Principles of Psychology*, vols 1 and 2. New York: Hot.

Jaspers, K. (1963) *General Psychopathology*, vol. 1. Baltimore, MD: Johns Hopkins University Press.

Jaspers, K. (1964) 'Psychologie der Weltanschauungen', in M. Friedman (ed.), *The Worlds of Existentialism*. London: University of Chicago Press.

Jones, E. and Nisbett, R. (eds) (1972) *Attribution: Perceiving the Causes of Behaviour*. Morrison, NJ: General Learning Press.

Jourard, S. (1964) *The Transparent Self: Self-Disclosure and Well-Being*. Princeton, NJ: Van Nostrand.

Karlsson, G. (1993) *Psychological Qualitative Research from a Phenomenological Perspective*. Stockholm: Almqvist and Wiksell International.

Kaufman, W. (1980a) *Discovering the Mind: Goethe, Kant, and Hegel*. New York: McGraw-Hill.

Kaufman, W. (1980b) *Discovering the Mind: Nietzsche, Heidegger, and Buber*. New York: McGraw-Hill.

Kaufman, W. (1980c) *Discovering the Mind: Freud versus Adler and Jung*. New York: McGraw-Hill.

Kaye, J. (1995) 'Postfoundationalism and the language of psychotherapy research', in J. Siegfried (ed.), *Therapeutic and Everyday Discourse as Behaviour Change*. Norwood, NJ: Ablex.

Kearney, R. (1986) *Modern Movements in European Philosophy*. Manchester: Manchester University Press.

Kegan, R. (1982) *The Evolving Self: Problem and Process in Human Development*. London: Harvard University Press.

Kelley, H. and Stahelski, A. (1970) 'The inference of intention from moves in the prisoner's dilemma game', *Journal of Experimental Social Psychology*, 6: 401–19.

Keyes, D. (1981) *The Minds of Billy Milligan*. New York: Random House.

Kirschenbaum, H. and Henderson, V.L. (1990) *Carl Rogers Dialogues*. London: Constable.

Kleinke, C., Staneski, R. and Pipp, S. (1975) 'Effects of gaze, distance, and attractiveness on males' first impressions of females', *Representative Research in Social Psychology*, 6: 7–12.

Knorr-Certina, K.D. (1981). *The Manufacture of Knowledge*. Oxford: Pergamon Press.

Kocklemans, J.J. (1967) *A First Introduction to Husserl's Phenomenology*. Pittsburgh, PA: Duquesne University Press.

Koestenbaum, P. (1973) 'Phenomenological foundations for the behavioral sciences', in F. Severin (ed.), *Discovering Man in Psychology: A Humanistic Approach*. New York: McGraw-Hill.

Koestler, A. (1964/1975) *The Act of Creation*. London: Pan.

Koestler, A. (1980) *Bricks To Babel*. London: Hutchinson.

Koffka, K. (1935) *Principles of Gestalt Psychology*. New York: Harcourt Brace.

Kohler, W. (1929) *Gestalt Psychology*. New York: Liveright.

Kondo, D.K. (1990) *Crafting Selves*. London: University of Chicago Press.

Kvale, S. (1994) 'Ten standard objections to qualitative research interviews', *Journal of Phenomenological Psychology*, 25 (2): 147–73.

Kvale, S. (1996) *InterViews*. London: SAGE Publications.

Kvale, S. and Grenness, C.E. (1967) 'Skinner and Sartre: toward a radical phenomenology of behavior?', *Review of Existential Psychology and Psychiatry*, 7: 128–48.

Laing, R.D. (1960/1970) *The Divided Self*. Harmondsworth: Penguin.

Laing, R.D. (1961/1971) *Self and Others*. Harmondsworth: Penguin.

Laing, R.D. (1967) *The Politics of Experience and the Bird of Paradise*. Harmondsworth: Penguin.

Laing, R.D. (1982) *The Voice of Experience*. Harmondsworth: Penguin.

Laing, R.D. and Esterson, A. (1964/1971) *Sanity, Madness and the Family*. Harmondsworth: Penguin.

Laing, R.D., Philipson, H. and Lee, A. (1966) *Interpersonal Perception: A Theory and a Method of Research*. New York: Springer.

Langer, E. and Abelson, R. (1974) 'A patient by any other name... clinician group difference in labeling bias', *Journal of Consulting and Clinical Psychology*, 42: 4–9.

Lawson, E. (1971) 'Hair color, personality, and the observer', *Psychological Reports*, 28: 311–22.

Lee, N. and Mandelbaum, M. (eds) (1967) *Phenomenology and Existentialism*. Baltimore, MD: Johns Hopkins University Press.

Lieberman, E.J. (1985) *Acts of Will: The Life and Work of Otto Rank*. New York: Free Press.

Linehan, M.M. (1993) *Cognitive-Behavioral Treatment of Borderline Personality Disorder*. New York: Guildford Press.

Lodge, D. (2004) 'Goodbye to all that', *The New York Review of Books*, LI (9): 39–43.

Luchins, A. (1957) 'Primacy-recency in impression formation', in C. Hovland, W. Mandell, E. Campbell, T. Brock, A. Luchins, A. Cohen, W. McGuire, I. Janis, R. Feierabend and N. Anderson, *The Order of Presentation in Persuasion*. New Haven, CT: Yale University Press. pp. 33–61.

Luria, A.R. (1969) *The Mind of a Mnemonist*. London: Jonathan Cape.

McCall, R.J. (1983) *Phenomenological Psychology*. Madison, WI: University of Wisconsin Press.

McGrath, W.J. (1986) *Freud's Discovery of Psychoanalysis: The Politics of Hysteria*. Ithaca, NY: Cornell University Press.

Macquarrie, J. (1972) *Existentialism*. Harmondsworth: Penguin.

Madison, G. (2002) 'Illness… and its human values', *Existential Analysis*, 13 (1): 10–30.

Mahrer, A.R. (1996) *The Complete Guide to Experiential Psychotherapy*. New York: Wiley.

Mahrer, A.R. (2000) 'Philosophy of science and the foundations of psychotherapy', *American Psychologist*, 55 (10): 117–125.

Mair, K. (1992) 'The myth of therapist expertise', in W. Dryden and C. Feltham (eds), *Psychotherapy and its Discontents*. Milton Keynes: Open University Press.

Mannheim, B. (1966) 'Reference groups, membership group and self image', *Sociometry*, 29: 265–79.

Manz, W. and Lueck, H. (1968) 'Influence of wearing glasses on personality ratings: cross-cultural validation of an old experiment', *Perceptual and Motor Skills*, 27: 704.

Marcus, M. (1976) 'The power of a name', *Psychology Today*, 10 (5): 75–6.

Marcuse, F.L. (1959/1971) *Hypnosis: Fact and Fiction*. Harmondsworth: Penguin.

Maslach, C. (1974) 'Social and personal bases of individuation', *Journal of Personality and Social Psychology*, 29: 213–14.

Maslow, A.H. (1968) *Toward a Psychology of Being*, 2nd edn. Princeton, NJ: Van Nostrand.

Maslow, A.H. (1971) *The Farther Reaches of Human Nature*. New York: Viking.

Masson, J.M. (1985) *The Complete Letters Of Sigmund Freud to Wilhelm Fliess, 1887–1904*. London: Belknap Press.

May, R. (ed.) (1958) *Existence: A New Dimension in Psychiatry and Psychology*. New York: Basic Books.

May, R. (1969a) *Existential Psychology*, 2nd edn. New York: Random House.

May, R. (1969b) *Love and Will*. New York: W.W. Norton.

May, R. (1981) *Freedom and Destiny*. London: W.W. Norton.

May, R. (1983) *The Discovery of Being*. London: W.W. Norton.

Mazis, M. (1975) 'Antipollution measures and psychological reactance theory: a field experiment', *Journal of Personality and Social Psychology*, 31: 654–60.

Medcof, J. and Roth, J. (1979/1984) *Approaches to Psychology*. Milton Keynes: Open University Press.

Mehrabian, A. (1968) 'Inference of attitude from the posture, orientation, and distance of a communicator', *Journal of Consulting and Clinical Psychology*, 32: 296–308.

Merleau-Ponty, M. (1962) *The Phenomenology of Perception*. London: Routledge and Kegan Paul.

Merleau-Ponty, M. (1964) *The Primacy of Perception*. Evanston, IL: Northwestern University Press.

Merton, R. (1957) *Social Theory and Social Structure*. Glencoe, IL: Free Press.

Middlebrook, P.N. (1980) *Social Psychology and Modern Life*, 2nd edn. New York: Knopf.

Midgley, M. (1996) 'One world – but a big one', *Journal of Consciousness Studies*, 3 (5–6): 500–14.

Midgley, M. (1999) 'Being scientific about ourselves', *Journal of Consciousness Studies*, 6 (4): 85–98.

Milgram, S. (1974) *Obedience to Authority: an Experimental View*. New York: Harper and Row.

Miller, J. (1978) *The Body in Question*. London: Jonathan Cape.

Mishkin, M. and Forgays, D.G. (1952) 'The tachistoscopic recognition of English and Jewish words', *Journal of Experimental Psychology*, 65: 555–62.

Misiak, H. and Sexton, V.S. (1973) *Phenomenological, Existential, and Humanistic Psychologies: a Historical Survey*. New York: Grune and Stratton.

Mitchell, D. (2002) 'Is the concept of supervision at odds with existential thinking and therapeutic practice?', *Existential Analysis*, 13 (1): 91–7.

Moja-Strasser, L. (1996) 'The phenomenology of listening and the importance of silence', *Journal of the Society for Existential Analysis*, 7 (1): 90–102.

Moran, D. (2000) *Introduction to Phenomenology*. London: Routledge.

Moray, N. (1959) 'Attention in dichotic listening: affective cues and the influence of instructions', *Quarterly Journal of Experimental Psychology*, 11: 56–60.

Morgenstern, J. and Longabaugh, R. (2001) 'Mechanisms of CBT model unknown', *Brown University Digest of Addiction Theory and Application*, 20 (9): 4–5.

Morris, B.B. (1971) 'Effects of order and trial on necker cube reversals under free and resistive instructions', *Perceptual and Motor Skills*, 33: 235–40.

Moustakas, C. (1994) *Phenomenological Research Methods*. London: SAGE Publications.

Nagel, T. (1998) *The Last Word*. New York: Oxford University Press.

Neimeyer, R.A. and Mahoney, M.J. (eds) (1995) *Constructivism in Psychotherapy*. Washington, DC: American Psychological Association.

Neirenberg, G. and Calero, H. (1971) *How to Read a Person Like a Book*. New York: Hawthorn Books.

Neisser, U. (1967) *Cognitive Psychology*. New York: Appleton.

Neisser, U. (1976) *Cognition and Reality: Principles and Applications of Cognitive Psychology*. New York: Freeman.

Nielsen, S.L. and Sarason, I.G. (1981) 'Emotion, personality and selective attention', *Journal of Personality and Social Psychology*, 41: 945–60.

Nisbett, R. and Wilson, T. (1977) 'The halo effect: evidence for unconscious alteration of judgement', *Journal of Personality and Social Psychology*, 35: 250–6.

Olson, C. (2000) *Zen and the Art of Postmodern Philosophy*. Albany, NY: SUNY Press.

Ott, H. (1994) *Martin Heidegger: a Political Life*. London: Fontana Press.

Owen, I.R. (2002) 'Towards an intentional analysis of consciousness?', *Existential Analysis*, 13 (2): 237–65.

Parks, D. (1999). 'Unlocking the mind's manacles', *New York Review of Books*, October 7: 43–8.

Passini, F. and Norman, W. (1966) 'A universal conception of personality structure?', *Journal of Personality and Social Psychology*, 4: 44–9.

Penfield, W. and Perot, P. (1963) 'The brain's record of auditory and visual experience', *Brain*, 86: 595–697.

Pribram, K.H. (1971) *Languages of the Brain: Experimental Paradoxes and Principles in Neuropsychology*. Englewood Cliffs, NJ: Prentice-Hall.

Pribram, K.H. (1976) *Consciousness and the Brain*. New York: Plenum.

Ray, M. (1946) 'The effect of crippled appearance on personality judgements'. Unpublished master's thesis, Stanford University, CA.

Rennie, S. (2001) 'The phenomenology of the call of conscience', *Existential Analysis*, 12 (1): 107–21.

Revelli, S. (1998) 'The story of Miss U: an attempt at existential phenomenological analysis', *Journal of the Society for Existential Analysis*, 9 (1): 82–97.

Ricoeur, P. (1970) *Freud and Philosophy: an Essay on Interpretation*. New Haven, CT: Yale University Press.

Rock, I. (1984) *Perception*. New York: Scientific American Books.

Rogers, C. (1942) *Counseling and Psychotherapy*. Boston, MA: Houghton Mifflin.

Rogers, C. (1951) *Client-Centred Therapy*. New York: Houghton Mifflin.

Rogers, C. (1961) *On Becoming a Person*. Boston: Houghton Mifflin.

Rogers, C. (1964) 'Toward a science of the person', in T.W. Wann (ed.), *Behaviorism and Phenomenology: Contrasting Bases for Modern Psychology*. Chicago, IL: University of Chicago Press. pp. 109–40.

Rogers, C. and Stevens. B. (1967) *Person to Person: the Problem Of Being Human*. New York: Real People Press.

Rosen, S. (1984) Private communication.

Rosenthal, R. (1966) *Experimenter Effects in Behavioral Research*. New York: Appleton-Century-Crafts.

Rotter, J. (1966) 'Generalized expectancies for internal versus external control of reinforcement', *Psychological Monographs*, 80 (1): 609.

Rowan, J. (1976) *Ordinary Ecstasy: Humanistic Psychology in Action*. London: Routledge and Kegan Paul.

Rowan, J. (1998) 'Letters', *The Psychologist*, 11 (12): 578.

Rowan, J. (2001) 'Existential analysis and humanistic psychotherapy', in K. Schneider, J.F.T. Bugenthal and J. Fraser Pierson, *The Handbook of Humanistic Psychology: Leading Edges in Theory, Research, and Practice*. London: SAGE Publications. pp. 447–64.

Ruitenbeek, H.M. (ed.) (1962) *Psychoanalysis and Existential Philosophy*. New York: Dutton.

Russell, B. (1946/1961) *History of Western Philosophy*. London: George Allen and Unwin.

Ryan, E. and Carranza, M. (1975) 'Evaluative reactions of adolescents toward speakers of standard English and Mexican-American accented English', *Journal of Personality and Social Psychology*, 31: 855–63.

Ryback, D. (1972) 'Existentialism and behaviorism: some differences settled', *Canadian Psychologist*, 13: 53–60.

Sacks, O. (1985) *The Man who Mistook his Wife for a Hat*. London: Pan.

Sacks, O. (1995) *An Anthropologist on Mars*. London: Picador.

Sanford, R.H. (1935) 'The Effects of abstinence from food upon imaginal processes: a preliminary experiment', *Journal of Psychology*, 2: 129–36.

Sartre, J.P. (1947a) *The Age of Reason*. London: Hamish Hamilton.

Sartre, J.P. (1947b) *The Reprieve*. London: Hamish Hamilton.

Sartre, J.P. (1948) *Existential Psychoanalysis*. New York: Philosophical Library.

Sartre, J.P. (1950) *Iron in the Soul*. London: Hamish Hamilton.

Sartre, J.P. (1956/1991) *Being and Nothingness: an Essay on Phenomenological Ontology*. London: Routledge.

Sartre, J.P. (1984) *The Freud Scenario*. London: Verso.

Sartre, J.P. (1989) *No Exit and Other Plays*. New York: Vintage Books.

Schaap, C., Bennun, I., Schindler, L. and Hoogduin, K. (1993) *The Therapeutic Relationship in Behavioural Psychotherapy*. New York: John Wiley.

Schachter, S. (1964) 'The interaction of cognitive and physiological determinants of emotional state', in L. Berkowitz (ed.), *Advances in Experimental Social Psychology*, vol. 1. New York: Academic Press.

Schachter, S. and Singer, J. (1962) 'Cognitive, social and physiological determinants of emotional state', *Psychological Review*, 69: 379–99.

Schneider, D. (1973) 'Implicit personality theory: a review', *Psychological Bulletin*, 79: 294–309.

Schneider, K., Bugenthal, J.F.T. and Fraser Pierson, J. (eds) (2001) *The Handbook of Humanistic Psychology: Leading Edges in Theory, Research, and Practice*. London: SAGE Publications.

Schreiber, F.L. (1973) *Sybil*. New York: Warner Paperback.

Seligman, M. (1974) 'Submissive death: giving up in life', *Psychology Today*, 7 (12): 80–5.

Seligman, M. (1975) *Helplessness: on Depression, Development, and Death*. San Francisco, CA: Freeman.

Shaffer, J.B.P. (1978) *Humanistic Psychology*. Englewood Cliffs, NJ: Prentice-Hall.

Sherrington, C.S. (1941) *Man on His Nature*. London: Macmillan.

Shotter, J. and Gergen, K.J. (1989) *Texts of Identity*. London: SAGE Publications.

Sigall, H. and Ostrove, N. (1975) 'Beautiful but dangerous: effects of offender attractiveness and nature of the crime and juridic judgement', *Journal of Personality and Social Psychology*, 31: 410–14.

Sizemore, C. and Pittillo, E. (1977) *I'm Eve*. New York: Doubleday.

Skinner, B.F. (1971) *Beyond Freedom and Dignity*. New York: Knapf.

Smith, B. and Woodruff Smith, D. (eds) (1995) *The Cambridge Companion to Husserl*. Cambridge: Cambridge University Press.

Snyder, M. and Swann, W. (1978) 'Behavioral confirmation in social interaction: from social perception to social reality', *Journal of Experimental Social Psychology*, 14: 148–62.

Sorokin, P. (1947) *Society, Culture, and Personality: Their Structure and Dynamics*. New York: Harper.

Sortie, J. (1988) Private Communication.

Sperling, G. (1960) 'The information available in brief visual presentations', *Psychological Monographs*, 74: 498.

Spinelli, E. (1989) *The Interpreted World: an Introduction to Phenomenological Psychology*. London: SAGE Publications.

Spinelli, E. (1994) *Demystifying Therapy*. London: Constable.

Spinelli, E. (1997) *Tales of Un-Knowing: Therapeutic Encounters From an Existential Perspective*. London: Duckworth.

Spinelli, E. (2001) *The Mirror and the Hammer: Challenges to Therapeutic Orthodoxy*. London: SAGE Publications.

Spinelli, E. (2003) 'The existential-phenomenological paradigm', in R. Woolfe, W. Dryden and S. Strawbridge (eds), *Handbook of Counselling Psychology*, 2nd ed. London: SAGE Publications. pp. 180–98.

Spinelli, E. (forthcoming) *Selves-in-Relation*. London: SAGE Publications.

Spranger, E. (1928) *Types of Men*. Halle: Neimeyer.

Steele, R.S. (1982) *Freud and Jung: Conflicts of Interpretation*. London: Routledge and Kegan Paul.

Steiner, G. (1978) *Heidegger*. Glasgow: Fontana.

Stern, D.N. (1985) *The Interpersonal World of the Infant: A View from Psychoanalysis and Developmental Psychology*. New York: Basic Books.

Stern, D. (1985) *The Interpersonal World of the Infant*. New York: Basic Books.

Stern, D.N. (2004) *The Present Moment in Psychotherapy and Everyday Life*. New York: W.W. Norton.

Stevens, R. (ed.) (1996) *Understanding the Self*. London: SAGE Publications.

Strasser, F. (1999) *Emotions: Experiences in Existential Psychotherapy and Life*. London: Duckworth.

Strasser, F. and Strasser, A. (1997) *Existential Time-Limited Therapy: the Wheel of Existence*. Chichester: Wiley.

Strawson, G. (1997) 'The self', *Journal of Consciousness Studies*, 4 (5–6): 405–28.

Szasz, T. (1970) *Ideology and Insanity*. Harmondsworth: Penguin.

Szasz, T. (1974) *The Myth of Mental Illness*, revised edn. New York: Harper and Row.

Tesser, A., Gatewood, R. and Driver, M. (1968) 'Same determinants of gratitude', *Journal of Personality and Social Psychology*, 9: 233–6.

Thorndike, E. (1920) 'A constant error in psychological ratings', *Journal of Applied Psychology*, 4: 25–9.

Valle, R.S. and King, M. (1978) *Existential-Phenomenological Alternatives for Psychology*. Oxford: Oxford University Press.

Van Haute, P. (1995) 'Fatal attraction: Jean Laplanche on sexuality, subjectivity and singularity in the work of Sigmund Freud', *Radical Philosophy*, 73: 5–12.

Van Kaam, A.L. (1966) *Existential Foundations in Psychology*. Pittsburgh, PA: Duquesne University Press.

Varela, F. (1996) 'Neurophenomenology', *Journal of Consciousness Studies*, 3 (4): 330–49.

Varela, F., Thompson, E. and Rosch, E. (1993) *The Embodied Mind*. Cambridge, MA: MIT Press.

Verinis, J. and Roll, S. (1970) 'Primary and secondary male characteristics: the hairiness and large penis stereotypes', *Psychological Reports*, 26: 123–6.

Wann, T.W. (ed.) (1964) *Behaviorism and Phenomenology: Contrasting Bases for Modern Psychology*. Chicago, IL: University of Chicago Press.

Warnock, M. (1970/1979) *Existentialism*. Oxford: Oxford University Press.

Watts, A.J. (1957/1974) *The Way of Zen*. Harmondsworth: Penguin.

Wells, G. and Harvey, J. (1971) 'Do people use consensus information in making casual attributions?', *Journal of Personality and Social Psychology*, 35: 279–93.

White, M. (1995) *Re-authoring Lives: Interviews and Essays*. Adelaide: Dulwich Centre Publications.

Wilber, K. (ed.) (1982) *The Halographic Paradigm and Other Paradoxes*. London: Shambhala.

Wolin, R. (ed.) (1993) *The Heidegger Controversy: a Critical Reader*. London: MIT Press.

Wolf, D. (1999) 'Heidegger's conscience', *Journal of the Society for Existential Analysis*, 10 (2): 54–62.

Wollheim, R. (1984) *The Thread of Life*. Cambridge, MA: Harvard University Press.

Wolman, B.B. (1981) *Contemporary Theories and Systems in Psychology*, 2nd edn. London: Plenum.

Woodside, A. (1972) 'A shopping list experiment of beer brand images', *Journal of Applied Psychology*, 56: 512–13.

Wright, B.A. (1960) *Physical Disability: A Psychological Approach*. New York: Harper and Row.

Wylie, R., Miller, P., Cawles, S. and Wilson, A. (1979) *The Self-Concept: Theory and Research on Selected Topics*, vol. 2. Lincoln, NB: University of Nebraska Press.

Yalom, I. (1980) *Existential Psychotherapy*. New York: Basic Books.

Yandell, B. and Insko, C. (1977) 'Attribution of attitudes to speakers and listeners under assigned-behavior conditions: does behavior engulf the field?', *Journal of Experimental Social Psychology*, 13: 269–78.

Yardley, K. and Honess, T. (eds) (1987) *Self and Identity: Psychosocial Perspectives*. Chichester: John Wiley.

Young, S. (1993) 'Everything is what it is, not something else', *Journal of the Society for Existential Analysis*, 4: 13–18.

Zahavi, D. (1998) 'Beyond empathy: phenomenological approaches to intersubjectivity', *Journal of Consciousness Studies*, 8 (5–7): 151–67.

Zaner, R.M. (1970) *The Way of Phenomenology*. New York: Pegasus.

Zeki, S. (1993) *A Vision of the Brain*. Oxford: Oxford University Press.

Zeki, S. (2000) *Inner Vision: an Exploration of Art and the Brain*. Oxford: Oxford University Press.

Zimbardo, P. (1969) 'The human choice: individuation, reason, and order versus deindividuation, impulse, and chaos', in W.J. Arnold and D. Levine (eds), *Nebraska Symposium on Motivation*, vol. 17. Lincoln, NB: University of Nebraska Press.

Zimbardo, P., Haney, C., Banks, W. and Jaffe, D. (1972) 'The Psychology of Imprisonment: Privation, Power, and Pathology'. Unpublished paper, Stanford University, CA.

Zukav, G. (1980) *The Dancing Wu-Li Masters: an Overview of the New Physics*. London: Fontana.

Index

'abnormal' behaviour 9
absolute truths problem 8, 11
abstract art 10
acceptance and commitment therapy
    (ACT) 200
accessibility of past events 188
accommodation/assimilation 68
accuracy of self-analysis 81
   see also correctness of interpretations
ACT *see* acceptance and commitment
   therapy
actions versus being 164–5, 170
active interpretation 153, 210
actor-observer differences 64
adolescence 165–6
adult perceptions 74
affective state 69
after-life 114
agnosia 41–2
AI *see* artificial intelligence
aims of subject area 33–4
alienation 158, 160
altered states 115
ambiguous figures 38–9, 46–7, 49–55, 95
angst (anxiety) 72, 82, 115–16, 154–6
anguish 118
anorexia nervosa 85
anti-medical stance 156–7
anti-rationalism 104
anxiety (angst) 72, 82, 115–16, 154–6
apodicticity 50
appearances 11
approximations of reality 133
arrested development 165
artificial intelligence (AI) 197
artwork 10
Asch, Solomon 66
assimilation/accommodation 68
assumptions *see* biases
attention 27
   see also selective attention
attitudes 146–7
attraction 29
attractiveness 62
attribution theory 199–200
attuning to clients 150–1

authenticity 110–16, 145, 183
autonomous identity 165, 169
awareness of being 106–7

'bad faith' 120–2, 158
'bad' versus 'good' self 164–6
Bandura, Albert 195
Bartlett, Sir Frederick 96
Bateson, Gregory 174–5
behaviour 68, 77, 177
behaviourism 194–6
being versus actions 164–5, 170
being-for-itself 118
being-for-others 119–20
being-in-itself 118–19
being-in-the-world 29, 107–8, 145–6, 159–60
beings/Being distinction 106–8
beliefs
   mutuality 120
   non-finality 114
   re-examination 154
   self-perception 78, 85
Bergson, Henri 96–7
biases
   ambiguous figure studies 41–5
   formation 210
   object perception 52–3, 56
   suspending 20–5, 133–4
   see also expectations; experience;
     interpretations
Binswanger, Ludwig 147
bio-genetic factors 156–7, 166–8
bio-physical explanations 177
bodily control 84
Boss, Medard 190
'bracketing' 20, 117, 133–4, 150–2
   see also biases
Brentano, Franz 14, 15
brightness constancy 39–40
Buber, Martin 123–5

categorization of experience 68
causality 134, 188–9
CBT *see* cognitive-behavioural therapy
central traits 66
challenging expectations 150–1

change, personal 75, 86–90
chaos theory 189
childhood fears 162
childhood trauma 91
choice 112–13
    see also ownership of behaviour
Christina (Oliver Sacks study) 84–5
client-therapist relations 146, 148,
    150–2, 181, 191–2
clustering of data 136, 140
co-constitutionality 133
'cocktail party phenomenon' 47
cognitive flexibility 57
cognitive revolution 177
cognitive schools 197
cognitive-behavioural psychology
    197–200, 211
cognitive-behavioural therapy
    (CBT) 199–201
Cohen, John 177
Cohn, Hans W. 110
Colaizzi, Paul 136–7
collaborative research 135, 142
communication 73
compelling events 86–90, 111
conditional presentation 57
conflict 118–20, 154
congruence 172
consciousness
    behaviourism 194, 196
    cognitive behaviourism 197
    exclusion from research 187
    interpretative action 15
    phenomenology 133–4, 204
consciousness-independence 5
constancy in perception 39
constructivist systems 199
contextual factors 46–7, 64–5, 131
control 72, 84
    see also ownership of behaviour
'core self' 75–6, 80–1, 89–90
'correctness' of interpretations 8–10, 114
'correlational poles' *see* noema
    and noesis
counter-culture 178
critical overview 202–18
cultural factors 8, 63
'curing' processes 145

dasein 107–8, 112
death anxiety 154–5, 192
defensive strategies 154–5, 158–60, 169
defining phenomena 134
'delusions' 8–9
demand characteristics 50
denial 77, 82, 92, 110, 116, 157

depth/distance perception 43, 44
Descartes, René 36
describing experience 20–1, 26, 153
description rule 20–1, 173
Deurzen, Emmy van 147
dialectical behaviour therapy 199–200
dialogue 133
Dilthey, Wilhelm 128, 176
directional focus *see* noema
    and noesis
disclosure 133
disease model 156–7
dissociated identity *see* multiple
    personalities
dissociation 146–7, 190
Dr P (Oliver Sacks study) 41–2

Eagleton, Terry 216
Eastern philosophies 94
ego psychology 177–8
Eigenwelt worldview 147
emotion 198
empathy 171–2
engulfment fear 160
enrichment of perception 46
environmental stimuli 194–5, 209–10
epoché rule 20, 173
equal reality rule 25
equalization rule *see* rule of
    horizontalization
essence 103
Eve White study 90
existence 5, 103, 106–9, 115
existential phenomenology 7, 103–27
existential psychotherapy 143–75
    aims 145
    attitudes 146–7
    client 149–50
    modes of enquiry 148–9
    principles 144
    therapist 150–4
existentialism *see* existential
    phenomenology
existentials 112–16, 203
expectations 45–7
    see also biases; future expectations
experience
    categorization 68
    describing 26, 153, 20–1
    exploration 145–6
    foci 16–18, 131
    humanistic perspective 182
    'I' assumption 27–8
    immediacy 148, 151, 175
    individual 12
    ineffability 27

experience *cont.*
  interpretative nature 16
  knowledge 15
  meaninglessness 9–10
  object perception 45
  ownership 110
  phenomenological view 31–2, 131, 182
  physical/mental interaction 12
  reconstituting 150
  sharability 17–18, 30–1, 73, 171
  straightforward versus reflective 26–7
  structure 131–2
  timelessness 27
  uniqueness 18, 12–13, 40, 71,
      203, 211–12
  unity 172
  variants 19
  see also biases; interpretations;
      past experience
experiential focus *see* noema and noesis
experimenter bias 195
explanation versus understanding
      109, 128–31
explanations of behaviour 64, 177
exploratory methods 134, 145–6
externalising 78, 89, 92

facial expressions 59, 63
facticity of existence 118–19
'false self' 184
familiarity effects 57
family 164–6
fears 160–2
figure/ground phenomenon 48–50, 71,
      95, 133
filtering stimuli 48, 70, 97
first impressions 66, 68
'fitting' of experience 68
flashbacks 99–100
fluidity of the self 102
foci of experience *see* noema and noesis
form perception 43–4
foundational structures 132, 142
fragmentation 158, 165, 169
free association 191
freedom 105, 117–18, 195
Freud, Sigmund 126, 188, 193
Fromm, Erich 72
fundamental attribution error 64
future expectations 69–71

Gestalt psychology 35–6, 176–7
'givens' 12, 17, 107–9, 111, 154
  see also existentials
'good' versus 'bad' self 164–6

Grossmann, Reinhardt 205–6
gryphon 206

Haber, Ralph 97–8
Hall, G. Stanley 177
hallway/pyramid illusion 50–5
halo effect 65
Heidegger, Martin 7, 105–12
hierarchies of significance 21–2, 27
horizontalization rule 21–2, 173
horror films 161
Hughes, Howard 159
human encounter/potential
      movement 178
human versus natural sciences 109,
      128–31, 189
humanistic psychology 176–85
Husserl, Edmund 6, 13–14, 32,
      132, 202–3
hypnosis 81–2
hypochondria 21

the 'I' 27–30, 209
  see also the self
'I-focused' inquiry 148
'I-It' versus 'I-You' relations 123–4
'I-not-I' concept 133
ideologies 147–8
idiot savants 98
illusions *see* ambiguous figures
immediacy of experience 148,
      151, 175
impermanence of the self 82–3
implicit personality theories 65
implosion fear 160
inauthenticity 110–16, 158
inclusion 124
inclusionary/exclusionary rule 25
individual experience 12
individualism critique 130
individuals versus persons 123
ineffability of experience 27
infant perceptions 74
inference 35–41, 59–61
infinite regress 206–7
innate perception 43–4, 49
insignificant memories 97
integration 183
intentionality 14–16, 18, 202
inter-relations
      cognitive-behavioural therapy 200
      conflict 119–20
      existence 125, 149, 150
      reality 130–1
      reflection 105

inter-relations *cont.*
  self/other 124, 203
  subject/object 202
  worldviews 146
interaction 12, 14–18, 66–7, 73
interactionist models 79
internalising 78
interpersonal attraction 29
interpersonal theories 193–4
interpretations of reality
  biochemical imbalances 167
  cognitive-behavioural psychology 197
  'correctness' 8–10, 114
  experience 16
  invariant mental structures 9
  memory 100–2
  object-based 15
  person perception 67
  plasticity 12–13, 18
  processes 7–8
  sharability 9, 17–18, 30–1, 73
  uniqueness 12–13
  see also biases; experience; reality
interpretative methodologies 129–30
interview techniques 136
intolerance 166
introspectionism 208–9
invariant structures
  figure/ground phenomenon
      30–1, 48–50
  meaning attribution 9, 10, 12, 17–18
  self-consciousness 83
invincibility belief 154–5

James, William 76, 177
Jaspers, Karl 151

Kant, Immanuel 6, 36
Kaye, John 129
Kearney, Richard 117, 119
Kierkegaard, Sören 104–5
knowledge 15

labelling theory 157–8
Laing, R.D. 157–68
language 94, 130
learned helplessness 78
linear causality 134, 188–9, 212
listening to clients 146
literature 104, 116
Locke, John 36
love 72
LSD effects 167
Luria, Alexander 98
lying 93, 122

marriage guidance 71–2
meaning
  extraction 136, 140, 192
  facticity 118–19
  natural versus human science 129
  psychotherapy 144
meaning attribution
  abstract art 10
  behaviour 82
  choice 112–13
  experience 7–8
  figure/ground phenomenon 49
  novel stimuli 45
  reflection 27
meaningless experience 9–10, 114, 118
medical intervention 161–2
medical models 156
memory 95–102, 197
mental frameworks 10, 12, 211
mental illness models 156–8
mental/physical interaction 12
methodologies 129–30, 135–41
Milgram, Stanley 87–9
Miller, Jonathan 83–4
Mitwelt worldview 147
mood 69
morality 122–3
motivational state 47
multiple personalities 90–4, 158
mutuality of being 120

names 63
narrative models 79–80
natural science 212
  versus human sciences 109,
      127–31, 189
nausea 122
Naven rituals 175
neurobiology 68
Nietzsche, Friedrich 104–5, 214
noema and noesis 16–18, 131, 171,
      186, 198, 203
non-existent objects 205–6
non-intentional phenomena 205
non-originators of behaviour 78
non-verbal behaviour 63
'normal' behaviour 9
normality assumptions 158
North American psychology 179–80
novel stimuli 45, 53

obedience to authority 87–9
object perception 35–58
  aspects 43
  biases 41–5

object perception *cont.*
  constancy 39, 43
  context 46–7
  depth and distance 43, 44
  everyday experience 56–8
  expectations 45–7
  filtering 48
  form 43–4
  inference 37–41
  motivational state 47
  organization 36, 41–5
  phenomenological method 51–8
  sensation 37–8
  size 44
  theories 35–6
  variability 39
object relations theory 177–8, 193
object-based interpretations 15
object/subject inter-relation 202
  see also intentionality
objective observation 212
objective reality 5, 11, 13, 132–3, 195, 213
observability of stimuli 195
obstacles to therapy 153
ontic aspects of existence 108–9
ontological aspects of existence 108–9
ontological insecurity 158–61
openness 53–4, 115, 133, 150–2
  see also suspending biases
operational definitions 134
organization of perception 36, 41–5
originators of behaviour 78
origins of phenomenology 6
'otherness' 124–5
'others' 149
overextension of phenomenology 213–15
ownership of behaviour 77, 92
  see also choice; control
ownership of experience 110

'paranoid delusions' 8–9
passive reaction 194
past experience 69, 188–9
past-present-future relationships 189
Penfield, Wilder 98–9
perception *see* biases; experience;
    interpretations; object perception;
    person perception; self-perception
perceptual set 46
permanence of memory 97–100
person perception 59–74
  anxiety 72
  central traits 66
  facial expressions 63
  figure/ground phenomenon 71

person perception *cont.*
  first impressions 66, 68
  infants versus adults 74
  inference 59–61
  interactive variables 66–7
  interpretation 67
  names 63
  non-verbal behaviour 63
  past experience 69
  physical appearance 59, 61–2
  possessions 63
  projectional variables 65
  psychological research 61–7
  re-interpretation 72
  self-awareness 71
  strangers 70
  uniqueness 71
  voice 63–4
  wants 70
person-centred therapy 169–74
persons versus individuals 123
petrification fear 160
phantom limb effect 85
phenomena, definition 6
phenomenological method 19–34
  consequences 26–31
  Husserl 6, 203
  object perception 51–8
  person-centred therapy 172–4
  practice 22–5
  psychological research
        133–4, 203
  summary 31–2
phenomenological research 128–42
  example study 137–41
  methodology 135–41
  objectives 131–2
  principles 131–5
  versus traditional research 132–41
phenomenology
  development 13–14
  existential 7, 103–27
  fundamental issues 14–18
  origins 6
  rationale 5
  reality concept 7–8, 11–13
  transcendental 7, 11, 31, 103
philosophical critique 205–7
photographic memory 98
physical appearance 61–2
physical reality 12, 13, 147
  see also objective reality
physical/mental interaction 12
physics 13
Piaget, Jean 68, 200–1

plasticity of interpretations 18
positive regard 170–1
possessions 63
post-post structuralism 215
postmodernity 215
power 77, 154–5
preconceptions *see* biases
prejudices *see* biases
'prisoners and guards' study 86–7
projectional variables 65
proprioception 83–6
psychoanalysis 68, 116, 126, 187–94
psychological critique 207–13
psychological research
  limitations 25, 207
  memory 96
  person perception 61–7
  phenomenological psychology
    32–4, 55–6, 67–74, 126–7,
    132–41, 186–201
  the self 75–6
psychotherapy 128–9
  see also existential psychotherapy
punishment 162, 163
pure sensation 45

qualitative data 135, 196
question formulation 138–9, 153

rational-emotive behaviour therapy
  (REBT) 69
rationalizing behaviour 68, 81, 93
'rationally-dependent selves' 80–1
raw matter 12
re-interpretation 12–13, 72, 107
'real self' 184
reality
  approximations 133
  cultural variations 8
  elusiveness 117
  inter-relational 130–1
  language 130
  objective 5, 11, 13, 132–3, 195, 213
  phenomenology 7–8, 11–13
  physical substance 12
  subjective 11
  see also interpretations of reality
REBT *see* rational-emotive behaviour
  therapy
recall of memories 96
reciprocal determinism 195
reconstitutive inquiry 150
reconstruction of the self 93, 101
reductionism 129, 176–7
reflection 82–3

reflective versus straightforward
  experience 26–7
relation between stimuli 43
relationships, human 72
relativism 216
reliability 130
religious conflict 120
respect for clients 151, 163
responsibility 105, 153
  see also ownership of behaviour
ritualistic behaviour 162–3
Rogers, Carl 168–74, 180
role enactment studies 86–7
rote memory 98
Rowan, John 134, 181, 184
rule of description 20–1, 173
rule of epoché 20, 173
rule of horizontalization 21–2, 173

Sacks, Oliver 73–4
satiation or fatigue theory 49–50
Sartre, Jean-Paul 113, 116–23
schemata *see* mental frameworks
schismogenesis 174–5
schizoid condition 158–9, 164–8
scientific method 25, 129, 134, 212
scientific status 212–13
security/insecurity 159
selective attention 47–50
the self
  boundary extension 85–6
  'characteristics' approach 76–9
  'components' approach 76–9
  fluidity 102
  impermanence 82–3
  models 79–81
  phenomenological versus humanistic
    perspectives 183–4
  psychological research 75–6
  splitting 158
  see also core self
self and others
  boundaries 58
  inter-relationship 71, 133, 203
  mutual dependence 29–30, 120
  splitting 158
self-actualization 118, 169, 182–3
self-awareness 71, 75
  see also the 'I'
self-concept 169
self-deception 81–2, 121–2
self-defence 154–5, 158–60, 169
self-esteem 80
self-fulfilling prophecies 62, 65, 138
self-investigation 136–7, 145, 152

self-perception 75–102
self-preservation 159–63
   see also defensive strategies
sensation versus perception 37–8
sensory stimuli 15–16, 26, 48, 70, 97
sexual intercourse 28
shadowing studies 47
Shaffer, John 178
shame 119
sharability of experience 17–18,
   30–1, 73, 171
significance hierarchies 21–2, 27
significant others 147, 166
similarity of interpretations 9
size perception 44
social constructionist models 79
social context 157–8
social relations 147
Soviet Union 157–8
splitting of the self 158
Spranger, Eduard 176
stereotyping 64
stimulus theory 35–6
storage of memories 96
'stories' in therapy 171
straightforward versus reflective
   experience 26–7
strangers 70
stroke injuries 84
structure of experience 131–2
subject/object inter-relation 202
   see also intentionality
subjective reality 11
subjectivity 209
surrealist art 10
suspending biases 20–5, 133–4
   see also openness
symptoms 147–8, 154–5

technique versus understanding 144
temporality of the self 102
tension reduction 9–10
theorizing 25
theory exclusion 169
therapist-client relations 146, 148,
   150–2, 181, 191–2
'they-focused' inquiry 148
'they-self' 110
thrownness 113–14
timelessness of experience 27

transcendental phenomenology 7, 11,
   31, 103
transference relationship 191
translation of stimuli 15, 16
trauma 91
'truths' 8, 11, 135

Uberwelt worldview 147–8
'ultimate rescuer' 155–6
Umwelt worldview 147
uncertainty of existence 115
unconditional presentation 57
unconscious processes 189–90
understanding 109, 128–31, 144, 176–7
unidirectional causality 188–9, 195
unification of perception 41–5
unification of psychology 200–1
uniqueness of experience 12–13, 18,
   40, 71, 203, 211–12
unity of experiences 172
universality of fears 161

validity 130
variability in perception 39
variable isolation 134
variants of experience 19
verifiability 130, 136, 141, 196, 212
vision studies 44, 49
voice 63–4

wants 70
Warnock, Mary 121
'ways of being' 108–9, 149–51
'we-focused' inquiry 148, 149
wholeness 183
workaholism 155
World Trade Centre attacks 111
worldviews 145–6, 202

Yalom, Irvin 154–5
'you-focused' inquiry 148

Zimbardo, Philip 86–7

Compiled by INDEXING SPECIALISTS
(UK) Ltd., Regent House, Hove Street,
Hove, East Sussex BN3 2DJ. Tel: 01273
738299. E-mail: richardr@indexing.co.uk.
Website: www.indexing.co.uk.